Journal of Camus Studies
2013

www.camus-society.com

www.camus-us.com

Journal of Camus Studies
2013

General Editor

Peter Francev

Camus Society
2013

Journal of Camus Studies

The purpose of the *Journal of Camus Studies* is to further understanding of the work and thought of Albert Camus.

The material contained in this journal represents the opinions of the authors and not necessarily those of the Albert Camus Society or anyone affiliated with the society.

Book Design: Helen Lea
Cover Design: Simon Lea

Contents

Introduction

In November 2013, the Albert Camus Society US and Albert Camus Society UK held its 6th annual joint-conference in Bloomsbury, London. After the success of the 2012 conference, the organizers decided that it was best to have a two-day conference in order to accommodate the increasing number of conference speakers. The end result is this collection of essays.

In October we will be coming out with a special edition of the *Journal of Camus Studies* because of an extraordinary number of submissions. These will not be articles from the 2013 joint conference, but reponses from our call for papers. The 2015 journal will be 'back-on-track', so to speak, coming out in March of 2015 and will contain conference essays and independent solicitations.

We would like to welcome Eric Berg as the new Book Review Editor as of the 2014 journal. Eric Berg is associate professor of philosophy and religion at MacMurray College, and is the editor for Protestant theology and doctrine at the scholarly journal, *Religious Studies Review*. Under his editorship, the book review section will become a permanent and valuable feature of the *Journal of Camus Studies*.

Peter Francev
President of the Albert Camus Society US

Simon Lea
President of the Albert Camus Society UK

Absurdism: The Second Truth of Philosophy

by Kimberly Baltzer-Jaray

Abstract

When one surveys the history of early modern/modern philosophy, specifically the ideas and theories that fall within the domain of metaphysics and epistemology, one quickly realizes the presence of the absurd, sitting there like a pink elephant in the room, unacknowledged or at times purposely ignored. Descartes may have uncovered the indubitable primary truth - I think, therefore I am - but Camus called out what I believe is the indubitable secondary truth of philosophy - human attempts to know everything and the purpose of it all are met with a silent, indifferent, impenetrable universe that defeats every attempt. This is why practically every treatise written during the period inevitably fails or must admit God into the picture as the ultimate explanation and designer (and the inevitable notion of how small our minds are in comparison to God comes about to explain why we are having a hard time figuring the world out). From Bacon to Berkeley, rationalism to empiricism alike, we see attempts to identify the boundaries of human knowledge for the purposes of accuracy in science and to have truths built on certainty, and we see failure happen over and over. I believe this was due to the fact that none were daring enough to see the absurd at work, and what they sought was truly impossible. That is until Kant came along, who I would argue was the first to really sniff out and speak of the absurd, and when he did this he was met with fierce opposition and misinterpretation. Everyone wanted to flee from the absurd and/or deny it existed at all, rather than come to terms with it, accept it, and move on or revolt against it in personal authentic ways.

In this paper, I will discuss the presence of absurdism in the history of philosophy, demonstrating that it is not simply an existential or literary notion, but rather the key to the problems of metaphysics and epistemology. In fact, it is core to the philosophical discipline itself and philosophical inquiry. This will hopefully lead to or in the very least inspire a 'Camus renaissance', where we can start to appreciate the significance of his contribution in a much more accurate light.

* * *

The story of the nature of reality and whether we know it or not is an old one; the Pre-Socratics were asking it long before René Descartes, John Locke and Immanuel Kant. But I prefer to begin with Descartes since he infamously wrote in his *Discourse On Method* (1637) and again later in his *Meditations On First Philosophy* (1641): I think, therefore I am. This is of course what philosophers refer to as the 'first truth' of philosophy; that which cannot be doubted and that from which all inquiry springs forth – I am "a thing that thinks ... a thing that doubts, understands, affirms, denies, wants, refuses, and also imagines and senses."[1] Sadly, what came after this jewel was pretty lackluster: the commitment to strict methodological doubt gave way quickly to "Nature is my teacher and God is no deceiver", and God's constant intervening as the ad hoc solution to communications between the will and the body (and for causal interaction what so ever). But in the positing of the indubitable first truth he gave us not only the point of departure – the "I" that thinks from within the inner scull sanctum – but also a boundary problem that desperately needed to be settled. We knew the starting position, the origins of subjective experience if you will, but where does the world of our 'knowledge' extend to and end? This question sat at the very intersection of metaphysics and epistemology, and it resulted in a debate that would rage on for centuries. It also, in my opinion, forms part of the dialogue with the absurd, which I will discuss further in a moment.

After Descartes, many philosophers attempted to find and define this outer boundary of human knowledge, often in the name of science – for improved methods, for better clarity, true accomplishable goals, etc. On some occasions it was claimed finding this boundary could improve philosophy as a discipline, by doing away with vague language and empty, meaningless concepts. And then concerning metaphysics specifically the question of the boundary often was used in an attempt to prove or disprove whether it could be a science or not. Regardless of 'why' they wished to do it a pattern

---

[1] René Descartes, *Meditations On First Philosophy*, accessed 7 January 2014, http://www.earlymoderntexts.com/pdfs/descartes1641.pdf, pg. 5.

emerged when philosophers attempted to establish where this boundary of human knowledge was. Allow me to illustrate.

A first, prime example of what I am speaking about can be seen in the epistemological work of John Locke. He writes in his *Essay Concerning Human Understanding*, "My purpose ... is to enquire into the origin of certainty and extent of human knowledge, and also into the grounds and degrees of belief, opinion, and assent"[2] and to do this he must inquire into the nature and powers of the understanding. The hopeful result of this enquiry is the discovery of its powers, including "how far they reach, what things they are adequate to deal with, and where they fail us."[3] Furthermore, "If I succeed, that may have the effect of persuading the busy mind of man to be more cautious in meddling with things that are beyond its powers to understand; to stop when it is at the extreme end of its tether; and to be peacefully reconciled to ignorance of things that turn out to be beyond the reach of our capacities."[4] Now it is important to recall that Locke was an empiricist and so he didn't believe in the notion of the mind possessing any innate principles; your mind at birth is a blank slate, objects of sensation produce ideas and so it is experience that furnishes the mind with everything it needs to ground knowledge. So, when we take into account his philosophical affiliation and what he said in the introduction to his *Essay* (stated above), it is rather brow-raising that his discussion ends up containing things like Substance (that 'which I know not what'; three types of Substance include God, Finite Spirits and Matter) and knowing the existence of God – things which we cannot experience with the senses directly and thus the understanding cannot really grasp for knowledge creation. To reiterate, these admissions contradict the intentions he stated and the results he hoped to achieve, and stranger yet are in direct opposition to the foundations of empiricism. Locke originally argued the boundary for human knowledge was what could be perceived/sensed, thus experienced, and then he quickly admitted things into the mix that couldn't be experienced proper (and made them explanations or causes of things). Given Locke was a very intelligent man it really does make one ask: what the heck is going on here?

---

[2] John Locke, *Essay Concerning Human Understanding*, accessed 7 January 2014, http://www.earlymoderntexts.com/pdfs/locke1690book1.pdf, pg 1.
[3] Locke, pg. 1.
[4] Locke, pg. 1.

Another fine example is George Berkeley, the Irish Immaterialist and Bishop of Cloyne. In the introduction to *The Principles of Human Knowledge*, he writes: "... as soon as we depart from sense and instinct to follow the light of a higher principle – i.e., to reason, meditate, and reflect on the nature of things – a thousand doubts spring up in our minds concerning things that we previously seemed to understand fully."[5] His purpose then is to attempt to discover the underlying sources of our doubtfulness, uncertainty, and the state of contradiction that so many philosophers have fallen into: is it natural weakness, misuse of our faculties?; Or is it unclear language?; or bad reason? Thus, this investigation must involve, "a strict inquiry into the first principles of human knowledge, to sift and examine them on all sides..."[6] and even at this early point Berkeley thinks false principles might be to blame rather than our faculties or abilities. Specifically, he cites language and the use of abstract ideas as problems (e.g., substance, unity). Berkeley criticizes those materialist philosophers before him; those who believed in the idea that material substance/objects exist even when not perceived by anyone. He outright rejects the idea of unperceived things existing in the world. Philosophically this makes him an idealist and an immaterialist. Further, he writes, "Unless we take care to clear the first principles of knowledge from being burdened and deluded by words, we can reason from them forever without achieving anything; we can draw consequences from consequences and never be the wiser."[7] Once again we have a statement about the need to 'clean house' in philosophy.

But what he ends up arguing seems to defeat his own comments in the introduction about language: Berkeley ends up tweaking and somewhat abusing the meaning of 'existence' so that it becomes intimately tied to perception, in fact relying on perception of people or God to obtain whatsoever. He posits that no things exist independently of minds – his infamous motto "to exist is to be perceived."[8] Existence is now no longer the common sense, simple idea of something outside ourselves 'being there', it now means that this something is there because it is perceived to be present by a mind (ours, and if all else fails God's): "The table that I am writing on *exists*, that is, I see and feel it; and if I were out of my study I would still say that it existed, meaning that if I were in my study I would perceive it, or that

---

[5] George Berkelely, *The Principles of Human Knowledge*, accessed 7 January 2014, http://www.earlymoderntexts.com/pdfs/berkeley1710.pdf, pg. 1.
[6] Berkeley, pg. 1.
[7] Berkeley, pg. 10.
[8] Berkeley, pg. 11.

some other spirit actually does perceive it .... They couldn't possibly exist out of the minds or thinking things that perceive them."[9] Existence, to be spoken about meaningfully amongst persons, is rather subjective (i.e., we can talk about the tree in the yard as existing because we both see it) and no longer objective (i.e., we cannot talk about other planets or species no one has experienced, or even theoretical physics): he states that it is an outright contradiction to say that there are things that exist independent of us and unperceived.[10]

With his rejection of materialism, he's made all perceptible qualities (i.e., colour, extension, shape, motion, etc.) as only ideas in the mind, not outside it in the thing or as the product of a sensory union between mind and object, and thus he leaves us with really no explanation of what is the first moment of perception like (how does it all start before we get accustomed to things). He criticized others before him for not describing how the process of perception works, how objects outside of myself create ideas or impressions inside my mind, but he has left us in no better state since he too has failed to explain how perception actually works. Perception is an intentional relationship, meaning that it's perception 'of' something, and Berkeley has really manipulated what this 'of' is. In arguing against materialism and yet not wanting to say that when I close my eyes everything is annihilated, he has left us in a position where the process of perception is rather confused, one-sided, and against common sense, but more importantly discussing the existence of something is rather convoluted (like a bad language game). Which is ironic because he stated in his introduction that he wished to clean out the verbal controversies of philosophy, the very weeds that hinder the growth of true and sound knowledge.[11] Regardless of contradictions, Berkeley's philosophical position on perception has placed the boundary of human knowledge at the eye sockets. What? I won't even get into the discussions of how God, who is described like a great voyeur in the sky. But, I ask the same question again, what the heck is going on?

And last but not least, there is David Hume, the Scottish Skeptic and Empiricist. He rightly called shenanigans on much of philosophy dealing with metaphysics and epistemology, and he cast doubt on things like our ideas of necessary connection, the self, power, the existence of God, even the accuracy of our own experience (our mind seems to have little command

---

[9] Berkeley, pg. 11.
[10] Berkeley, pg. 12.
[11] Berkeley, pg. 9.

over itself). His psychological investigations revealed that our minds seemed to prefer and possess lots of habits, and the connections amongst our ideas could be boiled down to resemblance, contiguity, and cause and effect.[12] Unlike Locke and Berkeley, Hume strictly limited human knowledge to sense-experience. In doing such, he argued that metaphysics couldn't be a science (things like God, freedom, and immortality were outside our knowledge scope; more like beliefs or opinions) and he cast a lot of doubt on human ability to actually acquire valid and truthful knowledge about the world: what we really know pales in comparison to what we think we know or can possibly know. The inductive reasoning we use every day is practical and helps us survive, but it's foundationless and based on past experience more than truth or objectivity according to Hume. Truth may be had in mathematics and in logic since they could be proved by demonstration and reliably so, but outside in the world of mankind there was only induction, and causal reasoning. There was no guarantee that the sun would rise up tomorrow, or that I wouldn't wake up as an insect like Gregor Samsa did in Franz Kafka's *The Metamorphosis*. All I had to go with for expectations of tomorrow is what I experienced today and yesterday, and that isn't sound, certain reasoning.

But in doing this, he essentially threw out the baby with the bathwater. He cast so much doubt on human cognition and knowledge acquisition that philosophy seemed fruitless and foolish, one could even say natural science and theoretical physics were too, and even attempting to understand the world around us seemed utterly futile. As much as I admire Hume for his militant cleaning of the philosophical closet, it feels like too much has been pitched out – it's unsettling in barrenness and it is even hard to not become fatalistic. Once again, what the heck is going on?

I could name others and go on but I believe these three suffice for making my point. As I mentioned earlier, there is a pattern here. Each speaks of how others before him went wrong and lays out some ideas or a plan as to how to fix this so truth and certainty can be had, and then when that crucial moment of discussing what we can actually know about the world around us (that much sought after boundary of human knowledge) they do everything they can to avoid it and retreat: God or substance become used as the band-aid explanation for mysteries of existence, or it is argued that somehow our natural mental abilities/capacities are lacking or we misapplied them, or we

---

[12] David Hume, *Enquiry Concerning Human Understanding*, accessed 7 January 2014, http://www.earlymoderntexts.com/pdfs/hume1748.pdf

use bad language and empty concepts, or there is the grand denial that we can have any knowledge of reality at all and so we should give up. Philosophers like these seem to go to a lot of trouble to avoid something, and this something is what Camus calls the absurd. What I call the second truth of philosophy.

The absurd, for Camus, has two sources: the universe and death[13]. The first is the notion that absurdity lies in the chaos and irrationality of the universe, a universe that is not oriented toward our concerns but is rather benignly indifferent to our aspirations and endeavors. Twists of fate, strange patterns of behavior, and unpredictable events are all glimpses of the absurd. These also serve as evidence that there is no God, predetermined divine design or absolute purpose present in the universe. The universe is totally silent when we ask questions and demand answers.[14] As fellow existentialist Sartre would say, everything exists for no reason at all, an existence without necessity and without definition. To exist is simply *to be there*.

So, why do philosophers like Locke, Berkeley and Hume want to avoid this or seem to do their best to dance around it? Because it's very unsettling; recognizing and contemplating the absurdity present in the universe, realizing the crucial role it plays in the boundary of human knowledge, creates a tension that is extreme and at times difficult to accept. It can feel unnerving, terrifying, frustrating, or paralyzing; it enhances other existential moods like anguish (feeling the heaviness of freedom, man is alone with no excuse) and abandonment (hand in hand with anguish; God does not exist, so we ourselves decide our own being and there is nothing to tell you how you ought to be or what to do). The absurd cannot be settled; it will not be overcome or ignored. It demands the dropping of illusions, like the idea that man's ability to reason makes him able to conquer the world and be the master over Mother Nature, or the idea that God created this world for us

---

[13] Albert Camus, *The Myth of Sisyphus and Other Essays*. Trans. Justin O'Brien (New York: Vintage International, 1991), pgs. 51-65. Camus also tells us that death is a source of absurdity, since it negates any aspirations and achievements; it destroys any meaning we have created and importance we give to things, and this means that all human desires, goals, and achievements are irrational. Every single person on this earth knows that they will die at some point, and in the face of this fact they continue to spend every day creating meaning, collecting things, aspiring, and desiring, and for Camus that is absurdity in its clearest form. Death is the great equalizer; everyone from Charles Manson, to the Pope, to President Obama, to the Dalai Lama will come to the same end—nothingness. Living each day to the fullest and creating meaning for your self is a revolt against death and the extinction it brings.
[14] Camus, pgs. 51-53.

and has a big plan we all necessarily follow. If philosophers want to know the nature of reality, and have a real understanding of what we know about this world we are thrown into, then they must recognize the presence (and the reality) of the absurd – they must see that there will be things we cannot know and we must live with that tension, that mystery. Don't make stuff up to reconcile the unknowns of the absurd, don't ignore it, and don't run away from it. So, what should a philosopher do? For one thing, be like Kant and call it out.

In his magnum opus *The Critique of Pure Reason*, Kant begins like so many others: talking about the state of things in philosophy (metaphysics and epistemology), and how he thinks he has a better answer to the question of the limits of human knowledge (and if metaphysics can be a science).[15] In short, Kant, taking cues from Hume's skeptical comments, sought to show that a merger between Rationalism and Empiricism was the best road for philosophy. He sought to explain how coming to an understanding of how the external world affects our senses and how our mind shapes the sensory content it receives could help clarify what we can know. Most importantly, investigating in this way could go a long way to proving if metaphysics, namely, enquiries into things that are beyond tangible experience like God, freedom, the soul, and immortality, could be the objects of science at all. In doing this, he did something unlike his predecessors; he accepted the presence of the absurd and gave it a name – Noumena.

One of the most significant and controversial notions Kant introduced is the distinction between phenomena and noumena: the conception of a gap between how something appears to a person and how it is in-itself, or to put it another way, how the mind assembles the cognition of an object from the sense data provided could differ from how the object actually is in the world.[16] For example, Kant thought that objects must be perceived in space and time, and that space and time are fundamental for experience. Hence, space and time are not only psychologically prior, but also logically prior to experience. According to Kant, humans have pure forms of space and time hardwired in their minds, in the Faculty of Sensibility, and so all sensory

---

[15] Immanuel Kant, *The Critique of Pure Reason*. Trans. Werner S. Pluhar (Indianapolis: Hackett Publishing Company, 1993), B295-315; A 235-260, pgs. 303-322. For Kant, metaphysics cannot be a science because what metaphysics seeks to discover and describe cannot be experienced with our senses. Thus, we cannot ever *know* in the strictest sense the true nature of things like God, freedom, the soul, and immortality. However, he does think that our reason gives us sufficient evidence to believe in all three.

[16] Kant, A34–49; B50–73, pgs. 88–104.

stimuli are processed through them. What this means, in the simplest of terms, is that when experience begins, the first intuitions consist of (1) there are things outside of myself (a primal distinction between me and not me; my feeling of embodiment against the world), and (2) that I can feel my conscious mind process data sequentially (I feel my mind being aware in a series of time rather than as some chaotic mass). The extension of this notion is that Kant recognized that objects themselves do not necessarily exist in space and in time the identical way we perceive them, or at all. He also acknowledges that it is highly possible that things in the world exist in dimensions we cannot perceive, have colors our eyes cannot distinguish, are made of textures our touch cannot sense, and have tastes for which we have no receptors. Kant's point is that we have to accept that our experience of the world is limited to the capacities we have. We have to admit that objects may have more intrinsic features than we can perceive and these are aspects we simply cannot know. For Kant, the noumena will never be seen or understood, no matter the amount of training in philosophy you have or how hard you analyze all the phenomena of a thing. It's simply an issue of cognitive and biological limitations. This is the limit of human knowledge. Kant's noumena, I would argue, is the first true recognition of the absurd (in philosophy).

The beauty of this distinction is that it is largely epistemological in nature; it speaks to what we can know using the faculties we possess, and where the limits of our knowledge are. However, it does have ontological consequences in that objects themselves retain the possibility of having qualities we cannot sense or know; the world can have its mysteries and chaos, and that's fine. Because of the way we are biologically and psychologically constructed and have evolved, we cannot or may not ever be able to know everything about the world around us. Not every question has an answer; not every mystery can be solved. Unlike Locke and Berkeley, Kant doesn't rely on substance or God to address the absurd, nor does he become the skeptic and deny much of our knowledge like Hume. The absurd for him is a fact of life; see it, understand it, live with it, and move on. Noumena, like Camus's notion of the absurd, are silent, indifferent, impenetrable aspects of the universe that defeat every attempt we make to understand them. They may be the underlying sources of phenomena, but that doesn't imply they are knowable, predictable, or logical.

Kant's distinction caught a lot of attention and he endured a lot of criticism for it. Most of his critics were Empiricists (one of his main critics, Feder, took a position closer to Locke). Most felt Kant's phenomena-noumena distinction reinstated a Platonic or dualistic framework, where people mentally construct their own reality, they said he was just another Berkeley Idealist.[17] What this implied was that people had no ability to have any real, objective knowledge of the world around them whatsoever– everyone had their own subjective versions of knowledge, thus reality.[18] For some critics, the difference between the phenomenal and the noumenal worlds was so vast; it was like having two different plains of reality on earth. They felt this was damaging to science as much as philosophy. They didn't agree with our knowledge being of appearances only, they didn't like being told they had no access to things themselves, which they felt was necessary to avoid idealism and have viable knowledge of the world: they basically screamed out, "How can we live in a world in which we cannot know anything?" In short, these Empiricist critics of Kant couldn't deal with the presence of the absurd and the unsettling tension it brings. They would do anything to avoid it and make it go away.

As I mentioned earlier, death is the second source of absurdity for Camus. Death negates any and all human aspirations and achievements; it destroys any meaning we have created and importance we give to things, and this means that all human desires, goals, and achievements are irrational. Every single person on this earth knows that they will die at some point, we cannot control when death will come, and in the face of this fact they continue to spend every day creating meaning, collecting things, aspiring, and desiring, and for Camus that is absurdity in its clearest form. Death is the great

---

[17] Brigitte Sasson, *Kant's Early Critics: The Empiricist Critique of the Theoretical Philosophy* (Cambridge: Cambridge University Press, 2007).

[18] Kant's theory was highly and hotly debated because other philosophers (mainly empiricists) felt that Kant was telling them that we didn't have access to reality inasmuch as he asserts that noumena affect our senses but remain completely out of our reach. Some even suggested that noumena occupy a different world. They saw Kant as saying that noumena existed but that we couldn't know they did, which is a complete contradiction and quite ridiculous sounding. They also did not like the idea of faculties or intuitions being innate in the mind, that dreadful word 'a priori'; because empiricists, like John Locke, saw the mind as a blank slate imprinted upon and shaped by experience. For Kant, much of what shapes experience, enables experience to happen at all and the way we have it, some things like faculties, pure intuitions, pure concepts, etc. must be logically and necessarily in the mind prior to experience. These a priori entities in the mind are, however, meaningless without the data provided to them by experience; without sensory information they have nothing to work with, nothing to process, nothing to do. Cognition, then, is a beautiful handshake between the external world and the internal workings of the mind – a merger between the empiricist and rationalist views – at least on the epistemological side of things. Because cognition can only be of experiential things, knowledge bears the same boundary: we can only *know* something if we can empirically experience it (i.e., if sensory data is provided to our mind to process).

equalizer; everyone from Charles Manson, to the Pope, to President Obama, to the Dalai Lama will come to the same end—nothingness. However, he does not advocate despairing over this or committing suicide; both are a denial of freedom, responsibility and of defining one's essence, and moreover suicide is an acceptance at its extreme and a reconciling of the absurd. In a section titled 'Absurd freedom,' Camus writes:

> Living an experience, a particular fate, is accepting it fully. Now, no one will live this fate, knowing it to be absurd, unless he does everything to keep before him that absurd brought to light by consciousness. Negating one of the terms of the opposition on which he lives amounts to escaping it. To abolish conscious revolt is to elude the problem. The theme of permanent revolution is thus carried into individual experience. Living is keeping the absurd alive. Keeping it alive is, above all, contemplating it... One of the only coherent philosophical positions is thus revolt. It is a constant confrontation between man and his own obscurity.[19]

The response Camus proposes is one of rebellion – revolt gives life its value.[20] Go down kicking and screaming; make your life so meaningful it is as if to stick the finger to death (just as Sisyphus did to the gods as he rolled the boulder daily – a strong sign of, "you cannot defeat my will"). He says, "it is essential to die unreconciled and not of one's free will ... The absurd man can only drain everything to the bitter end, and deplete himself. The absurd is his extreme tension, which he maintains constantly by solitary effort, for he knows that in that consciousness and in that day-to-day revolt he gives proof to his only truth, which is defiance."[21] I think this response offered by Camus is an excellent one for philosophers as well, in the situation of realizing the presence of the absurd in the universe.

Philosophers need to be ever aware of the role absurdity plays in the universe at large and in particular concerning the boundary of human knowledge: Like the absurd man Camus describes in his *The Myth of Sisyphus*, philosophers need to acknowledge the absurd is present, live that tension, and not let it stop them from creating work that brings meaning and truth to their lives and that of others. However, this doesn't mean creating ad hoc solutions, strange illusions or language games, since to do such things is an avoidance of the absurd and a denial of one's freedom and project. It

---

[19] Camus, pgs. 53-54.
[20] Camus, pg. 55.
[21] Camus, pg. 55.

means being like Kant – seeing it, calling it out, and then doing what can in the face of it (having philosophy, not committing suicide or running away).

Philosophers are also affected physically by death just like everyone else: it extinguishes all the meaning they've created, all the ideas they've thought up and contemplated, and any importance given to affiliations, figures or arguments. The only way philosophers can 'beat death' is to become immortal through their printed works. And let's face it, I think most would prefer to be remembered for brilliance and depth of truth rather than their mistakes and foolishness. Confronting the absurd and philosophizing in the face of it is one way to obtain the former and avoid the latter.

Works Cited

Berkeley, George. *The Principles of Human Knowledge.* Early Modern Texts. Web. 11 April 2014.

Camus, Albert. *The Myth of Sisyphus and Other Essays.* Trans. Justin O'Brien. New York: Vintage International, 1991.

Descartes, René. *Meditations On First Philosophy.* Early Modern Texts. Web. 11 April 2014.

Hume, David. *Enquiry Concerning Human Understanding.* Early Modern Texts. Web. 11 April 2014.

Locke, John. *Essay Concerning Human Understanding.* Early Modern Texts. Web. 11 April 2014.

Kant, Immanuel. *The Critique of Pure Reason.* Trans. Werner S. Pluhar. Indianapolis: Hackett Publishing Company, 1993.

Sasson, Brigitte. *Kant's Early Critics: The Empiricist Critique of the Theoretical Philosophy.* Cambridge: Cambridge University Press, 2007.

Lessons in Contrast from *The Fall*: From Lucidity to Opacity

by Eric B. Berg

In this paper I will outline and illuminate a stark difference in topography in Albert Camus's work; primarily focusing on the sharp difference between the topography in *The Fall* and most, if not all, other works by Camus. I will argue Camus uses topography in *The Fall* to demonstrate opacity as opposed to lucidity. The topography in the narrative of *The Fall* delivers a sense of confusion to the reader that is intentional, it illuminates our place in nature when we try and force meaning on nature, thus bringing his concept of the absurd to the reader's attention.

The Fall is one of Camus's most challenging works with allusions to his own personal life littered throughout the work, published after a literary dry-spell, the strong use of Christian theological language, and the challenge of tying the early themes to this work, make the novella a complex piece for scholars of his work. Many have seen the character of Jean-Baptiste Clamence as a self-mocking portrait painted by Camus of himself at this time. *The Fall* grew from a short story *L'Exil et le Royaume* and it appears to have been written quickly, started in the fall of 1955 and finished by March of 1956. The text was anxiously received by fans and critics alike, flamed the desire for a conversion to Christianity by some, and refreshed his reputation among most on an international level.

General topography in *The Fall*.

Many readers, when reading through Camus's works, are struck by the fact that *The Fall* does not take place in the Mediterranean. Some readers are happy with a change of topography, others miss the sun and light of the Mediterranean. Either way, the change is notable for such an intentional author; this change of location in *The Fall* is worth a closer look by my view.

The word "topography" itself is a fantastic word for this study; it comes from the Greek *topos* "place" and *graphos* "to write". To write about a place; it is a fitting word to use as a lens to study the works of Camus. The field of topography studies the surface details of a place, the altitude, vegetative, other physical features, and also considers the "artificial" or human engineered changes to a place. Camus attacks his writing with a terrific eye for place using this definition of topography. The natural environment is very prominent in his work, as are the human additions and alterations to each place. Even in the very early works like his adaptation of the play *La Temps du mépris* in 1935 when stage design became very important for the young Camus, thus incorporating topography intentionally into his works of theater and continued this attention to topography into his essays and novels. He wanted the play to have a physical impact on the patron, as the topography does to his readers in his later works. This early attention to topography is never forgotten and comes to maturity in *The Fall* as a contrast to the other works. Place is very important in his work, most readers of Camus come away from each work with a very clear sense of the "place" where the narrative happened. In *The Stranger* we are treated to a wonderful North African urban and beach place, in *The Plague*, a clear picture of Oran in 194_, and in *The Fall*, a dark, wet, Amsterdam. He narrows the topography of his work to particular settings. Think of Meursault's apartment in *The Stranger* (taken from memories of his youth in Algiers) describe for the reader in detail, and for this paper on *The Fall*, recall the bar named Mexico City in Amsterdam. Camus paints it well: "...enthroned at Mexico City, above the drunks and pimps."[1]

The Fall takes place in Amsterdam, and by contrast (considering just the novels or novellas) *The Plague* takes place in Oran, Algeria, and *The Stranger* also takes place in Algeria. Most of his short stories and essays take place on the Mediterranean, and of these short stories, the stories that are most dependent on place, like *Nuptials at Tipasa* and *Summer*, the place is described in great detail and most are set in North Africa. Camus writes in *Nuptials at Tipasa*, " In the spring Tipasa is inhabited by the gods and the gods speak in the sun and the scent of absinthe leaves in the silver armor of the sea, in the raw blue sky..."[2] There are many differences in the topography between North Africa and Amsterdam and these are the differences I wish to explore for their value to his literary corpus.

---

[1] Albert Camus, *The Fall* (New York: Vintage, 1991), 129.
[2] Albert Camus, *Lyrical and Critical Essays* (New York: Vintage, 1968), 65.

Amsterdam is located in Western Europe as opposed to North Africa, it sits on the Atlantic proper as opposed to the Mediterranean, it is built on a series of canals as opposed to a port on a beach or rising above the sea, it is portrayed by Camus as dark as opposed to the brilliant light of the Mediterranean. The weather is a variety of rain, fog, and even snow in the end, as opposed to heat and light. Most of the scenes in *The Fall* take place at night as opposed to the sunlight of day in the rest of the works, and finally, many of the scenes take place in a bar with an intentionally confusing name, as opposed to wandering the streets of a city or outside. Furthermore, Camus bring the reader's attention to the low physical position of Amsterdam in *The Fall* and this contrasts with the Mediterranean coast, especially Algiers, where the cliffs and the inhabitants of these cliffs rise and soar above the sea. Amsterdam sits at an average altitude of one meter above sea level, most of the city's inhabitants live below sea level; Oran for instance, sits at 101 meters above and Algiers rises to a maximum of 424 meters above sea level. Towards the end of *The Fall*, Camus takes the opportunity to really describe the macro-feature of Amsterdam: it is flat. Camus writes of the water surrounding Amsterdam: "On this flat monotonous, interminable water whose limits are indistinguishable from those of the land?"[3] He contrasts this strongly with the Mediterranean where geographical features stick out so there is "no confusion possible".[4] I argue that the topography of *The Fall* takes on opacity and the Mediterranean takes on lucidity: not meaning, but an openness to the world. Amsterdam does the opposite, it closes off the opportunity for lucidity and represents the condition of modern humans.

Camus has a habit of using the weather as a natural element to add emphasis to a scene, to add drama to a point delivered, and uses it as a literary device to call attention to a shift in position or course of a narrative. For example, the sermons in *The Plague* are sharply illuminated by the weather conditions when they are delivered. When Father Panloux delivers each sermon in *The Plague*, Camus frames the sermon with intense weather conditions. For the second sermon, the thunderstorm actually dominates and starts to take over. For more on this particular use of weather in Camus see my paper "Panloux's Turn: An Analysis of the Sermons in *The Plague*", published in *The Journal of Camus Studies*.

---

[3] Camus, *The Fall*, 108-9.
[4] Ibid., 97.

In *The Fall*, Camus uses the weather to set a mood over the narrative that contributes to the philosophical argument he is creating in the narrative. The argument illuminates the absurd by way of topography; the confusion and resulting inability (for both the characters, and more importantly the reader) to become lucid in *The Fall*. The whole book is dark: most scenes take place at night or in a dark bar, the city is draped in fog, rain, and snow. The main character is very dark in many respects. Jean Baptiste has a confusing name with heavy Christian references that are never made clear, he is a moral mess, a social pariah, a bigot, a racist, an elitist, duplicitous, and in the end we are never quite sure if he is speaking to someone else or just wandering the city, alone and crazy. Darkness, fog, and rain all contribute to opacity. As a reader our perspective is limited to the immediate and our surroundings are shrouded in darkness and various weather conditions. Even the narration of *The Fall* limits our perspective, we can never be sure who is actually in the conversation. By contrast, some of the most moving passages of his other works take place in brilliant sunlight and contribute to lucidity in the characters. For example in *Nuptials at Tipasa* Camus writes, " ...I am fulfilling a truth which is the sun's..."[5] In the play *The Misunderstand* (or *Cross-Purposes*) from 1944, Camus uses the character Martha to speak frankly about Europe, Martha says "I, too, am tired, tired to death of these narrow horizons".[6] Giving the audience and readers of the paly a perspective on the horizon of Europe mirrored in *The Fall*. Martha continues while speaking to her mother with her contrast between Europe and the Mediterranean, "...it was you who brought me into the world in a land of clouds and mist, instead of a land of sunshine"[7] The vision is not in terms of a static dichotomy but a spectrum of opacity to lucidity and returning to opacity. He has the ability to move sunlight to the other end of the spectrum and cause blindness and opacity (if you will) by too much illumination (killing scene in *The Stranger*) By contrast, the narration in text like *The Stranger* is clear and the reader need not struggle with the Kierkegaardian tricks employed in *The Fall*. Either way, Camus is working with light, perspective, and horizon to give the characters and the reader lucidity or opacity in their view of the world and the situation at hand. The weather, horizon elevation, and night and day are wonderful tools to use in the novel as they are elements that fit into the category of facticity, we cannot change them, they come to us as an external factor. Despite our attempts to control or rid them, they are ever-present and determine our field of vision, the more we fight, the harder the realization that they are ever-present and stand

---

[5] Camus, *Lyrical and Critical Essays*, 69.
[6] Albert Camus, *Caligula and 3 Other Plays*, (New York: Vintage, 1968), 99.
[7] Ibid.

outside our control. The idea of the absurd for Camus comes to the forefront for the reader.

As early as page ten in the O'Brien translation of *The Fall* fog sets in on Amsterdam and Jean-Baptiste begins his topography laden narrative about where he lives. Jean-Baptiste claims to live in the Jewish Quarter of the city, or now, the "old Jewish Quarter" as the Nazi atrocities have changed the physical and ethnic makeup of the city. Jean-Baptiste lives in a very sad part of the city, the site of "one of the greatest crimes against humanity".[8] The human marks made on the topography are very hard to miss, yet come to us by negation. The city has absconded with something, there is evidence and memory of the Jewish Quarter, yet it is gone. The topography (recalling the all-inclusive definition I proposed) is bleak, the human marks on this section of the city are tragic, morally corrupt, and exist as a ghost; very dark. The human changes made on the city are dramatic and clear, yet there is a need to forget and a desire to shift blame to others. This section of the city lives with a tragic past, as does Jean-Baptiste, and the effort to forget is futile mirroring the absconded art in Mexico City. Camus ends this narrative with the news that it has rained the last few days.

In a macro-description of Amsterdam, he describes "these people"[9] as being "hemmed in by fog, cold lands, and steaming sea."[10] He paints a claustrophobic scene for the city of Amsterdam. By contrast, the cities of North Africa and the topography of those cities are not as claustrophobic and seem more open. In *Nuptials at Tipasa* he paints a picture of an Algerian village: "The village we pass through to get there already opens on the bay. We enter a blue and yellow world..."[11] And, in *The Misunderstanding* Martha speaks of Europe: "Too many bleak years have passed over this little spot of Central Europe, and they've drained all warmth out of this house."[12] and desires to live in "a land of endless sunshine beside the sea."[13] concluding that "This Europe of yours is so sad.".[14] The tight physical setting of Amsterdam limits the vision of people living in Amsterdam and parallels nicely with the limited vision the characters have, and most importantly, the limited vision of the reader. The

---

[8] Camus, *The Fall*, 11.
[9] Ibid.,12.
[10] Ibid.
[11] Camus, *Lyrical and Critical Essays*, 65.
[12] Camus, *Caligula and 3 Other Plays*, 96.
[13] Ibid., 84.
[14] Ibid.

fog, unnaturally low altitude, and darkness, are topographical literary tools to limit the perspective of people in Amsterdam, they cannot get up and out into the sun, into an elevated position to see the horizon and have clarity. The characters in *The Fall* suffer from this, Jean-Baptiste's inherited and twisted morality, his false sense of superiority, his status as an alien in the city limit him. And, most interestingly, the confusion over who exactly Jean-Baptiste is talking to in *The Fall*, creates a confusing and very limited perspective for the reader. Camus writes: "Everything horizontal, no relief; space is colorless, and life is dead."[15] It sees clear from an epigraph attached to an early edition of *The Fall* that the character of Jean-Baptiste is a composite of his generation, and thus a carefully and intentionally constructed character to deliver the impression of opacity in the face of the absurd to the reader. Lottman writes; "Camus quotes Lermontov about that novel':...indeed a portrait, but not of that man: it is the assembling of the defects of our generation in all the fullness of their development.'"[16]

Camus's early study of the works of Søren Kierkegaard are present here, especially Kierkegaard's (actually Vigilius Haufniensis) *The Concept of Anxiety*. In *The Concept of Anxiety* Kierkegaard attempts to physically demonstrate to the reader the concept of anxiety as opposed to fear. He makes the language (originally in Danish but the English version does the trick as well) so spiraling and confusing, yet on a track to the point of the distinction between fear and anxiety that the reader can occasionally follow the argument and can become a bit sea-sick when reading *The Concept of Anxiety* by Kierkegaard. I argue that Camus effectively employs a similar literary device in *The Fall* limiting the reader's perspective and literally demonstrating opacity.

After the discussion of the woman's suicide in Paris in *The Fall*, the weather is described as "hard to breathe, air is heavy."[17] The psychological claustrophobia is setting in on the reader; the tremendous guilt that is figuratively squeezing Jean-Baptiste is mirrored by the weather. "Heavy" air, haunted by the suicide, confused by the voices of children laughing (he does not know who is talking to him, we do not know who he is talking to), driven to Amsterdam by this; the over-the-top duplicity of Jean-Baptiste makes the condition of the reader opaque. This literary device surprisingly does not drive readers away, it does engage them with the author more. The

---

[15] Camus, *The Fall*, 72.
[16] Herbert Lottman, *Albert Camus*, (Garden City: Doubleday, 1969), 591.
[17] Camus, *The Fall*, 43.

"heavy" air presses in during this scene, the character being haunted by an event in the past that is ever present and intentionally confuses the timeline. The "ghosts" of children laughing lends a fantasy element to throw the reader off, and the frustrating duplicity of Jean-Baptiste does not allow the reader a clear view of who we are dealing with. We cannot, and should not trust Jean-Baptiste. He openly admits that he has "lost that lucidity to which my friends used to enjoy paying respects."[18] The inability to trust him lends instability to the reader's position and works to cloud our vision. It seems he moved to Amsterdam to hide and yet simultaneously amplify his suffering, to judge others and to be judged, his character has the subtle ability to draw in each reader and indicts them with similar guilt, as this I believe was Camus's intent.

Camus describes the canals of Amsterdam as "stagnant waters, the smell of dead leaves".[19] Think back to the recent scene of the woman plunging to her death in the Seine in Paris (Pg. 39 in the O'Brien) By contrast, the water of the Mediterranean is so alive and brilliant full of sea smell and not death. In *Nuptials at Tipasa*, Camus describes the Mediterranean: " The hills were framed with trees, and beyond them stretched a band of sea on which the sky, like a sail becalmed, rested in all its tenderness. I felt a strange joy in my heart..."[20] In *The Misunderstanding* Martha speaks of the waters of the Mediterranean: "In that southern land, guarded by the sea, to which one can escape, where one can breathe freely, press one's body to another's' body, roll in the waves..."[21] The connection between the dead woman in the Seine in Paris and the smell of the canals of Amsterdam is unmistakable. Whereas the Mediterranean gives rise to the prototypical free human in touch with nature and herself, Amsterdam is a low point, the settling of humans into a stagnant pool of their own making and polluted by their choices. The quartering off the Jewish Ghetto and the subsequent moving of the Jewish population to concentration camps give a stench to Amsterdam and European humanity of the 20th century, like Amsterdam, we are so confused we allow things like Auschwitz to happen.

The city of Amsterdam imposes itself on nature, recapturing land from the sea and controlling the water through canals. Amsterdam makes no effort to fit in with the natural environment; it forces its will on nature. It is an

---

[18] Ibid., 73.
[19] Ibid., 43.
[20] Camus, *Lyrical and Critical Essays*, 71.
[21] Camus, *Caligula and 3 Other Plays*, 125.

artificial construction as opposed to an ancient city that hangs on a hill above the sea. Camus writes in *The Fall*: "...the Zuider Zee is a dead sea...With its flat shores, lost in fog, there's no saying where it begins or ends."[22] By sharp contrast he writes of the Mediterranean: " In the Greek archipelago I had the contrary feelings...No confusion possible; in the sharp light everything was a landmark."[23] This description of Amsterdam, and by contrast, the Greek coast is particularly telling for my argument as he deliberately contrasts the two using topography and the result is a contrast between clear vision (lucidity) and being lost in a fog (opacity). In *The Wind at Djemila* Camus speaks of Mediterranean lucidity connected to topography. He writes, "Between the columns with their now lengthening shadows anxieties dissolve into the air like wounded birds. And in their place came an arid lucidity.[24]

Clearly, Amsterdam is linked to hell in Dante, he writes: " ...a capital of waters, and fogs, girdled by canals, particularly crowded, and visited by men from all corners of the earth."[25] and "Have you noticed that Amsterdam's concentric canals resemble the circles of hell?"[26] The use of concentric circles and humans wandering around these circles, often drunk, in search of vices of all sorts brings a clear mood and ethos to the setting of the novel. Camus remarked that Amsterdam was "...ugly, and to be there was punishment: appropriate surroundings for his judge penitent."[27] The city itself is painted as dark and wet: "damp air...at this extremity of Europe"[28], bathed in artificial neon light, with a great mix of people, some local and some aliens, wishing to be anonymous, as they wander around the city. Amsterdam is painted by Camus's pen as a dark, wet, confusing, city with a mixed temporary population of Europeans. Language barriers abound as " He speaks nothing but Dutch"[29] and sometimes for no good reason as "he merely grunts."[30] Social and economic barriers are enforced as the bartender is referred to as a "worthy ape"[31] in the city allowing for more miscommunication. Ethnic barriers are reinforced by way of a tradition of slavery in Amsterdam; "the house belonged to a slave dealer."[32] All of these

---

[22] Camus, *The Fall*, 97.
[23] Ibid.
[24] Camus, *Lyrical and Critical Essays*, 76.
[25] Camus, *The Fall*, 138.
[26] Ibid., 14.
[27] Lottman, Albert Camus, 592.
[28] Camus, The Fall, 144.
[29] Ibid., 3.
[30] Ibid., 4.
[31] Ibid., 3.

artificial barriers imposed by humans add to confusion, lack of communication and understanding among the population, and leads to opacity for the population and for the reader. Language separates, social and economic barriers keep people apart, ethnic barriers abound, sailors add a transient ethos to the city, and the ex-pat community adds another level of transitory population and a feeling of (French in this case) superiority. A city that has imposed its will on nature and has a sad and divided recent past and present. The Arab/French division is clearly a strong theme in Camus's Mediterranean works, but, by my view, lends itself to his strong political feelings and lays the groundwork for reform in Algeria. The barriers in Amsterdam are similar but multitude and are derived from murky and unclear sources. By contrast, the division exists in Algeria have a common source that is quite clear.

Narrowing the topography to a specific location, *The Fall* opens in a bar called "Mexico City". It is an ironic name that adds to the character of the novel, the city, and region Camus is painting a picture of for the reader. Mexico City is a mixed bag, not European but set in Europe, Not Mexican but named as such, a local bar full of non-local sailors and ex-pats, a bartender that has no language skills, even in Dutch, once adorned by art, but stolen art that is now missing. The bar is described as like a "primeval forest, heavy with threats."[33] It is painted as dark, threating, duplicitous, and odd. It also has the curious distinction of at one time housing a fairly famous and valuable stolen work of Christian art and now has a hollow empty place above the bar. Like Augustine's restless heart, the bar is without its anchor piece. Like the city, it has a past that is recalled *via negative*. Apparently the bar actually existed in the 1950s and in 1954 (Lottman pp. 565-6) Camus took a tour of Amsterdam with a friend and sought out the dark side of the city. Between October 4 and 7 of October Camus visited The Netherlands and wandered the streets of Amsterdam in a cold rain, bringing those impressions to the reader of *The Fall*.

In conclusion; I have argued that Camus uses topography as a literary device to bring the feeling of opacity to the reader via the characters and the setting in *The Fall*. This is in contrast to his other works where there is a tendency to elevate to lucidity in the Mediterranean topography, but I do not argue that that is the central or only theme of the other works. I argue that one primary use by Camus (there are secondary and tertiary uses also) of *The*

---

[32] Ibid., 44.
[33] Ibid., 3.

Fall is one of contrast, to bring absurdity into sharp relief for the reader of Camus in contrast to the other works, using topography as the literary device to do that task. Camus uses the elements listed below to contrast with elements in his other works to bring the reader a better understanding of the concept of the absurd, a central theme in his work. He uses the topography of The Netherlands and Amsterdam in particular to bring the absurd into sharp contrast by way of opacity in *The Fall* and moments of lucidity in the other works.

The Fall	**Other works**
Far Western Europe	North Africa
Cold light	Warm light
Atlantic Ocean	Mediterranean Sea
Canals	Beach
Stagnant water	Living water of the Mediterranean
Night	Day
Rain, fog, snow	Heat and light
Abnormally low altitude	Above sea-level altitude
Many inside scenes	Dominated by outdoor scenes
Confusion regarding narrator	Clarity of narration
Flat	Horizon Features
Main character Parisian	Main characters North African
Opacity	**Lucidity**

Works Cited

Camus, Albert. *Caligula and 3 Other Plays*. Trans. Justin O'Brien. New York: Vintage, 1968. Print.

——. *Lyrical and Critical Essays*. Trans. Ellen Conroy Kennedy. New York: Vintage, 1968. Print.

——. *The Fall*. Trans. Justin O'Brien. New York: Vintage International, 1991. Print.

Lottman, Herbert R. *Albert Camus*. Garden City: Doubleday &, 1979. Print.

Accepting the Absurd

by Kurt Blankschaen

A fundamental tenet of Existentialism is the Absurd: the world is without inherent or objective meaning and attempts to create meaning will eventually wash away. Since meaning is a human concept the Absurd is not something found out in the world; it conditions the way we relate to the world. This paper surveys some of the ways Existentialists have responded to the Absurd and assesses the consequences of adopting each view. These responses characterize the Absurd as a constraint to be avoided, evaded, or broken though. Sartre, in his early literary work, provides an unsettling account of how the Absurd disrupts life and examines the fallout of our first encounter with the Absurd. Sartre's gritty representation complements Camus's presentation of the Absurd in *The Myth of Sisyphus* because Camus minimally describes how the Absurd enters into our life. While Sartre's work supplements Camus's discussion of the Absurd, Sartre seems to still conceive of the Absurd as something to be resisted or overcome. Camus proposes, instead, that we simply accept the Absurd as a starting point. Sisyphus, the Absurd hero, acts as a model of someone who has successfully internalized the Absurd.[1]

This essay has three basic parts. The first section surveys some of the more influential Existentialist responses, specifically Heidegger, Nietzsche, and Dostoevsky. I examine how each account confronts and negotiates with the Absurd. Though there is no explicit mention of the Absurd in each thinker's work, the idea is cashed out in other ways. Heidegger uses our anxiety towards death to talk about our way to evade confrontation with meaninglessness. Nietzsche's encouragement to project our values into the world presupposes a canvas of value that we can write over. Dostoevsky's Underground Man rejects mathematical or scientific determinism on the grounds that rational laws invalidate choice; since choice is what enables

[1] I want to thank Theodra Bane for her helpful comments throughout the paper, Travis Timmerman and Kenneth Pike for helping me get started, and the Albert Camus Society for great suggestions regarding the details and direction of the paper.

meaning the Underground Man unflinchingly presents the irrational side of how people make decisions. Camus, however, argues that since the Absurd is simply a fact about the way we interact with the world, there is no need to feel anxious about it, to desire to overcome it, or even a panicked attempt to spite it. Camus's decision to simply accept the Absurd as a fact about our condition empowers people to choose meaning, life, and, if we are like Sisyphus, happiness in an otherwise overwhelming existence.

The second section focuses on the connection between Sartre and Camus. Sartre and Camus are typically linked by being close friends who collaborated on the same ideas and then had a nasty falling out. Unless the work is specifically about their relationship, the scholarly focus is more about how Sartre's later work is drastically different than Camus's. But this narrative overlooks the important ways Sartre's early literary work can help complement the underdeveloped aspects of Camus's position, especially in *The Myth of Sisyphus*. *Nausea* is usually selected to show Absurdist influences in Sartre's work, but his short story *The Wall* helps show the even at this early stage, Sartre has a different conception of Absurdity that foreshadows the later philosophical divergence between Sartre and Camus.

In the final section I develop why Camus makes Sisyphus an Absurd hero. This heroism is not a dramatic display of bravery, but rather a quiet courage to accept his interaction with the world as it is—devoid of inherent meaning—and expect nothing more. Sisyphus retains his heroism each time he retrieves his boulder. Sisyphus is a model for coping beyond the initial impact of the Absurd in our lives; just as Sisyphus never fails to renew his task, so too can we rebuild a meaningful existence. Sisyphus' return to his boulder shows us that we do not need to be anxious about meaninglessness or desire to overcome it. Sisyphus chooses to begin again, because of, not in spite of, the conditions he finds himself in; we too are capable of that choice. Camus cryptically concludes *The Myth of Sisyphus* with "one must imagine Sisyphus as happy." But must I imagine Sisyphus as happy because if the Absurd hero cannot find joy in his task, then what hope do I have? Or, must I imagine Sisyphus as happy because once I accept the world as he does, it is absurd to be sad? Camus's presentation of the Absurd offers a better way forward for people to construct meaning in their lives. Instead of despairing in an Absurd world, Camus's account gives us life, hope, and meaning and does so without any of the costs of the other major Existentialist responses.

Other Existentialist Responses

This section surveys a few of the more influential Existentialist responses to the Absurd. I start with Heidegger, then move to Nietzsche, and conclude with Dostoevsky. In no way do these responses represent the Existentialist canon, but they do provide a fairly good account of three main Existentialist responses to the Absurd: (1) evasion, (2) overcoming, or (3) resistance. While all of these responses are plausible, they come with fairly steep structural costs. I compare the costs of adopting each thinker's view and then explain why Camus's account avoids those problems.

One important way Heidegger differs from Camus is over a concern about metaphysics. For Heidegger, our encounter of the Absurd through anxiety is just the stepping off point into a deeper labyrinth of questioning. Heidegger saw this encounter as not just an opportunity for self-reflection and authenticity, but also as way to dig deeper into what grounds metaphysics. But Camus points out in *The Myth of Sisyphus* that Heidegger does not think that this encounter is particularly enjoyable. Heidegger believes, according to Camus, that "the only reality is 'anxiety' in the whole chain of beings." [2] Our primary motive for acting, as Camus understands Heidegger, is not because we want to create meaning in our lives, but because we are anxious about an encounter with the Absurd.

Anxiety towards death means something special in Heidegger's mouth. Heidegger is careful to point out we are not afraid of death, we are anxious of it. Heidegger makes this distinction because we can only "become afraid in the face of this or that particular being that threatens us in this or that particular respect," [3] but death does not threaten us in the same way a mugger might; Heidegger argues that death threatens everything all at once, but never manifests as any one particular threat. Heidegger concludes that our anxiety, not our fear, towards death tells us something deeper. Since anxiety does not attach to any one specific thing, "the indeterminateness of that in the face of which and for which we become anxious is no mere lack of determination but rather the essential impossibility of determining it." [4] We cannot determine the source of our anxiety not because we are too

---

[2] Albert Camus, *The Myth of Sisyphus and Other Essays*. Trans. Justin O'Brien. New York, NY: Vintage International, 1991), p. 24.
[3] Martin Heidegger, *Basic Writings*, ed. David Krell. New York: NY (Harper Perennial Modern Thought, 2008), p. 100.
[4] Ibid. 100-01.

overwhelmed or confused, but because there is simply no way to determine it; anxiety, as Heidegger understands it, never localizes. Instead, "anxiety reveals the Nothing."[5] But this revealing is not all at once; we do not directly confront Nothing, but only catch glimpses of it when we are in states of anxiety.

Understanding what Heidegger means by "nothing" is a monumental task that I cannot undertake here, but the basic idea is that Nothing is not a thing; it is not just the negation of beings, but, rather, the ground of possibility for any being to exist at all. Even this description is misleading, as Heidegger thinks Nothing is not simply a logical function or a grammatical remark—Nothing is being that is never qualified into any particular existent. A major hurdle we have in even understanding Heidegger is that our thought process has been screwed up to a point where we cannot understand Nothing and so describe it as a grammatical or logical operation. Further, we cannot even understand how to pose questions to inquire about Nothing. A further consequence of this encounter is that once we glimpse Nothing as the ground of Being, that is what makes Being even possible at all, we then understand that there is no rational structure holding the world as it is together. This lack of structure in the world signals that we are not *now* confronted with a world without organizing principles, but that we have *always* been in a world without these principles.

In order to safeguard our encounter with Nothing we continually use everyday activities to evade this confrontation. This evasion "requires that we actively complete the transformation of man into his *Dasein* that every instance of anxiety occasions in us, in order to get a grip on the Nothing revealed there as it makes itself known. At the same time this demands that we expressly hold at a distance those designations of the Nothing that do not result from its claims."[6] This concealment of anxiety is not something that occurs after we have encountered Nothing; Heidegger claims that since Nothing is the ground of being our anxiety is perpetually with us, hidden underneath our *Dasein*.[7] *Dasien* is specifically a human understanding of existence conditioned in the here and now and can range from any ordinary activity to any extraordinary endeavor. Thus, *Dasein* enables people to choose between a living authentically or in conformity. Since there is nothing structuring *Dasein* there is no "correct" way to live; someone living

---

[5] Ibid. 101.
[6] Ibid. 102.
[7] Ibid. 106.

authentically pursues projects or activities not as a way to avoid thinking about death, but because she has transcended that purpose altogether. Living a life in conformity means simply trying to relate to other people and relate to the world as they do. Heidegger thinks that we only really create meaning when we try to live authentically—if *Dasein* is unconstrained then we have a blank canvas. If pressed, Heidegger wouldn't deny that lives in conformity have meaning, but would instead characterize that meaning as pre-chewed, artificial, or inauthentic. But whatever meaning we create is only a temporary solution to mask anxiety, or how we encounter Nothing, which is always with us. If Nothing is as Heidegger describes it, then it may be the ground of being, but if Nothing is only possibility, then it is not anything in actuality and if it is not actually anything, there it cannot have meaning in the relevant sense.[8]

One cost of Heidegger's position is the perpetual anxiety we have in negotiating with the Absurd. For Heidegger anxiety or angst is the perhaps the only sensible reaction to discovering that there is no, and never was an, overarching rational principle or justification for existence. Looking past the emphasis on metaphysics, Heidegger's account of anxiety and angst may come close to Camus's description of how people react to first uncovering the Absurd, but the suggested emotional responses soon diverge. If Nothing truly underwrites our experience with the world, then the Absurd is simply a fact. Facts only have the meaning we assign to them. The fact that certain cells react and behave in a different way when they are cancerous means little until we provide an interpretation. Most people interpret this new fact as terrifying, while others find it liberating and are now able to do all the things in life they were too afraid to do before. Camus simply asserts that the Absurd is just a fact about the way we interact with the world. If Nothing really does underlie existence, then it too, is just a fact. These facts have no more meaning than we assign to them, and so there is no more reason to be anxious about them than to celebrate them.

Though Nietzsche doesn't explicitly talk about the Absurd, he spends a lot of time developing the idea that there is no absolute or objective meaning in this world. Nietzsche cautions us that even though we inherit moral systems or philosophical paradigms, we should not uncritically accept them. Instead of relaying some timeless, objective, and inerrant truth, Nietzsche argues that these ways of thinking about or interacting with the world come from specific non-philosophical concerns. Certainly this struggle to jettison past

---

[8] I am grateful to Polo Camacho for his help and suggestions here.

influences, be they cultural, religious, or political, is a very difficult task, but the metaphor of overcoming runs rife through Nietzsche's work. The fact that we can overcome and replace these other ways of thinking suggests that they are not some kind objective representation of the way the world is. Thus, current of overcoming conventional ways of thinking and a desire to project our originality into the world are two ways Nietzsche negotiates with the Absurd, or lack of objective meaning in the universe.

Nietzsche has a sophisticated conception of struggle. Nietzsche undoubtedly praises struggle because it compels us to be creative, to be innovative, and, above all, to have an idea worth fighting for. Walter Kaufman takes great pains to debunk Nietzsche's inaccurate and unfortunate historiography. Traditionally Nietzsche's philosophy was edited and interpreted to support a will to power which looked more like a will to domination. Those who were able developed their talents and abilities to combat those who were weaker until the weaker submitted. But Kaufman points out that this interpretation of Nietzsche presupposes the deliberate and dishonest editing done by Nietzsche's sister and her husband.[9] A more nuanced and careful reading of Nietzsche suggests that competition between free spirits and those who are not afraid to experiment is designed to push each other to excel and be even more creative. Further, this conflict truly tests an individuals will and commitment to a project; we pay for our dedication to the amount we are willing to sacrifice at its altar.[10] But this sacrifice is due to our desire for self-development, not to outdo someone *per se*. Nietzsche thinks rivalries that are about one-upmanship are really expressions of *ressentiment* and distort the focus from oneself to a petty and spiteful obsession of another.[11] Thus, we overcome a rival not necessarily by defeating them in the traditional sense, but by being so advanced and beyond their ability to compete that we simply obviate competition, until we find a new, and worthy, competitor.

Nietzsche's desire to project originality butts up against his doctrine of the Eternal Recurrence. Nietzsche uses a simple thought experiment to illustrate its relevance for our decisions.[12] We are asked to consider our reaction to the

---

[9] Friedrich Nietzsche, *The Will to Power*. Trans. Walter Kaufmann and R.J. Hollingdale. New York: NY (Vintage International, 1967), p. xiii-xxix.
[10] Friedrich Nietzsche, *The Gay Science: With a Prelude in Rhymes and an Appendix of Songs*. Trans. Walter Kaufmann. New York: NY (Vintage Books, 1974), p. 280-83.
[11] Friedrich Nietzsche, *On the Genealogy of Morals*. Trans. Walter Kaufmann and R.J. Hollingdale, New York: NY (Vintage Books, 1967), p. 36-37.
[12] *The Gay Science,* 273-74.

proposal that we live the life we have chosen over and over again. If we despair at this proposal, we are not satisfied with our decisions, but if we have no regrets about what we have chosen or how we lived our life, then we should accept the proposal as a tremendous gift. While allowing us to critically examine what we are doing and why we are doing it, the thought experiment also brings out the fact that this life a just a fleeting moment in time. Further, the cosmological significance of the Eternal Recurrence is that all the decisions we have made have been made before and will be made again—there is no objective value to what we have chosen. Nevertheless, as the first response to the proposal shows, we do not have to despair if our life replays again and again—we simply have to make choices worth repeating. The ability to make choices worth repeating suggests a way to overcome the Absurd aspects in the Eternal Recurrence. The main way we can be satisfied with our own decisions is if they are *our* decisions. What Nietzsche means is that we have to reject past influences, even ones we are extremely attached to. This overcoming is perhaps the most difficult as we have to not just figure out which ideas, projects, or values are worth having, but also be vigilant in the ways others have influenced our value systems. These past values are often shaped and formed by friends, family, or others we hold in high esteem—to combat those values is to combat those people's influence on our lives. This cost is extremely steep, but allows us to own our decisions as our own.

Adopting Nietzsche's view point is both tempting and intoxicating, as it demands our attention and devotion, but it doesn't leave much room for enjoying the here and now. If I am always struggling to overcome this or that obstacle, or scrutinize my friendships to make sure we are constantly competing with one another to develop our talents, then I am not content with what I have now—I am always looking to have more. While Camus and Nietzsche agree that we need to create value and meaning in this world, Camus doesn't think we have to overcome the Absurd. There are other ways to give our lives meaning besides an ultimately futile struggle. In simply accepting the Absurd as the way we create meaning in the world, we are no longer in competition with it. If the Absurd threatens the way we create meaning we may, in a way, transcend it by simply accepting it.

Dostoevsky may seem out of place in the context of Heidegger and Nietzsche. Walter Kaufman states that he "can see no reason for calling Dostoevsky an Existentialist, but [he] does think that Part One of *Notes from Underground* is the best overture for Existentialism ever written,"[13] namely because the Underground Man's responses seems to capture the more visceral rejection of a Rationalist or determinism universe. *Notes from Underground* is written as a stream of consciousness journal; unlike other works that rely on polished prose or an editing an argument, the Underground Man simply shows us what an unfiltered and unrestrained though process looks like, and the opening lines don't paint a pretty picture: "I am a sick man…I am a spiteful man. I am an unattractive man."[14]

The Underground Man is concerned about how we find meaning in a world that is already determined by mathematical and scientific laws. Rationalist laws threaten meaning because they undermine the ability for someone to choose; if all of my decisions are already fixed, then it seems it doesn't matter what I choose because I couldn't have chosen differently. The Underground Man, however, rebels against this deterministic picture by asserting that mathematical or scientific laws only hold if the world is rational. Since humans are not wholly rational, those laws cannot determine human choice, thus saving human choice. Even if these choices are contradictory choices, poorly chosen, or extremely harmful, the Underground Man concludes that meaning obtains because he chose.

The Underground Man's solution is not as important as the way he understands the problem of determinism. The problem is framed like this

> The impossible means the stone wall! What stone wall? Why, of course, the laws of nature, the deductions of natural sciences, mathematics…Nature does not ask your permission, she has nothing to do with your wishes, and whether you like her laws or dislike them, you are bound to accept her as she is, and consequently all her conclusions. A wall, you see, is a wall.[15]

In this description we see the Underground Man taking a markedly different approach towards the Absurd than either Heidegger or Nietzsche. For Heidegger, encountering the Absurd was a fairly difficult task and came about only through anxiety; we spend most of our time trying to avoid it. Nietzsche's attempts at empowering originality are designed to overcome

---

[13] Walter Kaufman, *Existentialism from Dostoevsky to Sartre*. New York: NY (Plume Books 1975), p. 14.
[14] Fydor Dostoevsky, *Notes from the Underground, The Double, and Other Stories*. Trans. Deborah A Martinsen. New York: NY (Barnes & Noble Classics, 2003), p. 209.
[15] Ibid. 216-17.

the Absurd. But the Underground Man simply tries to break through the wall; his frantic attempts are irrational and quite painful. Instead of trying to go over the wall, the Underground Man uses himself as a battering ram. Even though the Underground Man succeeds in his goal, he clearly shows the irrational side of humanity, it is not really that desirable a life. For instance, just to prove that choice still exists, the Underground Man obsessively dwells on being able to bump into an officer and not have his shoulder give way. Not only does he fixate on this desire, he spends several months following the officer and trying to set up a chance to bump into him—further, he borrows against his salary to be able to afford a coat so he can appear to the officer as someone worthy enough to not give ground with his shoulder when they bump into each other. But when the melodramatic shoulder jousting happens, the officer doesn't even notice—months of planning, obsessing, and poor financial decisions made no difference.[16] Soon after this plan falls through the Underground Man meets some of his old classmates who he hasn't seen in years and doesn't particularly care for; nevertheless he insists on attending a farewell dinner with them for another classmate who he doesn't like. He borrows more money to attend a dinner he can't afford to spend time with people he doesn't like so he can fail to impress them with his mediocre job and modest salary that turns out to be wildly insufficient for these harebrained schemes.[17] Clearly, this plan, like the shoulder bumping plan, is crazy, and that may be the point the Underground Man is trying to make: if decisions don't make sense, then the deterministic laws cannot predict them.

The Underground Man's success comes at a fairly high cost. He himself admits that he is not happy with his life and further, no one else really wants to live like he does. There has to be a better way here. We do not need to spite the Absurd world as the Underground Man does—we can simply accept our relationship with the world is Absurd and leave it at that. Camus's account can also challenge determinism, but in a more roundabout way. The "fundamental question of philosophy," i.e. suicide, questions determinism because suicide often happens in spite of all the reasons not to commit suicide. People sometimes kill themselves even when they have everything going for them. If there is no sufficient reason to explain why individuals choose suicide, aside from the rationale offered by Camus, then it seems Camus's account can still challenge determinism by providing an example of non-rational or irrational choices that are made. Dostoevsky's

---

[16] Ibid. 243-53.
[17] Ibid. 257-78.

Underground Man diffuses irrationality to all of his choices, and the result is a pretty unpleasant life, while irrationality (in the motivation for suicide) localizes in only one decision, even if that decision is the most important one. Because Camus contains irrational decisions, his explanation of the Absurd seems to offer us better options for making good life decisions.

This section surveyed the responses to the Absurd by Heidegger, Nietzsche, and Dostoevsky. These positions are not summative of Existentialism, but they do provide a good sample of general attitudes towards the Absurd: evasion, overcoming, or resistance. Each of these general views offers a way to create meaning in a world devoid of objective meaning, but have fairly high structural costs. Camus's account, however, simply accepts the Absurd for what it is and then goes from there. Thus, his approach does not posit an ever present anxiety, a constant need to overcome, or a peevish desire to be noticed. Instead, Camus offers us a wider set of options for constructing meaning by simply accepting that meaning is temporary and only subjectively significant.

Sartre's Absurd

This section examines two of Sartre's early works, *The Wall* and *Nausea*. These works showcase a more unsettling picture of the Absurd that complement areas Camus leaves underdeveloped. Camus seems to be more concerned about the larger implications of accepting the Absurd condition while Sartre's work explores the experiences of first coming to terms with the Absurd. Despite the fruitful juxtaposition, however, Sartre's work casts the Absurd as something to be rejected or endured.

Sartre's early literary work provides uncomfortable examples of people confronting the Absurd. In *Nausea*, for instance, Antoine is content to go throughout his daily routine; he writes his book, he reads at the library, and he does fairly innocuous activities to fill the rest of his time. While all these workaday facts are happening, they have all already happened as well; Antoine's life has been going more or less the same for quite some time. But the novel starts off in the middle of a change that is hard to identify. Antoine is perplexed that ordinary objects and people begin to look foreign and he has to take a few seconds to even recognize what object he is actually looking at. His self-diagnosis is that "it is an abstract change without object," and he asks "am I the one who has changed? If not, then it is this room, this city and this nature; I must choose."[18]

Antoine's initial description of the Absurd is important because it shows two aspects of Sartre's position towards the Absurd: (1) it localizes either in an object or a subject and (2) and that Sartre prioritizes choice. Antoine initially believes that the change is either in him or in the world, for it must manifest somewhere. But this belief misunderstands the Absurd, for Camus is very careful to point out that the Absurd is not a thing in the world, but rather is simply a relationship between humans and the world. The objects people related to do not change and people do not undergo some kind of ontological transformation when they encounter the Absurd: all that changes is how people interact with those objects. In the second respect Antoine feels that his decision to locate this change in himself or in the object helps better understand it. Consider Antoine's remarks when he remembers picking up a stone: "I recall better what I felt the other day at the seashore when I held the pebble. It was sort of a sweetish sickness...it came from the stone, I'm sure of it, it passed from the stone to my hand. Yes, that's it, that's just it—a sort of nausea in the hands." [19] Here, we see a more indicative detail that further characterizes Sartre's conception of the Absurd: the Absurd is not a neutral fact to be accepted among other facts about the world because this fact induces nausea.

I think Sartre is quite right to highlight this emotive resistance or disgust towards the Absurd world as an initial reaction. The Absurd disrupts the idea of objective meaning in the world and if the narrative of objective meaning has been internalized for someone's entire life, then losing that sense of security would be disorienting and jarring. Antoine spends the rest of the novel watching this nausea metastasize to all the other aspects of his life; he quits writing the book he has spent a lot of time on, he becomes dissatisfied with his relationships, and wonders if he will ever find his way again. Contrast the way Sartre describes Antoine's struggle with the Absurd with Camus's brief description in *The Myth of Sisyphus*. Camus simply says that we have a routine and then one day we ask why we are doing that routine and gradually that "why?" radiates to other areas of our life until we are forced to question if we have been doing anything of meaning ever at all.[20] Camus summarizes the event as our choice between "suicide or recovery," but this disjunction seems too brief; someone just watched the world she built crumble under the weight of the Absurd.[21]

---

[18] Jean-Paul Sartre, *Nausea*. Trans. Lloyd Alexander. New York: NY (New Directions Publishing, 1964), p. 4.
[19] Ibid. 11.
[20] Camus, *The Myth of Sisyphus and Other Essays*, p.12-13.
[21] Camus does provide a more direct view of someone encountering the Absurd in *The Fall*,

Antione's recovery shows a key way that Sartre's early work differs from Camus's overall project. Antoine's abandonment of his prior projects and dejected wandering around town show a more realistic representation of the loss of meaning. Antoine doesn't seem to confront the choice Camus thinks he must—suicide or recovery—instead, Antoine muddles through, dazed and without any real purpose or motivation. Further, we see that the decision to rebuild meaning in the ruins of a past life is not some grand event, but rather in the spontaneous enjoyment of things. The most immediate example is Antoine's love of jazz—it is the first thing that quells his nausea, though he is not able to realize why. These brief moments of enjoyment lead to other meaningful acts, like deciding to leave the city and start over or standing up for the Self-Taught Man, which Antoine does not do from some sense of duty or overwhelming compassion for someone else, but simply because he wants to.[22] We don't get grand life projects in Absurd reconstruction, but then again, we may not need them.

We see a bit starker a picture of the Absurd in Sartre's *The Wall*. Some insurgents are captured and sentenced to death by firing squad in a few hours. The Absurd is front and center: whatever the prisoners do, they will die. Further, their actions won't be remembered except by the other people in the room who will die with them. So whatever they do, they cannot alter their fate. Yet in these last few hours the insurgents seem to carry on as if the death sentence was not there. The enclosed setting heightens the futility of their actions one way or another. Tom starts to exercise because he is cold, but he is no warmer when he's done and all that changed was he's more tired than when he started.[23] Pablo points out later that Tom is so afraid of the firing squad that Tom pisses his pants. Instead of simply admitting fear, Tom rebukes Pablo: "'it isn't true,' he said furiously. "I'm not pissing. I don't feel anything....I don't know what it is,' Tom said ferociously. 'But I'm not afraid. I swear I'm not afraid.'"[24] In normal contexts we might say there is reason to lie here, but no one else is going to find out about Tom's mishap—namely because the only one in the room who will not die at the firing squad is the doctor, and he doesn't seem to

---

but he is largely concerned with religious themes in a secular context, e.g. truth, innocence, confession, etc. Camus uses the Absurd as a lens for these issues, but the work is more about how these themes transform in an Absurd context rather than how an individual copes in an Absurd world.

[22] Sartre, *Nausea*, p. 164-69.
[23] Jean-Paul Sartre, *The Wall*. Trans. Lloyd Alexander. New York: NY (New Directions Publishing, 1975), p. 3.
[24] Ibid. 9.

particularly care—and if people did find out that Tom was afraid, it seems a fairly understandable reaction in light of a death sentence. Whether Tom admitted or denied what he did, it would not change what was in store for him.

The wall in the story further symbolizes Sartre's understanding of the Absurd. Pablo is interrogated before he is sent to the firing squad. Before he meet the officers, he realizes that he no longer cares about Concha, a woman he was involved with, and no longer is really dedicated to the cause he fought for. He doesn't abandon these commitments out of spite or to somehow reduce his fear towards his impending death. In fact, Pablo states that in letting the projects go, he feels calm. The wall acts not just as a constraint to actions, is something to be broken through like the Underground Man, but it is also the place where meaning stops and can go no further. In the context of the firing squad it has the added significance of being the place where life stops. But Pablo says that the wall is a jolting reminder that actions, meaning, or life end. He reflects and remarks that "in the state I was in, if someone had come and told me I could go home quietly, that they would leave me my life whole, it would have left me cold: several hours or several years of waiting is all the same when you have lost the illusion of being eternal." [25] In short, it is only through the sad and hurtful loss of illusion—of eternality, of objectivity, of whatever else—that we are finally free to rebuild our life. Camus doesn't talk about this repellent aspect of the Absurd, but I think Sartre is right to try and give us a full account of how difficult it will be to try and rebuild meaning in our lives.

Pablo's decision to lie to the captors seems to foreshadow some of Sartre's later work. After his rupture with Camus, Sartre spends more of his time trying to empower human choice and arguing for people to take a more active role in society, politics, morality, and religion. A hallmark of this attitude, to Sartre's chagrin, is his famous "Existentialism is a Humanism." There, and elsewhere, Sartre spends time developing ways people can take a more active way in creating meaning in their lives. He no longer seems to be concerned about the limits laid down by an Absurd wall, but rather is concerned about overtaking them. Pablo decides to lie to the interrogators not to spite them, to evade his sentence, or to even overcome the circumstances he finds himself in. Pablo lies because he simply wants to make fools out of his captors, not because he wants to try and buy Gris, the rebel commander, more time or safety; he lies simply because he wants to.

---

[25] Ibid. 12.

But there is something else to his motive—by lying for his own reasons Pablo also thinks he cheats the Absurd. Pablo's decision to reject the constraints placed on him seems to predict the lack of emphasis Sartre places on the Absurd in his later writing, but since this work is part of Sartre's early work, we are left with the Absurdly comical result—in trying to lie Pablo actually told the guards where Gris was hiding.

This section examined Sartre's account of the Absurd in his early literary works. This account covers areas Camus simply glosses over. Antione is sickened with the world once he uncovers the Absurd; he rebuilds his life gradually and slowly, but without a grand purpose. The insurgents in *The Wall* are slammed up against the Absurd because of their death sentence, but Pablo realizes that this fast approaching expiration date doesn't really matter—once he let go of the illusion of eternity, he realizes his death was always there. Sartre's depiction of the Absurd is complementary to Camus's description insofar as it talks about the here and now consequences of adopting an Absurdist mindset. One difference, however, is Sartre seems to evade the emphasis on suicide that Camus sees as fundamental to the Absurd. Perhaps this evasion is what later leads Sartre to downplay the Absurd in his later writings.

The Absurd Hero

This section explains why Camus considers Sisyphus the Absurd hero. The myth itself represents our Absurd condition in the universe. Sisyphus represents a model for people to look to, not just to survive, but live and create meaning in the world. Camus, perhaps intentionally, models Sisyphus ambiguously: is Sisyphus a hero because he always finds the strength to rebuild, or is Sisyphus a hero because once we accept the world as it is, there is no reason to not carry on?

The final section of *The Myth of Sisyphus*, also entitled "The Myth of Sisyphus," suggests that the myth itself is symbolic of our Absurd existence. Sisyphus as an ideal stand in for humanity. Camus tells us that "the gods had condemned Sisyphus to ceaselessly rolling a rock to the top of a mountain, whence the stone would fall back of its own weight. They had thought with some reason that there is no more dreadful punishment than futile and hopeless labor."[26] Camus characterizes the worry people have that living in

---

[26] Albert Camus, *The Myth of Sisyphus*, p. 119.

an Absurd world isn't that different from being condemned. One reason for this worry is that without objective meaning or purpose, then it seems like there isn't much of a point to life: if anything I do will ultimately wash away and there will come a time where it will be as if I never existed, then the motivation to go on may be a hard sell. In the context of the myth, we are like Sisyphus; he rolls his boulder up the mountain and we start projects, build relationships, and try to do a great many other things with the hope that they are important or, at least, that they matter. But neither one of us succeeds and so it appears that this existence is living out an Absurd sentence.

Despite his repetitive task, Sisyphus is a hero. Camus admires Sisyphus' heroism because he puts his entire being into trying push the rock up the hill. This struggle is not just intellectual, emotional, or physical, but rather tests every aspect of Sisyphus.[27] Just as Sisyphus pushes his rock up the hill, so too do people try to build meaning in their life. This struggle for meaning is often just as intense as Sisyphus' toil; getting a good job, building lasting friendships, or starting a family usually require multiple aspects of who we are and are often fairly challenging. The inevitable point of conflict for Sisyphus is that his rock will roll down the hill; Camus argues that our inevitable point of conflict for us is that we act with the belief that we are doing something objectively important or that what we do matters beyond our lifetime. Many actions outlast actors, but Ozymandias' inscription suggests that all actions have a shelf-life.

One possible objection to Camus might be that some people just never really encounter the Absurd. These people go through life without ever really wondering why and never watch the rock of meaning roll back down the hill. I think Camus could respond by saying that the Absurd conditions the way people interact with the world whether they recognize it or not. So whether or not someone breaks from the routine of "rising, streetcar, four hours in the office or factory, meal, streetcar, four hours of work, meal, sleep, and Monday, Tuesday, Wednesday, Thursday, Friday, and Saturday according to the same rhythm"[28] the Absurd still affects the way in which she relates to the universe—her actions won't last longer because she doesn't know about the Absurd.

---

[27] Ibid. 120-21.
[28] Ibid. 12-13.

Sisyphus is the Absurd hero because of how he reacts to the rock rolling down. In returning to the rock Sisyphus reflects on what happened. During his descent Sisyphus "knows the whole extent of his wretched condition...the lucidity that was to constitute his torture at the same time crowns his victory. There is no fate that cannot be surmounted by scorn."[29] We interpret the myth as tragic, Camus says, because Sisyphus is aware of what is happening—the repetitive nature of his work is demeaning because he never accomplishes anything. But the "lucidity" Camus attributes to Sisyphus may not be wholly tragic; after all, it "crowns his victory." Sisyphus is lucid about the way he interacts with the world: he knows his task is repetitive and never changes, but his awareness and, further, his acceptance of that fact frees Sisyphus because he recognizes the conditions he exists in to create meaning. He understands that the Absurd does not undercut or attenuate meaning; meaning has always been, and only ever was, subjective. Acceptance may seem an odd way to scorn something, especially because we typically think of "scorn" as some dramatic display of anger. But scorn does not always need to be showy to make a point. A woman can scorn a man's advances by simply ignoring whatever he does. She hasn't really displayed much emotion, but she has still scorned the advance. Sisyphus scorns his fate, his punishment, through acceptance. He does not expect the world to be different than it is, and so being condemned to an Absurd world looks a lot like simply existing in an Absurd world.

Sisyphus' heroism is marked by happiness. To rebuff the standard misreading of the Absurd—that a world without objective meaning would be too depressing—Camus insists that "happiness and the absurd are two sons of the same earth. They are inseparable. It would be a mistake to say that happiness necessarily springs from the Absurd discovery."[30] I think Camus is trying to point out that a very natural reaction to discovering the Absurd is depression, or sadness, or, even suicide. Finding out not that everything before the moment of revelation does not matter, but never did, is a heavy burden to bear. In truth, most reactions to the Absurd will resemble the characters in Sartre's work, but Camus says it doesn't have to be this way. We can be happy in an Absurd universe once we understand that we act because we find meaning in that action; that's all we need and all we ever needed. Sisyphus is there to help guide us through the depression, to choose meaning, happiness, and life. This reaction may not be our first, but it is something we can learn and something that will be highly subjective.[31]

---

[29] Ibid. 121.
[30] Ibid. 122.

The final words, "one must imagine Sisyphus happy,"[32] are ambiguous, and I see no sure way to decipher which interpretation is correct. If we treat Sisyphus as the Absurd hero or role model, then perhaps "must" is psychological; we must imagine him as happy because if the Absurd paragon was not happy to return to his iterated labor, then I have no chance to succeed. The other reading is that we must, by necessity, find Sisyphus happy because he has accepted the world as it is, indifferent to human actions or designs, and he has found happiness in whatever he assigned meaning to. We must imagine Sisyphus as happy because once we accept the way we interact with the world, it is Absurd to be sad. The psychological reading seems plausible to me because in many ways Camus is trying to figure out how we cope in an Absurd universe. As mentioned above, a standard criticism of Camus and many Existentialists is that the world they describe is simply too bleak to live in. One way to diffuse this criticism and help people accept their relationship with the world is to provide a model of someone who chooses life, even when there is no reason to. The necessity reading, that there is no reason to be sad in an Absurd universe, seems equally as plausible. If the Absurd is what people are worried about, then framing it as a fact about how humans interact with the world diffuses worries about life being too bleak. If the Absurd is a fact about our condition, then it only has whatever meaning we assign to it. Once we truly accept our Absurd condition, then there truly is no reason to be sad.

Even if we accept either reading, it seems odd to say Sisyphus is happy. One reason for doubting Sisyphus is happy is because we often think of happiness as smiling, having a good time, or enjoying something. Even more robust accounts of happiness, like Aristotle's, require that we have good habits, the rights goals, and a proper sense of self. In short, we when typically think of happiness, we don't think of someone like Sisyphus. We don't typically think of any of Camus's characters as being happy in the traditional sense. *The Stranger*, often taken with *The Myth of Sisyphus* to be Camus's philosophical signature, showcases Meursault, a man who is happy with parts of his life, but never in an public way. Sartre considered the works to be intimately linked; he thought

---

[31] While I spent much of the first section of this paper talking about how Camus differed from the other Existentialists, it is worth noting that there is common ground. Here, especially, we see Nietzsche's emphasis on the subjectivity of meaning. The motif of evading our encountering the Absurd with ordinary routines echoes Heidegger. The non-rational dimension of suicide shares the Underground Man's concern about determinism.
[32] Ibid. 123.

> *The Myth of Sisyphus* might be said to aim at giving us this *idea,* and *The Stranger* at giving us the feeling. The order in which the two works appeared seems to confirm this hypothesis. *The Stranger,* the first to appear, plunges us without comment into the 'climate' of the absurd; the essay then comes and illumines the landscape.[33]

We might think of Sisyphus giving us a theoretical model to look at while Meursault's character strips away the theoretical or mythic overtures. Sisyphus and his struggle exists in the abstract and we substitute our own struggle as rolling a rock up a mountain. But Meursault is more concrete and his struggles are more specific; we do not as readily identify with him. Hence, even though he exists within a society and knows all the proper social cues, he is still a stranger. Nevertheless, Meursault shows what Sisyphus only gestures towards; Meursault shows us how a new kind of happiness emerges in the Absurd. Meursault enjoys life in the present, but never overtly; his indifference towards events others take to be important, viz. his mother's death, Marie's talk of marriage, or his murder of the Arab, is misinterpreted by the other characters in the novel as Meursault being emotionally flat or absent. But Meursault is happy with his life because he dwells on the things he has chosen to have meaning, not the things others have dictated have meaning.

One reason for our doubt might be that we still have not fully accepted the Absurd; we still residually believe there is an objective standard of meaning or purpose in the world. So we doubt someone like Sisyphus could be happy because someone else who has not confronted the Absurd seems to be enjoying life a lot more. But this enjoyment is based on an illusion. Camus points out that we are perfectly content to live in our life of routine and things are going pretty well before we start seriously considering the Absurd. But just because we have not recognized the Absurdity of our condition does not mean it is any less Absurd. We tend to uncritically accept frameworks that give our lives some kind of objective meaning, but, when realized, the Absurd calls that very framework into question and the meaning we once took for granted, collapses. Being aware that this collapse was not due to our lack of trying, but was simply a fact about how we relate to the world, helps us understand that when the meaning we have previously built up collapses, we now have the opportunity to build again. Our creation

---

[33] Jean Paul Sartre, "An Explication of *The Stranger*," in *Modern Critical Interpretations: Albert Camus's The Stranger*. Ed. Harold Bloom. Philadelphia: PA. (Chelsea House Publishers, 2001), p. 95-106.

happens in the ruins of our previous life, and the ruins may be tragic, but we should be happy because the ruins are not the only thing there. We build because we think there is something worth building, even if is only matters to us. That, for Camus, is why Sisyphus is happy, and that is why we too can be happy.

Conclusion

This paper centered on Camus's response to the Absurd and compared the opportunity costs of adopting other views. I began by laying out a rough sketch of some of the other major responses Existentialists have proposed and then showed how those accounts were lacking in comparison with Camus's. Heidegger's position instills a perpetual state of anxiety, Nietzsche's work constantly urges people to improve and overcome, and the Underground Man suggests an irrational way of life that seems to interfere with most attempts at creating meaning for people. Camus's account differs because he simply accepts the Absurd as a starting point and then encourages people to build from there.

The second section developed the Absurd elements in Sartre's early literary work and compared them with Camus's account in *The Myth of Sisyphus*. Camus spends little time developing a detailed account of how people would actually react to uncovering the Absurd in their day-to-day lives. Contrariwise, when Sartre deals with the Absurd, he focuses on how people would react to uncovering a lack of objective meaning in the world. I think this connection is largely overshadowed by the emphasis on the later falling out between the two men. Despite the ways Sartre's early work can help develop our understanding of the Absurd, we still see early etchings of the later rupture; Antoine treats the Absurd as an illness, something to overcome, and Pablo treats the Absurd as a wall, something to be broken through. In either case, the Absurd is a constraint that is meant to be resisted, and this attitude definitely characterizes much of Sartre's later writings.

The third section discussed the role of Sisyphus as the Absurd hero. I argued that Sisyphus was a model for us in an Absurd universe because he totally internalizes his condition and does not wish it otherwise. In picking up the rock each time, Sisyphus chooses life and chooses to create meaning, even though he fully knows that whatever he creates is temporary. In accepting his condition, Camus concludes that we "must imagine Sisyphus as happy."

This conclusion is ambiguous because we may have a psychological need for a hero to show us how to do the impossible, that is to accept the Absurd, or because once we accept that our interaction with the world is Absurd, there is no reason to be sad. In adopting Camus's account of the Absurd, we are able to find ways to not just cope or resist the Absurd, but we are able to accept it as part of the human condition. Once we accept the Absurd as just a fact about how we relate to the world, we are in a better position to pursue whatever goals or life projects we have. We learn from Sisyphus that we carry on because the world is Absurd, not in spite of it.

Works Cited

Camus, Albert, *The Myth of Sisyphus and Other Essays*. Trans. Justin O'Brien. New York, NY: Vintage International, 1991

Dostoevsky, Fydor. *Notes from the Underground, The Double, and Other Stories*. Trans. Deborah A Martinsen. New York: NY, Barnes & Noble Classics, 2003.

Heidegger, Martin. *Basic Writings*, ed. David Krell. New York: NY. Harper Perennial Modern Thought, 2008.

Kaufman, Walter. *Existentialism from Dostoevsky to Sartre*. New York: NY, Plume Books 1975.

Nietzsche, Fredrich. *The Will to Power*. Trans. Walter Kaufmann and R.J. Hollingdale. New York: NY, Vintage International, 1967.

——. *The Gay Science: With a Prelude in Rhymes and an Appendix of Songs*. Trans. Walter Kaufmann. New York: NY. Vintage Books, 1974.

——. *On the Genealogy of Morals*. Trans. Walter Kaufmann and R.J. Hollingdale, New York: NY, Vintage Books, 1967.

Sartre, Jean Paul. *Nausea.* Trans. Lloyd Alexander. New York: NY, New Directions Publishing, 1964.

——. *The Wall*. Trans. Lloyd Alexander. New York: NY. New Directions Publishing, 1975.

——. "An Explication of *The Stranger*," in *Modern Critical Interpretations: Albert Camus's The Stranger*. Ed. Harold Bloom. Philadelphia: PA. Chelsea House Publishers, 2001.

Meursault and the Indifference of Death: A Logotherapeutic Perspective

by Peter Francev

For the absurd man it is not a matter of explaining and solving, but of experiencing and describing. Everything begins with lucid indifference. - Camus[1]

Often charged with being ambivalent, distant, indifferent, or callus, by critics who claim to understand his motives and lack of action, Meursault is, arguably, Camus's greatest and most psychologically challenging protagonist. In this paper, I plan to re-visit the first essay I wrote for the first Camus Society conference five years ago, examining the choices that Meursault makes, from the perspective of the psychotherapy of logotherapist Viktor Frankl whose seminal work, *Man's Search For Meaning*, will provide insight in his lack of sympathy towards his mother's death, his relationships, and his general malaise towards life.

'Maman died today. Or yesterday, maybe. I don't know.'[2] The opening lines of *The Stranger* are striking for a number of reasons: first, there is the unknowledgement of life's most definite certainty- death. Secondly, there appears to be a kind of reserved diffidence, on Meursault's part, towards his Maman. Thirdly, there is, one could argue, a marked callousness towards the ceasing of one's existence. I think, no matter which avenue we choose to examine, what is evident is Meursault's 'cool' and casual indifference.

The casual indifference is what psychotherapists define as an existential isolation which is a 'vale of loneliness', and a kind of 'unbridgeable gulf between the self and others' forming 'a separation from the world.'[3] It is this existential isolation which prevents Meursault from forming cohesive

---

[1] Albert Camus, *The Myth of Sisyphus* 94.
[2] Camus, *The Stranger* 3.
[3] Irvin D. Yalom, *Existential Psychotherapy* 355-356.

relationships with other individuals by preventing the growth and development of his closest and most intimate relationships. It has prevented Meursault from acquiring a sense of intimacy- whether it is the friendships with Emmanuel, Céleste, and Raymond, or the sexual intimacy with Marie. In each of these cases, he closes off himself from the other individual, thus, preventing an acquisition of a sensation of intimacy.

This can be seen in Meursault's relationship with Emmanuel. The day he returns to work, following Maman's funeral, the men catch the back of a truck and hitched a ride to Céleste's for lunch where Meursault is concerned with more trivial things such as: the last towel on the roll in the restroom, or the freighters in the harbor.

Upon arrival at Céleste's café, Meursault is asked if 'things were 'all right''.[4] He quickly, and somewhat quietly, dismisses Céleste's genuine concern for his well-being. He chooses to 'eat fast' and have 'some coffee.'[5] After finishing lunch, Meursault finds enough time to go home and take a short nap before going back to the office. This shows that there is a lucid indifference with which he either a) perceives the world, or b) goes on with his daily routines. Nevertheless, it is a consciousness with which he cannot avoid, and an indifference which he chooses to disregard out of fear of his cogniscent recognition.

Contrary to the 'casual' nucleus of his relationships, with Emmanuel and Céleste, there is matter of the examining the detailed relationships with Raymond and Marie.

Even though he does not explicitly state it, Meursault views Emmanuel and Céleste as 'weak' because they are not as physically 'strong' as Raymond; so, he finds himself gravitating towards Raymond and distancing himself from everyone else. Raymond represents everything that Emmanuel and Céleste are not; he is: impetuous, course, loud, apathetic and abusive. Because Meursault want to be like Raymond, he agrees to write the letter; and as he so blatantly puts it, '...it just came to me, but I tried my best to please Raymond because I didn't have any reason not to please him.'[6]

---

[4] Camus, *The Stranger* 26.
[5] Ibid., 26.
[6] Ibid., 32.

On the one hand, Meursault's repulsion to individuals who he does not see as 'strong', or 'masculine' is weak and, thus will have as little to do with them as possible and a garner kind of loathing towards them. In fact, this loathing, for the weak, will lead him to seek someone who he views as the opposite- the strong, or masculine. However, this repulsion is superficial and that it is not how he really view those individuals. In fact, Raymond's decision to abuse his mistress *should* have disgusted Meursault; yet, he chose consciously to ignore the threats towards the mistress, because he felt that if he objected, then he would be labeled 'weak' by Raymond.

Now that Meursault sees himself as weak, he finds himself isolated from the world around him; and it is this isolation which gives rise to the 'vale of loneliness', the 'unbridgeable gulf between the self and others" forming "a separation from the world.'[7] It is this existential isolation which prevents him from forming cohesive relationships with other individuals, but it is a conscious decision to prevent it. Otherwise Meursault will be forced to consciously acknowledge his separation from the rest of the world.

Meursault's relationship with Marie is quite a bit more complex. On the one hand, he desires to be with her- he craves the companionship- yet, he cannot commit to her repeated offers of marriage because there is fear- fear of the unknown, fear of commitment and the fear of admitting to happiness.

He fails to connect with men on a multi-layered and meaningful level because his father was absent from his life. As a young boy, he lacked a male role model and a father-figure. So, to compensate for this absence, he chose to associate himself with your 'ideal' man, someone who is strong and does not appear to be fearful- Raymond. This lends itself further to support the idea that it is because he admires Raymond, and because he is fearful of disappointing him, so that he agrees to author the letter to Raymond's mistress and, perhaps, head back to the beach and confront the Arab. It is the desire for companionship, coupled with the fear of disappointment which leads Meursault to kill the Arab.

As far as Marie is concerned: on the one hand, his desire to be with Marie is driven out of fear of the being alone, the need for companionship and, possibly, the dominant female in his life. On the other, Marie can be seen as a replacement for Maman. Subconsciously, Meursault's mind is divided on

---

[7] Yalom,, 356.

how he perceives Marie. On the conscious level, she is a constant companion who he recognizes as an equal, in sexual terms. For example, he does not objectify her, but rather subjectifies her making her the subject of sexual desire; he lays his head on her stomach[8], notices her hair in her eyes, and fondles her breasts at the cinema[9]. Each of these instances supports the idea that Meursault sees Marie as a companion and someone "more"- whether it is a sexual equal or an equal in a most lasting, more genuine relationship.

The flipside of the conscious desire towards Marie are Meursault's subconscious desires. He mentions that while out swimming with her, he pay particular attention to her breasts[10], and that when he lays your head on her stomach, he 'feel' her 'heart beating softly.'[11] Within the subconscious, there is the oedipal desire to be close to her sexually, which will provide the closeness with which Meursault seeks in a companion.

While the court will dismiss Meursault's intimate encounters with Marie as mistress as mere 'one-night stands', I, on the other hand, see significance. After the movie, Marie spends the night creating a desire; and it is the following morning where she leaves to go to her aunt's that we find Meursault consciously realizing that she is gone- missing from the bed- and yet, he chooses to roll over and 'tried to find the salty smell' of her hair on the pillow.[12] Meursault craves the intimacy of companionship which Marie provides, and it is a companionship that he could not and did not have with his mother.

However, there is also the desire to be close with Marie because she represents, oedipally, Maman. Marie is an oedipal symbol of Maman because she is a) a female and b) one with whom he tries to become intimate. His actions with her at the beach, and while swimming, are indicative of an infant's desires of his mother: the constant wanton of closeness, specifically the covetousness of being near her breasts which would be symbolic of motherhood and, to an extent, life-giving. This latter point, of the life-giving of Marie, brings me to a final position regarding

---

[8] Camus, *The Stranger* 20.
[9] Ibid., 20.
[10] Ibid., 19.
[11] Ibid., 20.
[12] Ibid., 21.

Marie and Meursault's subconsciousness, and that is the significance of her name.

Although he would never admit it, Meursault sees Marie as a kind of Mary, as in the Virgin Mary. The difference is that Marie is not a virgin, but she represents the saving qualities that a theist might find in the Holy Mother. While some see the Mary Mother of Christ as the epitome of compassion, love, kindness, or goodness, she symbolizes his idea of perfection. She is the saving grace of his life, and because she is as such, he embody hers with the qualities of perfection. He sees her as Maman, the Maman of his children, or the Maman of his dreams. She is how Meursault wishes his mother would have been to you: soft, supple, tender and kind. Marie has become the mother-figure that he seemed to have lacked.

There is a sense of insecurity with Meursault's fear of the unknown, because events are not definite, not planned, and he has no control over them. When it comes to marriage, the fear of commitment represents the definite, the life-long, where, again, he does not know what will happen. Yes, there is a possibility of being content and happy, but this will be overshadowed by the contentedness, or even that the happiness of marriage is not a guarantee. And if that is not enough, marriage to Marie would require having a dominate female in his life. This is something that he has not had in his life- and it scares him. Contrary to what some observers might believe, Maman was not the strong female in Meursault's life. This, I believe, is one of the reasons why he sent her to the home. He longed for a strong woman, who complimented him; but, he is fearful because he have never had a woman who represents strength.

His fear of happiness stems from the fact that it appears that happiness is foreign to Meursault. And since it is foreign, he does not know how to get along with it, so he dismisses and rejects happiness, even if it includes Marie.

Meursault's relationship with Marie is one where he use her as a coping mechanism for his isolation. As Martin Buber points out, 'A great relationship breaches the barriers of a lofty solitude, subdues its strict law, and throws a bridge from self-being across the abyss of dread of the universe.'[13] He benefits from his 'casual' relationship with Marie because

---

[13] Yalom, 363.

for the brief moments that they are together, through his projection of her, she affords him a bridge between loneliness and companionship. While with her, Meursault is something more than just 'Meursault the Dejected'; he gains a sense of self, and a kind of 'right side', which is 'often experienced as a surge of happiness when one feels a harmony between themselves and their place in the world.'[14]

Marie provides Meursault with harmony for himself, within himself and throughout the world. When he is in a state of disharmony between himself and the world, he slips into despair.[15] And it is this despair, which so many misinterpret as the absurd, which is so commonly defined as: '…the divorce between man and his life….'[16]

He has not divorced himself from the world, but merely 'slipped' into disharmony. The way we can assist a resurrection of Meursault is through logotherapy which 'tries to make the patient (or rather the individual) fully aware of his responsibilities,'[17] and its goal is to have the patient decide whether or not he is responsible for his actions. It is through responsibility that one can find meaning in life.

There are three ways to find meaning in one's life. First, one can create work or perform a deed; or experience something or encounter someone; or examine one's attitude towards unavoidable suffering.[18]

Since his first meeting with Marie, Meursault acknowledged that he 'had a thing for her at the time'[19] and that he was fairly certain that the feelings, or at least interest, were reciprocated as well. I propose to examine the experience as something more, as if it is not simply a fling or casual acquaintance, but rather something deeper, something more fulfilling.

Meursault's experiences of Marie occur on several levels: first, she is a co-worker; then, she becomes the object of interest (and yes, I am aware of the irony of Marie's 'objectification', as opposed to subjecification in this

---

[14] Simon Lea, 3.
[15] Ibid., 3.
[16] M.H. Abrams, 3.
[17] Viktor Frankl, 132.
[18] Ibid., 133.
[19] Camus, *The Stranger*, 19.

statement); and finally, Marie as transformed into his lover. Through the first two experiences, he encounters Marie on a superficial level; yet, once he confronts Marie on a sexual level, his relationship becomes more complex, and this is illustrated by the fact that Marie mistakes your sexual craving for something more- an indirect desire, or (sub)conscious wish on her part, for marriage.

Perhaps it is the very thought of marriage which terrifies Meursault; thus, his informal apathy towards Marie's wishes of marriage lead me to believe either a) his parents did not have a delightful relationship, which could explain his apprehensions towards marrying Marie because he would not want to go through the distress that his parents went through; or b) he just does not care.

It is of my opinion that apathy is not something trivial, but rather it is 'a strong psychological condition where emotions are blunted along with the feeling that no one could care anymore.'[20] The apathy with which he experiences is a kind of homeostasis, a tensionless existence where there is no meaning, and the outside world creates an existential vacuum, which is rendered his boredom.

Because his life is not challenged by Céleste and Emmanuel, he is bored with them. So, when he is around them, he feels nothing, as if your existence, at that moment, was suspended in a vacuum. Raymond provides a bit more stimulation through the desire to be like him. Hence, this desire to be like him leads to Meursault's desire to please him and, finally, to write the letter to his mistress and become involved with his domestic quarrel.

Finally, we come back to Marie who represents Meursault's savior, saving him from the dullness with which his life had become accustomed. When he is with her, he is not bored, nor does he show any signs of being bored- whether it is to dinner, the movies, or an intimate encounter. Since Marie alleviates boredom, she eases frustration to the point that it is as if Meursault is free from any sense of mental suffering which, like life and death, is eradicable. Logotherapy can facilitate the elimination of existential frustration.

---

[20] Frankl, 42.

Logotherapy is a therapy of the mind because it makes individual aware of his existential meaning. Once the individual is made aware of his existential meaning(lessness), he can reconcile the malady. The origin of existential frustration can be found in a) existence itself, b) the individual's meaning of existence, or c) the will to meaning in a personal existence, signifying that the individual chooses to ignore the self's sense of failure, leading to a life of despondency. Perhaps it is the frustration of finding one's meaning that arises from the problem of the will, which would punctuate a noögenic neurosis.

Noögenic neurosis is a different kind of psychological neuroses; rather than have their origin in the psychological, they are found in the noölogical (from the Greek *noös* for mind) dimension of human existence.[21] For Meursault, the feelings of meaninglessness come from the boredom that he faces and experiences on a daily basis. However, through his thoughts towards Marie, he begins to reconcile his life because Marie helps him find meaning through '… the simplest and most lasting joys: the smells of summer, …, a certain evening sky, Marie's dresses and the way she laughed.'[22]

By his own psychology, Marie is transformed into Meursault's savior. She helps him reconcile the meaninglessness in his life, which helps him discover his personal existential meaning through Maman. This is illustrated through Meursault's comprehension of Maman's desire to take Thomas Pérez as her 'fiancé', and that "'So, close to death, Maman must have felt free then and ready to live it all over again.'[23] Now, he finds himself opened 'to the gentle indifference of the world'[24] and that the culmination of his metamorphosis allows him to feel 'that [he] had been happy and that [he was] happy again.'[25] This is further proved by scholar Carl Viggiani, who argues that the 'main theme [of the novel] is death and the meaning of life comes out of a confrontation with death.'[26]

Meursault is confronted with death three times: Maman's death, the Arab's death and his impending execution. Because he lacks closeness with his

---

[21] Ibid., 123.
[22] Camus, *The Stranger*, 123.
[23] Ibid., 122.
[24] Ibid., 123.
[25] Ibid.
[26] Carl Viggiani, "Camus' L'Etranger" *PMLA* (New York: MLA, Dec. 1956) vol. 77, no. 5) 856-87.

mother, her death did not impact him in a way that the court and jury could understand. He goes to the home because he had an obligation to complete the cycle of bringing her there in life and seeing her there in death. The prosecution made a bigger issue out of the supposed indifference than should be allowed. They made him out to be a disheartened criminal, who was negligent towards his mother's well-being. However, in my opinion, the court failed to see that he was not a distraught son but, rather, one half of a mother and son who were not close with one another. The relationship with Maman was non-sequitur in regards to the Arab's murder.

When it comes to the shooting of the Arab, the court saw a premeditated crime.[27] The court failed to recognize that if the murder was premeditated, then it would have been planned methodically. However, the events which precede the Arab's murder are the following: Raymond (Meursault's supposed friend) was hurt; he looked up to him, and because he wanted to emulate him, subconsciously, Meursault admired Raymond; thus, to prove himself, he took the pistol, proceeded to go back to the beach where the Arab lay, and you 'shattered the harmony of the day', firing 'four more times at the motionless body where the bullets lodged without leaving a trace.'[28]

Subconsciously, the killing of the Arab asserted the friendship with Raymond and illustrated that Meursault was capable of being 'as much of a man' as he, through the macho-ness of taking someone else's life. However, the conscious effect of the murder is that each bullet 'was like knocking four quick times on the door of unhappiness.'[29]

At that precise moment, Meursault consciously acknowledged that the Arab's murder brings upon a sense of unhappiness into his life. For a brief moment, the overall unhappiness which had been repressed throughout his life came back furiously to the point of exploding into a 'trigger happy' rage. He was unable to prevent the repeated pull of the trigger because he was overcome by the unhappiness which had engulfed his life, which has diminished any rationality that he might have.

[27] Camus, *The Stranger*, 99.
[28] Ibid., 59.
[29] Ibid.

Weakened judiciousness, in any individual's situation, creates a kind of unease. And it is this unease, which he sensed within himself, at the time of the murder, was repressed as a coping mechanism through indifference. The indifference of the Arab's death signifies and, to an extent, symbolizes the pretended self-confident, brazen individual Meursault desired to become. However, it is nothing more than a façade for the foil that has become his forlorn and melancholic life, and this irritates him to the point of existential frustration.

Meursault's existential frustration becomes too much of an aggravation to cope with, so when the court reads the verdict and punishment of death, he does not think 'about anything anymore'[30] and that has nothing to say.

After the initial shock of the sentence, there is the abject acceptance of the inevitability of the circumstances. There is nothing more that Meursault can do, so he acknowledges and understands the inescapability of death albeit reluctantly because despite a willingness to understand, he just cannot 'accept such arrogant certainty. Because, after all, there was really something ridiculously out of proportion between the verdict of such certainty'[31] there is nothing more that can be done to alter the outcome, so he chooses to accept his fate which, again, provides him with a coping mechanism.

By coping with his situation, he transposes thoughts of his life, which seem to mean nothing to Meursault, and then he slowly initiates reflections on Maman's life. And it is here that the epiphany that 'There is no God. Life has no transcendent meaning, and it is not worth living, but it is all that we have; the only worthwhile afterlife would be one in which life on earth could be remembered.'[32]

Finally for, Meursault, 'The experience of death is the catastrophe that illuminates the human condition.'[33]; out of the shadows (of death), one's condition is elucidated for others to behold- not so much in terms of critiquing- so that the others might reflect upon the meaning of their own lives, and perhaps find meaning where none previously existed; and maybe

---

[30] Ibid., 107.
[31] Ibid., 109.
[32] Viggiani, 886.
[33] Ibid., 879.

it is the meaning that someone else finds that will help make his life meaningful, even after he is deceased from this earthly existence.

Works Cited

Abrams, M.H. "Absurd." *A Glossary of Literary Terms*, 9th ed. Boston: Wadsworth, 2009.

Buber, Martin. *Between Man and Man*. New York: Macmillan, 1965.

Camus, Albert. *The Myth of Sisyphus*. Trans. Justin O'Brien. New York: Vintage, 1954.

——. *The Stranger*. Trans. Matthew Ward. New York: Vintage, 1988.

Frankl, Viktor E. *Man's Search For Meaning*. New York: Pocket Books, 1985.

Lea, Simon. "Albert Camus and the Early Essays" excerpt. from *Existential Horror: Ethics and Society*.

Todd, Oliver. *Albert Camus: A Life*. Trans. Benjamin Irvy. New York: Knopf, 1997.

Viggiani, Carl. "Camus' L'Etranger." *PMLA* 77 (1956): 5.

Yalom, Irvin D. *Existential Psychotherapy*. New York: BasicBooks, 1980.

The Critique of Contemporary Philosophy in Camus's unpublished work 'L'Impromptu des Philosophes'

by Giovanni Gaetani

Se moquer de la philosophie, c'est vraiment philosopher.

BLAISE PASCAL, *Pensées*

One of the greatest creations of the human mind is the art of reviewing books without having read them.

GEORG CHRISTOPH LICHTENBERG, *Aphorisms*

Among all Camus's unpublished works, one in particular is too often forgotten by Camus scholars: *L'impromptu des philosophes*[1]. While a text like *Le premier homme* occupies a place of great importance in our comprehension of Camus's oeuvre, for *The Comedy of the Philosophers* (from now on just TCP) there is not even an entry in the most important bibliographies of Camus studies and French literature[2]. For this reason I have decided to write a paper in which I could analyse and comment appropriately this text, in order to, first, give a general overview of it and, second, to point out his relevance for Camus's critique of contemporary philosophy. Let us start with the first point.

---

[1] All the English translations from French are mine, since at the moment there is not an English edition of the text.

[2] For example, in the last update of the international bibliography of Camus studies collated by Raymond-Gay Crosier (http://www.clas.ufl.edu/users/gaycros/Bibliog.htm), as well as in some other main bibliographies of French literature. Only Michel Onfray in his last monograph on Camus (*L'ordre libertaire. La vie philosophique d'Albert Camus*, Paris, Flammarion, 2012) has dedicated a chapter to it, but evidently that is not enough.

Basic philological facts and short résumé

TCP has been published for the first time in 2006, in the second tome of the last edition of Camus's complete works, edited by Gallimard[3]. The French editors of the text had to work hard to find out the exact period in which Camus has wrote it: indeed, some sketches of TCP were wrote by Camus on six calendar pages of which the year is not visible; anyway, according to the dates, the text could have been written just in three possible periods – 1942, 1947 or 1952. The editors seems to be convinced that the second hypothesis (1947) is the most likely, essentially because in the *Notebooks* of that year there are plenty of critical observations on contemporary philosophy, especially on Sartre and Merleau-Ponty[4].

Although the text could be considered practically ready for the publication[5], Camus decided to avoid it, because he was seriously worried about the reactions of all his intellectual colleagues. Not satisfied with this precaution, he also put a pseudonym on the typescript (Antoine Bailly), so that no one could eventually attribute the text to him.

Let us have a look at the plot: the main character is Monsieur Néant, a weird fellow who pretends to be a well-known Parisian philosopher; the scene opens with his arrival at the house of Monsieur Vigne, the other main character, who is at the same time mayor and pharmacist of a small provincial town in France; Néant affirms that the philosophical works of Vigne are well-known in Paris, even if the author himself could swear that they have never been published (*sic!*); for Néant these are just details, what really matters is to practice his new profession, namely 'the salesman of new doctrines'; indeed, he came to Vigne's house just to teach him all the new great philosophical concepts in vogue in Paris, availing himself of a mysterious, voluminous book that he calls "the new Gospel" of which he considers himself 'the new Apostle'. From this point forward Néant is like a swollen river: no one can stop him from sustaining the most illogical

---

[3] Albert Camus, *Œuvres complètes*, Paris, Éditions Gallimard, 2006, tome II, pp. 769-791, notes by Raymond-Gay Crosier pp. 1376-1378.
[4] For example the following one: Albert Camus, *Œuvres complètes*, cit., II, p. 1091:
" Merleau-Ponty. Apprendre à lire. Il se plaint d'avoir mal été lu - et compris. C'est le genre de plainte auquel j'aurais incliné autrefois. Maintenant je sais qu'elle est injustifiée. Il n'y a pas de contresens ". For a closer examination of the philological particulars Cf. the important notes of Raymond Gay-Crosier in Albert Camus, *Œuvres complètes*, cit., II, pp. 1376-78.
[5] Camus even made a 40 pages long typescript with few handmade corrections, consultable at the *Centre de documentation Albert Camus* in Aix-en-Provence (CMS2. Ab11-01.03).

philosophical theories, using a meaningless and inconclusive language. The problem is that Monsieur Vigne seems to be totally delighted with them. He is really enthusiastic. No matter how hard his wife tries to bring him back to his senses: by then Monsieur Vigne is completely lost in Nèant's fool philosophy – for example, he strives to memorize and repeat the meaningless maxims of Néant and, worst, he almost divorces his wife, persuaded by Néant's strange ideas on love and engagement. Anyway, before the irreparable happens, the director of the local mental hospital comes on the scene to recapture Néant, who is clearly a mad and not at all a philosopher. This is in short the plot.

Analysis of the philosophical references

As we already underlined in the introduction, the sarcastic tone of TCP has a precise critical target, namely the hypocrisy of the contemporary philosophy – mainly the existentialism. More specifically what Camus really could not stand was the way in which philosophy was understood and performed by the French academic and intellectual *milieu*: a mix between an historical discipline, in which ideas are analysed and discussed with the typical detachment of an historian, and an intellectual *divertissement*, in which the philosopher can play with ideas as in a frivolous game – what Michel Onfray calls "la philosophie pour la philosophie", "philosophy for philosophy's sake"[6].

Indeed, for the contemporary philosopher the value of an idea is just relative and transitory: a new idea, more interesting and engaging, will always take the place of the former, like for fashion objects. That is, at least, the belief of Monsieur Néant: when he finds out that Vigne is still a believer, he does not advise him against religion through theoretical arguments or convincing reasonings; rather, he just affirms that "religion is not anymore in vogue in Paris among fashionable people"[7].

---

[6] Michel Onfray, *L'ordre libertaire. La vie philosophique d'Albert Camus*, Paris, Flammarion, 2012, p. 22: 'Comme il se trouve une tribu d'esthètes qui pratique l'art pour l'art, il existe une peuplade d'intellectuels qui pratique la philosophie pour la philosophie, comme un jeu d'enfants n'engageant à rien […]. Ce même jeu justifie aussi l'assimilation de la philosophie à un pur exercice de rhétorique dans lequel les sophisteries s'enchaînent pour prouver n'importe quoi.'

[7] Albert Camus, *Œuvres complètes*, cit., II, p. 773 : 'Cette religion, en tous cas, ne se porte plus du tout à Paris chez les gens qui sont à la mode.'

On the same line, Monsieur Néant proves himself to be a perfect disciple of existentialism, showing us his great philosophical capabilities: first, he argues with great calm that nothing in the world has a reason and it is just a matter of hazard; then, in order to dissolve the puzzlement of Monsieur Vigne, he affirms that 'the world is absurd because it is impossible to be explained' and that 'it is impossible to be explained just because it is absurd'[8] . *Chapeau!*

According to Camus, existentialist philosophers, especially Sartre and Heidegger, approach the absurd with an obsessive attitude that makes it a sort of idol to worship. We all know what the absurd was instead in Camus's eyes: just a necessary point of depart and not of arrival; an evidence to be surpassed, rather than a great revelation for the whole mankind. A dialogue of TCP explains Camus's critical point of view: when our presumed Parisian philosopher affirms that there is nothing more heroic than accepting the absurd, Vigne replies that in his opinion there is nothing so heroic in accepting what one cannot refuse. Surprisingly Néant agrees and says that 'this is exactly the advantage of this new philosophy': while before to be considered an hero some merits were needed, now one can become an hero without having done anything at all[9].

Anyway, beyond this kind of indirect references there are plenty of direct quotations strewn here and there in the text. The first one is about Heidegger: even if the name of the German philosopher is not mentioned, we are absolutely positive that Camus is referring to him. That is because in TCP Camus reuses the same argument from *The Myth of Sisyphus* concerning Heidegger's obsession for the sentiment of anguish – the original German term is *die Angst*. Let us compare the two passages: in the *Myth* Camus writes that for 'this professor of philosophy' anguish seems to be "much more important than all the categories in the world', so that "he thinks and talks only of it'[10]; likewise in TCP Monsieur Néant affirms that 'anguish is the best thing in the world', that 'there is nothing more

---

[8] *Ibidem*, p. 774.

[9] *Ivi*: 'Justement, c'est là qu'est tout l'avantage de cette nouvelle philosophie. Car auparavant, il fallait pour être héroïque avoir fait quelque chose, au lieu qu'aujourd'hui, et grâce à ces belles pensées, on est un héros tout à fait sans rien faire.'

[10] Albert Camus, *Œuvres complètes*, cit., I, p. 235 : " Ce professeur de philosophie écrit sans trembler et dans le langage le plus abstrait du monde que " le caractère fini et limié de l'existence humaine est plus primordiale que l'homme lui-même " [...] Ce souci lui parait à tel point dépasser en vérité les catégories du raisonnement, qu'il ne songe qu'à lui et ne parle que de lui".

consolatory than it' and that 'there is nothing worst than a life without it'; he even affirms that 'is just anguish that enables us to live'; the prove of it is that 'dead people does not feel any anguish at all'[11].

It concerns Sartre's quotations, the situation is more complex: already the name of the main character, Monsieur Néant, is a clear allusion to Sartre's *L'Être et le Néant*. And at least other three books of Sartre are directly mentioned all along the text: *Huis clos*, *Saint-Genet comédien et martyr* and *Les Chemins de la liberté*. In particular for this last one the sarcasm of Camus is unmistakable: talking about the right thing to do at the next election, Monsieur Néant suggests that,

> since to be free you have to fight for freedom during your life, and since to fight you need to be oppressed, you will declare your love for freedom and, at the same time, you will vote for those who want to suppress it[12].

Sartre's contradiction is mocked here: the same French philosopher who declared that 'man is condemned to be free' and who attributed the highest value to freedom is, at the same time, one of the most fervent supporter of the despotic and liberticidal regime of Soviet Union[13]. The fact that Sartre in 1956 condemned this same regime he used to glorify is, in my opinion, nothing but a countercheck of the intellectual hypocrisy criticized by Camus in TCP.

Indeed, it really seems that contemporary philosophers enjoy some absurd privileges: first, they can sustain one thing and its opposite without being accused of incoherence[14]; second, they can promote a certain philosophical

---

[11] Albert Camus, *Œuvres complètes*, cit., II, p. 780 : " Ah ! monsieur, rien n'est plus consolant que l'angoisse et il n'est rien de pire qu'une vie privée de cette vertu. En vérité, il est tout à fait impossible de vivre sans angoisse et c'est elle qui fait vivre au lieu qu'elle vous fasse le moindre mal. La preuve en est que le morts ne l'éprouvent point ".

[12] Albert Camus, *Œuvres complètes*, cit., II, p. 788 : " Eh ! bien, monsieur cela est fort simple, puisque vous ne sauriez être libre sans avoir lutté votre vie durant pour la liberté, puisque vous ne pouvez lutter que si vous êtes opprimés, vous proclamerez votre amour de la liberté et vous voterez en même temps pour ceux qui veulent la supprimer ".

[13] Using Tocqueville's words (letter to Madame Swetchine, 7th January 1856 in *Œuvres complètes*, Paris, Gallimard, 1991, XV, II), Camus defines Sartres and the progressivists " esprits "qui semblent faire du goût de la servitude une sorte d'ingrédient de la vertu" ". Cf. Albert Camus, *Œuvres complètes*, cit., IV, p. 1168.

[14] For an interesting overview of post-modernist philosophers' idiocies concerning their improper use of scientific concepts and their voluntary obscure and meaningless language Cf.

theory without being asked to 'preach it by example'[15]; third, they can criticize books without bothering to read it[16]; conversely, fourth, they can write everything they want, being sure that no one will ever read their whole books, being satisfied with a review of a journalist; at most, the only student who will zealously read their whole books will strive to find a meaning even where a meaning is absent[17].

Anyway, going back to the text, we could affirm that the only reasonable characters of TCP are the director of the mental hospital and Madame Vigne. This last one embodies the practical wisdom and the common sense facing the oddness of the two pseudo-philosophers. Indeed, she is the only one who strives to unmask their hypocrisy. In particular one dialogue is really interesting and funny at the same time: when Vigne argues again that nothing has a meaning, she replies with these words:

> since, as you say, nothing has a meaning, today you will not have dinner, while I will eat all alone this knuckle of ham, though persisting in error and ignorance[18].

Suddenly Vigne replies in turn that he must eat anyway, even though nothing has a meaning, and then, facing the inflexibility of Madame Vigne,

---

Alan Sokal, Jean Bricmont, *Fashionable nonsense, Postemodern intellectuals' abuse of science*, Picador, New York, 1998, first published in French under the title *Impostures intellectuelles* by Éditions Odile Jacob, 1997.

[15] Albert Camus, *The myth of Sisyphus*, Penguin, London, 2000, p. 14.

[16] Albert Camus, *Œuvres complètes*, cit., III, p. 603 : "Un écrivain écrit en grande partie pour être lu (ceux qui disent le contraire, admirons-les, mais ne les croyons pas). De plus en plus cependant, il écrit chez nous pour obtenir cette consécration dernière qui consiste à ne pas être lu. À partir du moment, en effet, où il peut fournir la matière d'un article pittoresque dans notre presse à grand tirage, il a toutes les chances d'être connu par un assez grand nombre de personnes qui ne le liront jamais parce qu'elles se suffiront de connaître son nom et de lire ce qu'on écrira sur lui. Il sera désormais connu (et oublié) non pour ce qu'il est, mais selon l'image qu'un journaliste pressé aura donnée de lui. Pour se faire un nom dans les lettres, il n'est donc plus indispensable d'écrire des livres. Il suffit de passer pour en avoir fait un dont la presse du soir aura parlé et sur lequel on dormira désormais ".

[17] Albert Camus, *Œuvres complètes*, cit., IV, p. 1087 : " Ceux qui écrivent obscurément ont bien de la chance : ils auront des commentateurs. Les autres n'auront que des lecteurs, ce qui, parait-il, est méprisable ".

[18] Albert Camus, *Œuvres complètes*, cit., II, p. 778 : " Eh ! bien, ce sera comme vous voudrez, et puisque rien ne sert de rien, vous ne souperez pas aujourd'hui tandis que je continuerai à croupir dans l'ignorance et dans l'erreur en mangeant toute seule ce jambonneau bien gras que Dieu, oui, Dieu lui-même, nous envoya ce matin ".

he invents with hesitation an embarrassing sophism which would convince no one:

> I need to to eat for your sake because, for what I know now, I am nothing without you and I have to become what I am, helping you to become what you are; from this it emerges that, being what I am, I have to do the same that you do, and you, being what you are, you must let me do what we need to do in order to be what we are. This is the reason why I must have dinner. Is it clear?[19]

> Madame Vigne is desperate but do not want to give up. At this point Monsieur Vigne asks Néant for help, who with no hesitation reports his favourite quote from his book: "Être en se faisant et faire que cela soit, c'est être à tout venant sans être quoi que ce soit"[20]. Madame Vigne is exhausted and runs away. The icing on the cake is that Monsieur Néant eats the knuckle of ham that she previously denied to his husband!

Referring to this dialogue, I would suggest an historical parallel between Néant and Vigne and those Sceptics who tried to deny Aristotle's law of non-contradiction[21]: both are two clear examples of conflict between theory and practice, between what they argue in words and what they actually do. Simplifying, while *theoretically* the Sceptics used to argue that "nothing is determined" and that everything is at the same time "so and not so", *in practice* they were acting like everything was instead determined. Against them Aristotle questioned:

---

[19] Albert Camus, *Œuvres complètes*, cit., II, p. 779 : " Sans doute, car (*il hésite – puis illuminé et très vite*) à ce que je sais maintenant, je ne suis rien sans vous et je me dois d'accomplir ce que je suis, en vous aidant à être ce que vous êtes, d'où il ressort qu'étant ce que je suis, je dois faire ce que vous faites et qu'étant ce que vous êtes, vous devez me laisser faire ce qu'il faut bien faire pour que vous et moi soyons ce que nous sommes. C'est la raison pour quoi je dois souper. Cela est-il clair ? ".

[20] Albert Camus, *Œuvres complètes*, cit., II, p. 780. I tried to translate it as follows : "To be in becoming and to let it happen, it is to be for everyone without being anyone".

[21] Apparently exaggerated, this parallel is indeed justified from the fact that Camus knew well the question about the law of non-contradiction in Aristotle – he even quoted in *The Myth* an entire passage from the *Metaphysics* with no advice. Cf. Albert Camus, *Œuvres complètes*, cit., I, p. 230. Cf. also the critique of Jean Grenier to Camus's interpretation of this Aristotle's passage, *Ibidem*, p. 1286 : " Votre dialectique est insuffisante et contraste avec la force de vos sentiments. Aristote dans la page que vous citez réfute les Sceptiques absolus et les dogmatiques absolus pour conclure qu'il existe certaines choses vraies et d'autres fausses – il dit donc le contraire de ce que vous lui faites dire ".

> For why does a man walk to Megara and not stay at home, when he thinks he ought to be walking there? Why does he not walk early some morning into a well or over a precipice, if one happens to be in his way? Why do we observe him guarding against this, evidently because he does not think that falling in is alike good and not good? Evidently, then, he judges one thing to be better and another worse.[22]

In TCP the same question is posed by Madame Vigne to his husband gone mad: if you really believe that nothing has a meaning, that life has no sense at all and that doing one thing is like doing its opposite, why in the end you want to have dinner? The answer is quite simple: all these nihilistic affirmations are just intellectual poses flaunted in bad faith. For two reasons: first, because these philosophers are inconsequent – indeed, if life has really no meaning at all then, coherently with this belief, they should commit suicide; second, because it is logically impossible to assert an absolute nihilism. A passage from *The Enigma* clarifies this point:

> Without getting to the bottom of things, one can at least mention that just as there is no absolute materialism, since merely to form this word is already to acknowledge something in the world apart from matter, there is likewise no total nihilism. The moment you say that everything is nonsense you express something meaningful. Refusing the world all meaning amounts to abolishing all value judgements. But living, and eating, for example, are in themselves value judgements. You choose to remain alive the moment you do not allow yourself to die of hunger, and consequently you recognize that life has at least a relative value[23].

At this point, it is time for conclusions: as we have seen, TCP can be considered a mere *divertissement* just for those who cannot see deeply inside

---

[22] Aristotle, *Metaphysics*, book IV, part IV, translated by W. D. Ross, The Internet Classics Archive, freely consultable at URL: http://classics.mit.edu/Aristotle/metaphysics.html

[23] Albert Camus, *Lyrical and Critical Essays*, Vintage Books Edition, 1970, pp. 159-160. For the French original text Cf. Albert Camus, *Œuvres complètes*, cit., I, pp. 605-606 : 'Sans aller au fond des choses, on peut remarquer au moins que, de même qu'il n'y a pas de matérialisme absolu puisque pour former seulement ce mot il faut déjà dire qu'il y a dans le monde quelque chose de plus que la matière, de même il n'y a pas de nihilisme total. Dès l'instant où l'on dit que tout est non-sens, on exprime quelque chose qui a du sens. Refuser toute signification au monde revient à supprimer tout jugement de valeur. Mais vivre, et par exemple se nourrir, est en soi un jugement de valeur. On choisit de durer dès l'instant qu'on ne se laisse pas mourir, et l'on reconnaît alors une valeur, au moins relative, à la vie.'

it; the aware reader can instead find in every passage an hidden reference to a certain philosopher or, more in general, to a strange attitude of contemporary philosophy. Behind the sarcastic tone and the fluency of the text, which by the way can be read easily in twenty minutes, Camus has left his personal witness against those literary and philosophical circles which have ostracized his person and banished his works in name of a presumed intellectual superiority.

Indeed, Camus truly never wanted to be part of this philosophical elite[24]. That is why he often refused the appellative of philosopher, like for example in 1945 in an interview to the French journal *Servir*[25]. But, as I elsewhere shown[26], this refuse was just a masking: reading carefully Camus's *Notebooks* it is easy to understand that he always wanted to be a philosopher, in his works as well in his life. In this perspective *The Comedy of the Philosophers* cannot but be a convincing countercheck of this will.

---

[24] According to the words of Bernard Henry-Levy's well-known article: " Camus est, de son propre aveu, un philosophe d'un genre particulier. C'est un philosophe qui, déjà, se moque des philosophes quand ils cèdent à l'académisme, la pompe, l'obscurité ". Cf. Bernard Henry-Levy, *Albert Camus, philosophe artiste*, Le Monde, 06/01/2010.

[25] As someone will maybe remember, the journalist opened the interview saying that "the name of Camus was often associated with the one of Sartre", as if he was a "disciple of the existentialist philosophy". At this point, Camus suddenly interrupted the journalist, using these words: 'I am not a philosopher. I do not believe in reason enough to believe in a system. What I do really care about is knowing how to behave" and, more precisely, how to behave when one does not believe either in God or in reason. I think it is not so difficult to read between the lines here. In my opinion Camus's first affirmation has not an absolute meaning: he is not saying "I am not a philosopher at all"; instead, he is suggesting that he is not a philosopher if with this word one means the existentialist philosophers like Sartre, Heidegger, Jaspers and so on. On the other hand, the task he recognizes as his own – "to know how to behave when one does not believe either in God or in reason" – is genuinely philosophical. Cf. Albert Camus, *Œuvres complètes*, cit., II, pp. 659-661

[26] *'Is Camus a philosopher?'* – conference presentation held in Budapest (Eötvös Loránd University) for the international conference *Camus in the 21th century*. Soon the acts of the conference will be published by the Centre for French Studies (CIEF).

Works Cited

For the French original text:

Camus, Albert. *Œuvres complètes*, Paris, Éditions Gallimard, 2006, tome II, pp. 769-791, notes by Raymond-Gay Crosier pp. 1376-1378.

Onfray, Michel. *L'ordre libertaire. La vie philosophique d'Albert Camus*, Paris, Flammarion, 2012 .

Weyembergh, Maurice. *Albert Camus, ou la mémoire des origines*, De Boeck universite, Paris-Bruxelles, 1998.

Amiot, Anne-Marie, and Jean-François Mattéi (editors), *Albert Camus et la philosophie*, PUF, Paris, 1997.

Guérin, Jean-Yves (editor), *Dictionnaire Albert Camus*, Laffont, Paris, 2009.

Faes, Hubert, and Guy Basset (editors), *Camus, la philosophie et le christianisme*, Cerf, Paris, 2012.

Absurdity, Creativity, and Constitution: Critical Observations on Camus's Critique of Husserl's Phenomenology in *The Myth of Sisyphus*

by George Heffernan

Abstract

Edmund Husserl (1859–1938), the founder of the phenomenological movement, and Albert Camus (1913–1960), the 1957 Nobel laureate for literature, were two of the leading thinkers of the 20th century. Despite Husserl's critique of what was in his time referred to as "philosophy of existence" (*Existenzphilosophie*), he never wrote anything about Camus's philosophy because due to historical circumstances alone he would hardly have had the occasion or opportunity to do so. For his part, despite his refreshing skepticism in regard to traditional academic philosophy, Camus singled out Husserl's phenomenology for what was by his standards a sustained critique in *The Myth of Sisyphus*. Given that Husserl argues that phenomenology owes its position as rigorous science to its eidetic character (as distinguished both from the empirical approach of psychology as a natural science and from the individual-personal approach of philosophy of existence as a human science), given that Camus focuses on Husserl's consistent and insistent essentialism, and given that his critique articulates the problems that a philosopher of existence may have both with existentialism and with phenomenology, it is remarkable that there has to date been virtually no philosophical literature examining and evaluating Camus's critique of Husserl. The present paper seeks to fill this void by sorting out the merits and demerits of what may be regarded as an exemplary existential but not necessarily existentialist critique of phenomenology.

1. Introduction: A lacuna in the literature

In *The Myth of Sisyphus*, Camus argues that what he calls "the absurd" is generated by the confrontation between human rationality and irrational reality ("l'absurde": 21, 28, 30–31, 54).[1] He asks whether the absurdity of existence dictates suicide and answers that from the fact that life has no meaning it does not follow that life is not worth living (3–4, 8, 119–123). Yet he argues that "the absurd walls" ("les murs absurdes": 10, 20, 22, 27) of the irrational world prevent human reason, which longs for a lucid and unitary understanding of existence, from attaining true knowledge of the self, the universe, or God. He criticizes various thinkers for committing "philosophical suicide" ("le suicide philosophique": 28–29, 41–42, 49–50, 54–55, 64), that is, for trying to bridge the gap between human understanding and incomprehensible reality by resorting to a cheap and easy leap to something transcendent, for example, the absolute, the divine, another life, another world, or forms, ideas, or essences. Thus Camus criticizes, without using the precise terms that would have to wait a while for their formal introduction, the thought of "the existentialists". In doing so, he refers to them as "the existentials" ("les existentielles": 41, 49, 65) and to their thought as "existential philosophy" ("la philosophie existentielle": 29, 59, 133), even talking in the plural of "the existential philosophies" ("les philosophies existentielles": 32, 104). Thus he attacks Kierkegaard, for example, for proposing that the absurdity of existence can be overcome by making "a leap" ("un saut"), that is, "a leap of faith", to a transcendent God who is supposed to give meaning to human life from beyond the world (25–26, 32–41). On the other hand, he does not blame but praise Nietzsche, for example, whom he regards not as "an existential" but as a kind of prophet of the absurd (64–65, 82, 93, 108–109, 137). According to Camus, then, "existential thought" ("la pensée existentielle": 36, 134–135) is characterized by an attitude that at least in the beginning faces the absurdity, anxiety, and despair of human existence, only in the end to deny, negate, or neutralize it by positing the possibility of some form of saving "leap" that spares human beings from the prospect of existential annihilation (33–38, 42, 46, 48, 50, 52–54, 59, 65, 91, 111, 130–132, 134–135, 200). All such attempts at escape, all such efforts to hide the absurd with various screens,

---

[1] Unless specified otherwise, parenthetical page references in the text are to the English translation *The Myth of Sisyphus* that was published by Knopf/Vintage (Camus 1955/1983). References to *Le Mythe de Sisyphe* ("*Sisyphe*") in the footnotes, on the other hand, are to the French text in the volume of the *Essais* that was published by Gallimard in the Bibliothèque de la Pléiade (Camus 1942/1965). Throughout, some quoted translations have been modified to render them more accurate.

all such meaning-bestowing strategies and sense-seeking tactics, Camus condemns as forms of "philosophical suicide" (28–29, 32, 35, 41–42, 49–50, 59). Thus the absurd contradiction between the human need for meaning and the cosmic fact of indifference remains irreducible, and only "the absurd human being" can grasp and live this harsh reality ("l'homme absurde": 37, 39, 41, 45, 49, 55, 57–92), albeit in the mode of a creative revolt against it ("la révolte": 10, 25, 38, 52–55, 60–66, 87–88, 93–118). "The absurd human being" is an embodiment of the will to understand, but his or her attempts at making sense of things may not be purchased at the price of decency, happiness, and truth (20–22). It is not a matter of "believing in order to understand" à la Augustine of Hippo ("crede ut intellegas": *Sermons* 43,4.7; 118,1; *Tractates on the Gospel of John* 29,6) or Anselm of Canterbury ("credo ut intellegam": *Proslogion* 1).

Yet Camus also criticizes, this time using the terms themselves, "phenomenology" ("la phénoménologie": 43), "phenomenological thought" ("la pensée phénoménologique": 44), and "the phenomenologists" ("les phénoménologues": 23, 26, 43). He attacks Husserl, for example, for taking refuge in a realm of essences behind phenomena that are supposed to bestow meanings on things (26, 43–50). Although he says that he is "not examining the philosophy of Husserl" (37–38, fn.),[2] it is clear that Camus's critique of Husserl's phenomenology involves a thematic, indeed, systematic, analysis of an essential element of that philosophy, namely, its resolute commitment to determinate essences. In fact, for Camus, the phenomenologists are members of "a whole family of minds related by their nostalgia but opposed by their methods or their aims", who have, "both on the logical plane and on the moral plane", persisted "in blocking the royal road of reason and in recovering the direct paths of truth" (23).[3] According to Camus, Husserl and the phenomenologists, "on the plane of method" and "by their very extravagances", "reinstate the world in its diversity and deny the transcendent power of reason", so that "the spiritual universe becomes incalculably enriched by them".[4] On their approach, for example, "the rose

---

[2] Cf. *Sisyphe*, 126: "On peut penser que je néglige ici le problème essentiel qui est celui de la foi. Mais je n'examine pas la philosophie de Kierkegaard, ou de Chestov ou, plus loin, de Husserl (il y faudrait une autre place et une autre attitude d'esprit), je leur emprunte un thème et j'examine si ses conséquences peuvent convenir aux règles déjà fixées. Il s'agit seulement d'entêtement."

[3] Cf. *Sisyphe*, 114: "De Jaspers à Heidegger, de Kierkegaard à Chestov, des phénoménologues à Scheler, sur le plan logique et sur le plan moral, toute une famille d'esprits, parents par leur nostalgie, opposés par leurs méthodes ou leurs buts, se sont acharnés à barrer la voie royale de la raison et à retrouver les droits chemins de la vérité."

[4] Cf. *Sisyphe*, 116: "Sur un tout autre plan, celui de la méthode, par leurs outrances mêmes,

petal, the milestone, or the human hand are as important as love, desire, or the laws of gravity".[5] Thus "thinking ceases to be unifying or making a semblance familiar in the guise of a major principle", but rather becomes "learning all over again to see, to be attentive, to focus consciousness, turning every idea and every image, in the manner of Proust, into a privileged moment" (26).[6] What is more, and "paradoxically" so, is that thus "everything is privileged" and "what justifies thought is its extreme consciousness".[7] Hence Camus regards Husserl's procedure as preferable to Kierkegaard's, in so far as it "negates the classic method of reason, disappoints hope, opens to intuition and to the heart a whole proliferation of phenomena, the wealth of which has about it something inhuman" (27).[8] "These paths", suggests Camus disjunctively, "lead to all sciences or to none".[9] This means, in turn, that "in this case the means are more important than the end", or that the method justifies the results, because "all that is involved is 'an attitude for understanding' and not a consolation" (27).[10] Yet what is decisive, according to Camus, is that Husserl's approach is disappointing because, although it aims to do all of these things "in the beginning", it fails to do any of them *in the end* (27).[11] Throughout, Camus's critical point is that, on Husserl's approach, the phenomenologists start out from a correct recognition of the fact that the universe is ruled by absurdity, antinomy, and anxiety, only to make the fatal mistake of wrongly abandoning their premises along the way in order to arrive at the questionable conclusion that consciousness can adopt "an attitude for understanding" the world and everything in it. In other words, if the world does not make sense, then consciousness makes sense of it by bestowing

---

Husserl et les phénoménologues restituent le monde dans sa diversité et nient le pouvoir transcendant de la raison. L'univers spirituel s'enrichit avec eux de façon incalculable."
[5] Cf. *Sisyphe*, 116–117: "Le pétale de rose, la borne kilométrique ou la main humaine ont autant d'importance que l'amour, le désir, ou les lois de la gravitation."
[6] Cf. *Sisyphe*, 117: "Penser, ce n'est plus unifier, rendre familière l'apparence sous le visage d'un grand principe. Penser, c'est réapprendre à voir, à être attentif, c'est diriger sa conscience, c'est faire de chaque idée et de chaque image, à la façon de Proust, un lieu privilégié."
[7] Cf. *Sisyphe*, 117: "Paradoxalement, tout est privilégié. Ce qui justifie la pensée, c'est son extrême conscience."
[8] Cf. *Sisyphe*, 117: "Pour être plus positive que chez Kierkegaard ou Chestov, la démarche husserlienne, à l'origine, nie cependant la méthode classique de la raison, déçoit l'espoir, ouvre à l'intuition et au cœur toute une prolifération de phénomènes dont la richesse a quelque chose d'inhumain."
[9] Cf. *Sisyphe*, 117: "Ces chemins mènent à toutes les sciences ou à aucune."
[10] Cf. *Sisyphe*, 117: "C'est dire que le moyen ici a plus d'importance que la fin. Il s'agit seulement 'd'une attitude pour connaître' et non d'une consolation."
[11] Cf. *Sisyphe*, 117: "Encore une fois, à l'origine du moins."

meaning on it. But this approach only yields "comprehension" at the cost of *consolation*.

By any measure, Edmund Husserl (1859–1938) and Albert Camus (1913–1960) must be counted among the intellectual and moral giants of the 20th century. The former is regarded as the founding father of the phenomenological movement in the precise sense (Franz Brentano [1838–1917] was a pioneering predecessor and Carl Stumpf [1848–1936] served as an experimental phenomenologist), and the latter has been viewed as the quintessential "existentialist" (*sit venia verbo*), at least in the popular but misleading sense of the word. Yet Husserl harbored strong reservations about and registered sharp disapproval of the intellectual orientation that in the German-speaking world of the 1920s and 1930s was referred to simply as "philosophy of existence" (*Existenzphilosophie*)—the English expression *existentialism*, the German *Existenzialismus*, and the French *existentialisme* all came later (Heffernan 2014). For his part, Camus both rejected phenomenology and denied being an existentialist. In fact, perhaps the only major thinker of the 20th century who did admit to being an existentialist was Camus's ally-turned-enemy, Sartre, and even he felt very early compelled to concede that the term "is being so loosely applied to so many things that it has come to mean nothing at all" (Sartre 1946/2007, 20).[12] In light of these developments, it is remarkable that there is virtually no scholarly literature focusing on the philosophical relationship between Camus and Husserl (an exception that proves the rule: Bielawka 1996 or Fiut 2009). Accordingly, the purpose of this paper is to examine Camus's critique of Husserl's phenomenology and to determine its philosophical merits and demerits. In Part 2, the basic points of Camus's critique of Husserl are laid out. In Part 3, the methodological limits of his critique are exhibited. In Part 4, the philosophical value of his critique is assessed. In conclusion, common ground between Camus and Husserl is located. It is worth noting that, for obvious reasons having to do with historical circumstances, there is no evidence that Husserl ever learned of or responded to Camus's criticisms.

---

[12] Cf. *L'existentialisme est un humanisme*, 25: "[…] et au fond le mot a pris aujourd'hui une telle largeur et une telle extension qu'il ne signifie plus rien du tout."

2. The points of Camus's critique of Husserl's philosophy in *The Myth of Sisyphus*

Camus's critique of Husserl's phenomenology is localized in *The Myth of Sisyphus* (Camus does not mention Husserl in the *Carnets/Notebooks*—cf. Camus 1963, 65, fn. 1), and it involves several major points. It is possible to organize the individual statements that express the particular points of the critique around six central themes, namely, intentionality, essentialism, logicism, intellectualism, rationalism, and evidence.

1. Intentionality. To begin with, Camus examines the theme of "the intention", to which has already been alluded, that Husserl emphasizes in his phenomenology (43).[13] Camus starts by claiming, probably counter-intuitively for many readers of Husserl, that "originally Husserl's method negates the classic procedure of reason" (43).[14] By this Camus means, to repeat himself, that "thinking", in the phenomenological sense, "is not unifying or making the appearance familiar under the guise of a great principle", but rather "learning all over again how to see, directing one's consciousness, making of every image a privileged place" (43).[15] In other words, "phenomenology declines to explain the world; it wants to be merely a description of actual experience" (43).[16] Thus phenomenology "confirms absurd thought in its initial assertion that there is no truth, but merely truths" (43).[17] For example, "from the evening breeze to this hand on my shoulder, everything has its truth" (43).[18] On this interpretation of the phenomenological approach, "consciousness illuminates [truth] by paying attention to it" (43).[19] Here Camus borrows a metaphor from Bergson (43): "Consciousness does not form the object of its understanding, it merely focuses, it is the act of attention, and, to borrow a Bergsonian image, it

---

[13] Cf. *Sisyphe*, 129: "J'examinerai seulement le thème de 'l'Intention', mis à la mode par Husserl et les phénoménologues. Il y a été fait allusion."

[14] Cf. *Sisyphe*, 129: "Primitivement, la méthode husserlienne nie la démarche classique de la raison."

[15] Cf. *Sisyphe*, 129: "Répétons-nous. Penser, ce n'est pas unifier, rendre familière l'apparence sous le visage d'un grand principe. Penser, c'est réapprendre à voir, diriger sa conscience, faire de chaque image un lieu privilégié."

[16] Cf. *Sisyphe*, 129: "Autrement dit, la phénoménologie se refuse à expliquer le monde, elle veut être seulement une description du vécu."

[17] Cf. *Sisyphe*, 129–130: "Elle rejoint la pensée absurde dans son affirmation initiale qu'il n'est point de vérité, mais seulement des vérités."

[18] Cf. *Sisyphe*, 130: "Depuis le vent du soir jusqu'à cette main sur mon épaule, chaque chose a sa vérité."

[19] Cf. *Sisyphe*, 130: "C'est la conscience qui l'éclaire par l'attention qu'elle lui prête."

resembles the projector that suddenly focuses on an image."[20] Yet, Camus observes, there is also a "difference" here, namely, "there is no scenario, but a successive and incoherent illustration" (43): "In that magic lantern all the pictures are privileged."[21] Alluding to the *epoché*, the signature act of "bracketing" or "suspension" that both characterizes Husserl's proper method and serves his own purposes, Camus writes (43): "Consciousness suspends in experience the objects of its attention. Through its miracle it isolates them. Henceforth they are beyond all judgments."[22] It is this "intention", according to Camus, that "characterizes consciousness" (43).[23] Yet, for Camus, "the word ['intention'] does not imply any idea of finality; it is taken in its sense of 'direction'; its only value is topographical" (43).[24] He continues (43–44): "At first sight, it certainly seems that in this way nothing contradicts the absurd spirit. That apparent modesty of thought that limits itself to describing what it declines to explain, that intentional discipline whence result paradoxically a profound enrichment of experience and the rebirth of the world in its prolixity are absurd procedures. At least at first sight."[25] Here one must remind oneself that, when Camus says that the performance of the *epoché* does not contradict "the absurd spirit", he then means this approvingly. That is, the phenomenological thought, namely, intentionality, is consistent with the absurd spirit. Yet the problem with the phenomenological approach, for Camus, is that this is the way it is, for Husserl, only "at first sight", but not *in the end*. The reason, according to Camus, is that Husserl seeks to transcend the psychological realm to transition to the metaphysical (44): "For methods of thought, in this case as elsewhere, always assume two aspects, one psychological and the other metaphysical. Thereby they harbor two truths. If the theme of the intentional claims to illustrate merely a psychological attitude, by which reality is

---

[20] Cf. *Sisyphe*, 130: "La conscience ne forme pas l'objet de sa connaissance, elle fixe seulement, elle est l'acte d'attention et, pour reprendre une image bergsonienne, elle ressemble à l'appareil de projection qui se fixe d'un coup sur une image."

[21] Cf. *Sisyphe*, 130: "La différence, c'est qu'il n'y a pas de scénario, mais une illustration successive et inconséquente. Dans cette lanterne magique, toutes les images sont privilégiées."

[22] Cf. *Sisyphe*, 130: "La conscience met en suspens dans l'expérience les objets de son attention. Par son miracle, elle les isole. Ils sont dès lors en dehors de tous les jugements."

[23] Cf. *Sisyphe*, 130: "C'est cette 'intention' qui caractérise la conscience."

[24] Cf. *Sisyphe*, 130: "Mais le mot n'implique aucune idée de finalité; il est pris dans son sens de 'direction', il n'a de valeur que topographique."

[25] Cf. *Sisyphe*, 130: "À première vue, il semble bien que rien ainsi ne contredit l'esprit absurde. Cette apparente modestie de la pensée qui se borne à décrire ce qu'elle se refuse à expliquer, cette discipline volontaire d'où procède paradoxalement l'enrichissement profond de l'expérience et la renaissance du monde dans sa prolixité, ce sont là des démarches absurdes. Du moins à première vue."

drained instead of being explained, nothing in fact separates it from the absurd spirit. It aims to enumerate what it cannot transcend. It affirms solely that without any unifying principle thought can still take delight in describing and understanding every aspect of experience. The truth involved then for each of those aspects is psychological in nature. It simply testifies to the 'interest' that reality can offer. It is a way of awakening a sleeping world and of making it vivid to the mind."[26] Generally, then, Camus examines a key aspect of the phenomenological approach to the acts and contents of consciousness, since that approach begins with acts *as* acts and contents *as* contents but ultimately seeks to determine the accuracy of the acts and the veracity of the contents. Specifically, too, Camus poses the problem of Husserl's appeal to essences (44): "But if one attempts to extend and give a rational basis to that notion of truth, if one claims to discover in this way the 'essence' of each object of knowledge, one restores its depth to experience. For an absurd mind that is incomprehensible."[27] Camus criticizes "this wavering between modesty and assurance that is noticeable in the intentional attitude", and claims that "this shimmering of phenomenological thought illustrate[s] absurd reasoning better than anything else" (44).[28] According to Camus, then, the teleological aspect of Husserl's notion of intentionality, that is, the orientation of intentional consciousness on verification and falsification, is, "for the absurd mind", "incomprehensible". Yet the question is whether and how "phenomenological thought illustrate[s] absurd reasoning" at all, and not "better than anything else". For phenomenology, according to Husserl, is not a skeptical enterprise that aims to serve the absurd spirit, but rather a rigorous science that seeks to make correct judgments about the truth of phenomena (Husserl 1987, 3–62: "Philosophie als strenge Wissenschaft" or

---

[26] Cf. *Sisyphe*, 130–131: "Car les méthodes de pensée, en ce cas comme ailleurs, revêtent toujours deux aspects, l'un psychologique et l'autre métaphysique. Par là elles recèlent deux verites. Si le thème de l'intentionalité ne prétend illustrer qu'une attitude psychologique, par laquelle le réel serait épuisé au lieu d'être expliqué, rien en effet ne le sépare de l'esprit absurde. Il vise à dénombrer ce qu'il ne peut transcender. Il affirme seulement que, dans l'absence de tout principe d'unité, la pensée peut encore trouver sa joie à décrire et à comprendre chaque visage de l'expérience. La vérité dont il est question alors pour chacun de ces visages est d'ordre psychologique. Elle témoigne seulement de l' 'intérêt' que peut présenter la réalité. C'est une façon d'éveiller un monde somnolent et de le rendre vivant à l'esprit."

[27] Cf. *Sisyphe*, 131: "Mais si l'on veut étendre et fonder rationnellement cette notion de vérité, si l'on prétend découvrir ainsi l' 'essence' de chaque objet de la connaissance, on restitue sa profondeur à l'expérience. Pour un esprit absurde, cela est incompréhensible."

[28] Cf. *Sisyphe*, 131: "Or, c'est ce balancement de la modestie à l'assurance qui est sensible dans l'attitude intentionnelle et ce miroitement de la pensée phénoménologique illustrera mieux que tout autre chose le raisonnement absurde."

"Philosophy as Rigorous Science"). Thus it remains to be seen whether Camus has valid and sound arguments for his position that "the absurd spirit" is better than and preferable to the phenomenological spirit that Husserl articulates. Merely "restoring depth to experience", cannot, after all, be, in itself, either good or bad.

2. Essentialism. In effect, Camus charges Husserl with a form of Neo-Platonism, saying that he "speaks likewise of 'extra-temporal essences' brought to light by the intention, and he sounds like Plato" (44).[29] He argues that on the phenomenological way of looking at things, "all things are not explained by one thing but by all things" (44–45).[30] Yet Camus says that he sees "no difference" here (45): "To be sure, those ideas or those essences that consciousness 'effectuates' at the end of every description are not yet to be considered perfect models. But it is asserted that they are directly present in each datum of perception. There is no longer a single idea explaining everything, but an infinite number of essences giving a meaning to an infinite number of objects."[31] As a result, "the world comes to a stop, but also lights up".[32] For Camus, Husserl's phenomenology is, the common understanding of it notwithstanding, not a kind of idealism, namely, transcendental idealism, but a form of realism (45): "Platonic realism becomes intuitive, but it is still realism."[33] Furthermore, Camus also suggests that Husserl "deifies" his essences and thus lands in a kind of "polytheism" (45): "Kierkegaard was swallowed up in his God; Parmenides plunged thought into the One. But here thought hurls itself into an abstract polytheism."[34] He even points out the apparently "absurd" (in Camus's "good" sense of the word) consequences of Husserlian essentialism (45): "But this is not all: hallucinations and fictions likewise belong to 'extra-temporal essences'. In the new world of ideas, the species of centaurs collaborates with the more modest species of metropolitan man."[35] Yet

---

[29] Cf. *Sisyphe*, 131: "Car Husserl parle aussi 'd'essences extra-temporelles' que l'intention met à jour et l'on croit entendre Platon."

[30] Cf. *Sisyphe*, 131: "On n'explique pas toutes choses par une seule, mais par toutes."

[31] Cf. *Sisyphe*, 131: "Je n'y vois pas de différence. Certes ces idées ou ces essences que la conscience 'effectue' au bout de chaque description, on ne veut pas encore qu'elles soient modèles parfaits. Mais on affirme qu'elles sont directement présentes dans toute donnée de perception. Il n'y a plus une seule idée qui explique tout, mais une infinité d'essences qui donnent un sens à une infinité d'objets."

[32] Cf. *Sisyphe*, 131: "Le monde s'immobilise, mais s'éclaire."

[33] Cf. *Sisyphe*, 131: "Le réalisme platonicien devient intuitif, mais c'est encore du réalisme."

[34] Cf. *Sisyphe*, 131: "Kierkegaard s'abîmait dans son Dieu, Parménide précipitait la pensée dans l'Un. Mais ici la pensée se jette dans un polythéisme abstrait."

[35] Cf. *Sisyphe*, 131: "Il y a mieux: les hallucinations et les fictions font partie elles aussi des

Camus also detects a certain ambivalence in Husserl's approach: "For the absurd man, there was a truth as well as a bitterness in that purely psychological opinion that all aspects of the world are privileged. To say that everything is privileged is tantamount to saying that everything is equivalent."[36] This psychological equivalence is, however, only one part of the picture, since the metaphysical equivalence is questionable (45): "But the metaphysical aspect of that truth is so far-reaching that through an elementary reaction he [the absurd man] feels closer perhaps to Plato. He is taught, in fact, that every image presupposes an equally privileged essence. In this ideal world without hierarchy, the formal army is composed solely of generals. To be sure, transcendence had been eliminated. But a sudden shift in thought brings back into the world a sort of fragmentary immanence which restores to the universe its depth."[37] According to Camus, then, Husserl's supposedly pure description of the contents of consciousness posits an essence for every phenomenon and thus entails a robust ontology that is hard to maintain. On this interpretation, Husserlian phenomenology is nothing more than a version of Platonic idealism, and as such it is vulnerable to the standard objections that have been leveled against it starting with Aristotle (*Nicomachean Ethics*, bk. I, ch. 6; *Metaphysics*, bk. VII, ch. 6). It is worth noting that Camus again charges Husserl with "restoring depth to the universe". And again the question that this critique raises is whether doing such a thing is bad, and, if so, why.

3. Logicism. At this point, Camus asks himself whether he has gone too far, that is, whether he has "carried too far a theme handled with greater circumspection by its creators" (45–46).[38] He answers by reading carefully the following assertions of Husserl, "apparently paradoxical yet rigorously logical if what precedes is accepted" (46): "That which is true is true absolutely, in itself; truth is one, identical with itself, however different the

---

'essences extra-temporelles'. Dans le nouveau monde des idées, la catégorie de centaure collabore avec celle, plus modeste, de métropolitain."

[36] Cf. *Sisyphe*, 131: "Pour l'homme absurde, il y avait une vérité en même temps qu'une amertume dans cette opinion purement psychologique que tous les visages du monde sont privilégiés. Que tout soit privilégié revient à dire que tout est équivalent."

[37] Cf. *Sisyphe*, 131: "Mais l'aspect métaphysique de cette vérité le mène si loin que, par une réaction élémentaire, il se sent plus près peut-être de Platon. On lui enseigne en effet que toute image suppose une essence également privilégiée. Dans ce monde idéal sans hiérarchie, l'armée formelle est composée seulement de généraux. Sans doute la transcendance avait été éliminée. Mais un tournant brusque de la pensée réintroduit dans le monde une sorte d'immanence fragmentaire qui restitue sa profondeur à l'univers."

[38] Cf. *Sisyphe*, 132: "Dois-je craindre d'avoir mené trop loin un thème manié avec plus de prudence par ses créateurs?"

creatures who perceive it, men, monsters, angels or gods."[39] (Cf. Husserl 1975, 125.) Here Camus concedes that he cannot deny that "reason triumphs and trumpets forth with that voice".[40] Yet he demurs (46): "What can its assertions mean in the absurd world?"[41] He counters that "the perception of an angel or a god has no meaning" for him, and that "that geometrical spot where divine reason ratifies [his own reason] will always be incomprehensible" to him (46).[42] At that very spot, too, Camus discerns, on Husserl's part, "a leap", and, "though performed in the abstract", it none the less means for him, Camus, "forgetting" just what he "does not want to forget" (46).[43] Indeed, Camus claims that he knows that he is then "faced with a metaphysics of consolation" when Husserl exclaims (46): "If all masses subject to attraction were to disappear, the law of attraction would not be destroyed but would simply remain without any possible application."[44] (Cf. Husserl 1975, 154.) Targeting the evidentiary basis of Husserl's assertions, a sensitive spot for the phenomenologist, Camus argues that, if he wants "to discover the point where thought leaves the path of evidence", then he has "only to reread the parallel reasoning that Husserl voices regarding the mind" (46): "If we could contemplate clearly the exact laws of psychic processes, they would be seen to be likewise eternal and invariable, like the basic laws of theoretical natural science. Hence they would be valid even if there were no psychic process."[45] (Cf. Husserl 1975, 154.) Thus Camus summarizes Husserl's position in a way that seems to reduce it to the absurd in his (Husserl's) own logical, rational sense (46): "Even if the mind were not, its laws would be!"[46] The point is, as Camus

---

[39] Cf. *Sisyphe*, 132: "Je lis seulement ces affirmations d'Husserl, d'apparence paradoxale, mais dont on sent la logique rigoureuse, si l'on admet ce qui précède: 'Ce qui est vrai est vrai absolument, en soi; la vérité est une; identique à elle-même, quels que soient les êtres qui la perçoivent, hommes, monstres, anges ou dieux.'"

[40] Cf. *Sisyphe*, 132: "La Raison triomphe et claironne par cette voix, je ne puis le nier."

[41] Cf. *Sisyphe*, 132: "Que peut signifier son affirmation dans le monde absurde?"

[42] Cf. *Sisyphe*, 132: "La perception d'un ange ou d'un dieu n'a pas de sens pour moi. Ce lieu géométrique où la raison divine ratifie la mienne m'est pour toujours incompréhensible."

[43] Cf. *Sisyphe*, 132: "Là encore, je décèle un saut, et pour être fait dans l'abstrait, il ne signifie pas moins pour moi l'oubli de ce que, justement, je ne veux pas oublier."

[44] Cf. *Sisyphe*, 132: "Lorsque plus loin Husserl s'écrie: 'Si toutes les masses soumises à l'attraction disparaissaient, la loi de l'attraction ne s'en trouverait pas détruite, mais elle resterait simplement sans application possible', je sais que je me trouve en face d'une métaphysique de consolation."

[45] Cf. *Sisyphe*, 132: "Et si je veux découvrir le tournant où la pensée quitte le chemin de l'évidence, je n'ai qu'à relire le raisonnement parallèle qu'Husserl tient à propos de l'esprit: 'Si nous pouvions contempler clairement les lois exactes des processus psychiques, elles se montreraient également éternelles et invariables, comme les lois fondamentales des sciences naturelles théoriques. Donc elles seraient valables même s'il n'y avait aucun processus psychique.'"

understands it, "that of a psychological truth Husserl aims to make a rational rule: after having denied the integrating power of human reason, he leaps by this expedient to eternal Reason" (46).[47] For Camus, then, Husserl's logical absolutism, which privileges the laws of human-neutral logic over the processes of human-natural thought, involves not an existentialist but an essentialist leap. This jump, according to Camus, avoids meaningful discourse about the absurd that arises out of the unbridgeable gap between the desire of human beings for meaning and the indifference of the world to meaning. In any case, the dispute between the claims of absurdity and the claims of rationality cannot be adjudicated by a dogmatic proclamation from either the one side or the other.

4. Intellectualism. In what probably does not represent a reference to the later Husserl's concept of the "life-world" (*Lebenswelt*), and in what probably does represent an allusion to his repeated emphasis on "the concrete" in the *Cartesian Meditations* (cf. Husserl 1950/1973[2], e.g., 60, 67–68, 97–99, 107–109, 117–118, 120–121, etc.; cf. also Husserl 2008), Camus says (46–47): "Husserl's theme of the 'concrete universe' cannot then surprise me."[48] Yet he adds a strong note of caution (47): "If I am told that all essences are not formal but that some are material, that the first are the object of logic and the second of science, this is merely a question of definition. The abstract, I am told, indicates but a part, without consistency in itself, of a concrete universal."[49] In fact, the "wavering" that Camus has already noted allows him to attempt to throw light on "the confusion of these terms" (47): "For that may mean that the concrete object of my attention, this sky, the reflection of that water on this coat, alone preserve the prestige of the real that my interest isolates in the world."[50] And Camus does not deny this.[51] On the other hand, he does affirm that "that may mean

---

[46] Cf. *Sisyphe*, 132: "Même si l'esprit n'était pas, ses lois seraient!"

[47] Cf. *Sisyphe*, 132: "Je comprends alors que d'une vérité psychologique, Husserl prétend faire une règle rationnelle: après avoir nié le pouvoir intégrant de la raison humaine, il saute par ce biais dans la Raison éternelle."

[48] Cf. *Sisyphe*, 132: "Le thème husserlien de l' 'univers concret' ne peut alors me surprendre."

[49] Cf. *Sisyphe*, 132: "Me dire que toutes les essences ne sont pas formelles, mais qu'il en est de matérielles, que les premières sont l'objet de la logique et les secondes des sciences, ce n'est qu'une question de définition. L'abstrait, m'assure-t-on, ne désigne qu'une partie non consistante par elle-même d'un universel concret."

[50] Cf. *Sisyphe*, 132–133: "Mais le balancement déjà révélé me permet d'éclairer la confusion de ces termes. Car cela peut vouloir dire que l'objet concret de mon attention, ce ciel, le reflet de cette eau sur le pan de ce manteau gardent à eux seuls ce prestige du réel que mon intérêt isole dans le monde."

[51] Cf. *Sisyphe*, 133: "Et je ne le nierai pas."

also that this coat itself is universal, has its particular and sufficient essence, belongs to the world of forms" (47).[52] According to Camus, all this means is "that merely the order of the procession has been changed" (47): "This world has ceased to have its reflection in a higher universe, but the heaven of forms is figured in the host of images of this earth."[53] So this "changes nothing", at least nothing essential, for Camus (47): "Rather than encountering here a taste for the concrete, the meaning of the human condition, I find an intellectualism sufficiently unbridled to generalize the concrete itself."[54] Thus, on Camus's interpretation of Husserl's attempt to retain the particular in his grasp for the universal, the best that happens is that the distinction between the concrete and the abstract gets blurred, and the worst that happens is that the concrete gets lost in the abstract. But this approach, for Camus, cannot do justice to the special, indeed, unique, character of the concrete particular. This is a new variation on the old theme, one of Husserl's favorites, that there can be no science of the particular. Yet there is no way to deal with the absurd, which primarily and ultimately confronts an individual living in a unique world, without knowledge of the particular.

5. Rationalism. Camus rejects what he regards as the attempts of both existentialists and essentialists to plaster over the absurdity of it all with their appeals to divinities and essences (47): "It is futile to be amazed by the apparent paradox that leads thought to its own negation by the opposite paths of humiliated reason and triumphal reason."[55] He draws a direct line from the great essentialist of the 20th century to the great existentialist of the 19th century (47–48): "From the abstract god of Husserl to the dazzling god of Kierkegaard the distance is not so great. Reason and the irrational lead to the same preaching. In truth the way matters but little; the will to arrive suffices. The abstract philosopher and the religious philosopher start out from the same disorder and support each other in the same anxiety. But the essential is to explain."[56] Thus, Camus argues, phenomenology departs from

---

[52] Cf. *Sisyphe*, 133: "Mais cela peut vouloir dire aussi que ce manteau lui-même est universel, a son essence particulière et suffisante, appartient au monde des formes."

[53] Cf. *Sisyphe*, 133: "Je comprends alors que l'on a changé seulement l'ordre de la procession. Ce monde n'a plus son reflet dans un univers supérieur, mais le ciel des formes se figure dans le peuple des images de cette terre."

[54] Cf. *Sisyphe*, 133: "Ceci ne change rien pour moi. Ce n'est point le goût du concret, le sens de la condition humaine que je retrouve ici, mais un intellectualisme assez débridé pour généraliser le concret lui-même."

[55] Cf. *Sisyphe*, 133: "On s'étonnerait en vain du paradoxe apparent qui mène la pensée à sa propre négation par les voies opposées de la raison humiliée et de la raison triomphante."

[56] Cf. *Sisyphe*, 133: "Du dieu abstrait d'Husserl au dieu fulgurant de Kierkegaard, la distance

its original path, which was not to explain but to describe (43).[57] Yet he also suggests that the human longing for a world that makes sense is stronger than the equally human striving to make sense of the world (48): "Nostalgia is stronger here than knowledge. It is significant that the thought of the epoch is at once one of the most deeply imbued with a philosophy of the non-significance of the world and one of the most divided in its conclusions. It is constantly oscillating between extreme rationalization of reality, which tends to break up that thought into standard reasons, and its extreme irrationalization, which tends to deify it."[58] Thus both phenomenology and existentialism emerge as strategies of avoidance discourse aimed at substituting nostalgia for absurdity (48): "But this divorce is only apparent. It is a matter of reconciliation, and, in both cases, the leap suffices."[59] Intentionally or not, Camus's concept of reason evokes the skepticism of "the French Socrates" (Montaigne 1967, 1991, II, 12) (48): "It is always wrongly thought that the notion of reason is a one-way notion. To tell the truth, however rigorous it may be in its ambition, this concept is nonetheless just as unstable as others. Reason bears a quite human aspect, but it is also able to turn toward the divine."[60] With respect to the tendency of reason to invent and apply principles that work for it in its attempts to understand the world, Camus, whose thesis for his *diplôme d'études supérieures* (University of Algiers, 1936) was entitled *Métaphysique chrétienne et Néoplatonisme* (*Christian Metaphysics and Neoplatonism*) (Camus 1936, 2007), establishes intellectual linkage all the way back to Neo-Platonism

---

n'est pas si grande. La raison et l'irrationnel mènent à la même prédication. C'est qu'en vérité le chemin importe peu, la volonté d'arriver suffit à tout. Le philosophe abstrait et le philosophe religieux partent du même désarroi et se soutiennent dans la même angoisse. Mais l'essentiel est d'expliquer."

[57] Cf. *Sisyphe*, 129: "Autrement dit, la phénoménologie se refuse à expliquer le monde, elle veut être seulement une description du vécu."

[58] Cf. *Sisyphe*, 133: "La nostalgie est plus forte ici que la science. Il est significatif que la pensée de l'époque soit à la fois l'une des plus pénétrées d'une philosophie de la non-signification du monde et l'une des plus déchirées dans ses conclusions. Elle ne cesse d'osciller entre l'extrême rationalisation du réel qui pousse à la fragmenter en raisons-types et son extrême irrationalisation qui pousse à le diviniser."

[59] Cf. *Sisyphe*, 133: "Mais ce divorce n'est qu'apparent. Il s'agit de se réconcilier et, dans les deux cas, le saut y suffit."

[60] Cf. *Sisyphe*, 133: "On croit toujours à tort que la notion de raison est à sens unique. Au vrai, si rigoureux qu'il soit dans son ambition, ce concept n'en est pas moins aussi mobile que d'autres. La raison porte un visage tout humain, mais elle sait aussi se tourner vers le divin." Cf. also Montaigne, *Apologie de Raimond Sebond*, 235: "J'appelle toujours raison cette apparence de discours que chacun forge en soi; cette raison, de la condition de laquelle il y en peut avoir cent contraires autour d'un même sujet, c'est un instrument de plomb et de cire, allongeable, ployable et accommodable à tout biais et à toutes mesures; il ne reste que la suffisance de le savoir contourner."

(48–49): "Since Plotinus, who was the first to reconcile it [reason] with the eternal climate, it has learned to turn away from the most cherished of its principles, which is contradiction, in order to integrate into it the strangest, the quite magical, one of participation. It is an instrument of thought and not thought itself. Above all, a man's thought is his nostalgia. Just as reason was able to soothe the melancholy of Plotinus, it provides modern anguish the means of calming itself in the familiar setting of the eternal."[61] Yet, as for Camus, so for "the absurd human being", nostalgia is incapable of soothing the pangs of absurdity: "The absurd mind has less luck. For it the world is neither so rational nor so irrational. It is unreasonable and only that."[62] Thus Camus understands Husserl as standing firmly and fully in the Neo-Platonic, anti-absurdist, rationalist-nostalgic tradition (48, fn.),[63] and he is especially hard on him in this regard (49): "With Husserl reason eventually has no limits at all. The absurd, on the contrary, establishes its limits since it is powerless to calm its anguish."[64] Thus, too, Camus understands Kierkegaard differently from Husserl, despite what, he claims, they have in common (49): "Kierkegaard independently asserts that a single limit is enough to negate that anguish. But the absurd does not go so far. For it that limit is directed solely at the reason's ambitions."[65] Hence his criticism of the existentialists, among whom he does not count himself, as abdicating reason in the face of the absurd (49): "The theme of the irrational, as it is conceived by the existentialists, is reason becoming confused and escaping by negating itself."[66] "The absurd", on the other hand, as it is understood by Camus and by "the absurd human being", "is lucid reason noting its limits" (49).[67] Camus clarifies the approach of the absurd human being thus (49): "Only at the end of this difficult path does the absurd man recognize his true motives.

---

[61] Cf. *Sisyphe*, 133–134: "Depuis Plotin qui le premier sut la concilier avec le climat éternel, elle a appris à se détourner du plus cher de ses principes qui est la contradiction pour en intégrer le plus étrange, celui, tout magique, de participation. Elle est un instrument de pensée et non la pensée elle-même. La pensée d'un homme est avant tout sa nostalgie. De même que la raison sut apaiser la mélancolie plotinienne, elle donne à l'angoisse moderne les moyens de se calmer dans les décors familiers de l'éternel."

[62] Cf. *Sisyphe*, 134: "L'esprit absurde a moins de chance. Le monde pour lui n'est ni aussi rationnel ni à ce point irrationnel. Il est déraisonnable et il n'est que cela."

[63] Cf. *Sisyphe*, 134 (fn.): "D'ailleurs ce n'est pas la seule contribution de Plotin à la phénoménologie. […]"

[64] Cf. *Sisyphe*, 134: "La raison chez Husserl finit par n'avoir point de limites. L'absurde fixe au contraire ses limites puisqu'elle est impuissante à calmer son angoisse."

[65] Cf. *Sisyphe*, 134: "Kierkegaard d'un autre côté affirme qu'une seule limite suffit à la nier. Mais l'absurde ne va pas si loin. Cette limite pour lui vise seulement les ambitions de la raison."

[66] Cf. *Sisyphe*, 134: "Le thème de l'irrationnel, tel qu'il est conçu par les existentiels, c'est la raison qui se brouille et se délivre en se niant."

[67] Cf. *Sisyphe*, 134: "L'absurde, c'est la raison lucide qui constate ses limites."

Upon comparing his inner exigency and what is then offered him, he suddenly feels he is going to turn away."[68] Camus also points out that, properly understood, Husserl should not, of course, need any nostalgia (49): "In the universe of Husserl, the world becomes clear and that longing for familiarity that man's heart harbors becomes useless."[69] The world of the existentialist, however, offers a different scenario (49): "In the apocalypse of Kierkegaard, that desire for clarity must be given up if it wants to be satisfied. Sin is not so much knowing (if it were, everybody would be innocent) as wanting to know. Indeed, it is the only sin of which the absurd man can feel that it constitutes both his guilt and his innocence. He is offered a solution in which all the past contradictions have become merely polemical games. But this is not the way he experienced them. Their truth must be preserved, which consists in not being satisfied. He does not want preaching."[70] Therefore Camus criticizes both the existentialist Kierkegaard and the essentialist Husserl, for he supposes that each refuses to take the reality of the absurd seriously enough, the former by appealing *nostalgically* to a divine command theory and a teleological suspension of the ethical, and the latter by appealing *rationalistically* to the possibility of eidetic intuitions of pure essences. One man's God is another man's essence, but in their nostalgia or rationality both fail to face reality, that is, absurdity.

6. Evidence. Finally, on a point that is very important but with which his thinking is not usually associated, namely, argumentative validity and epistemic justification, Camus says (49–50): "My reasoning wants to be faithful to the evidence that aroused it. That evidence is the absurd."[71] He continues (50): "It is that divorce between the mind that desires and the world that disappoints, my nostalgia for unity, this fragmented universe and the contradiction that binds them together."[72] Thus Camus describes the

---

[68] Cf. *Sisyphe*, 134: "C'est au bout de ce chemin difficile que l'homme absurde reconnaît ses vraies raisons. À comparer son exigence profonde et ce qu'on lui propose alors, il sent soudain qu'il va se détourner."
[69] Cf. *Sisyphe*, 134: "Dans l'univers d'Husserl, le monde se clarifie et cet appétit de familiarité qui tient au coeur de l'homme devient inutile."
[70] Cf. *Sisyphe*, 134: "Dans l'apocalypse de Kierkegaard, ce désir de clarté doit se renoncer s'il veut être satisfait. Le péché n'est point tant de savoir (à ce compte, tout le monde est innocent), que de désirer savoir. Justement, c'est le seul péché dont l'homme absurde puisse sentir qu'il fait à la fois sa culpabilité et son innocence. On lui propose un dénouement où toutes les contradictions passées ne sont plus que des jeux polémiques. Mais ce n'est pas ainsi qu'il les a ressenties. Il faut garder leur vérité qui est de ne point être satisfaites. Il ne veut pas de la prédication."
[71] Cf. *Sisyphe*, 134–135: "Mon raisonnement veut être fidèle à l'évidence qui l'a éveillé. Cette évidence, c'est l'absurde."
[72] Cf. *Sisyphe*, 135: "C'est ce divorce entre l'esprit qui désire et le monde qui déçoit, ma

effects that the principal existentialist and the principal essentialist have had on him (50): "Kierkegaard suppresses my nostalgia and Husserl gathers together that universe."[73] He comments on this unexpected turn of philosophical events (50): "That is not what I was expecting. It was a matter of living and thinking with those dislocations, of knowing whether one had to accept or refuse."[74] He emphasizes the essential, indispensable role of evidence in living and thinking, as well as in accepting or refusing (50): "There can be no question of masking the evidence, of suppressing the absurd by denying one of the terms of its equation. It is essential to know whether one can live with it or whether, on the other hand, logic commands one to die of it."[75] Here Camus picks up on and gives a new twist to the motif with which he began the work (50): "I am not interested in philosophical suicide, but rather in plain suicide. I merely wish to purge it of its emotional content and to know its logic and its integrity. Any other position implies for the absurd mind deceit and the mind's retreat before what the mind itself has brought to light."[76] Therefore it is hard to avoid the conclusion that Camus is accusing Husserl—and Kierkegaard too, though in a different manner—of philosophical suicide. This is very clear from the following observation of Camus on Husserl, in which Camus's passage seems to involve a reference to the Introduction to Husserl's *Cartesian Meditations*, though it is not clear which passage is meant (50): "Husserl claims to obey the desire to escape 'the inveterate habit of living and thinking in certain well-known and convenient conditions of existence', but the final leap restores in him the eternal and its comfort."[77] Thus Camus sees a significant difference between Husserl and Kierkegaard in this regard (50): "The leap does not represent an extreme danger as Kierkegaard would like it to do. The danger, on the contrary, lies in the subtle instant that precedes the leap. Being able to remain on that dizzying crest—that is integrity and the rest is subterfuge."[78] In conclusion, Camus remarks (50): "I know also that

---

nostalgie d'unité, cet univers dispersé et la contradiction qui les enchaîne."
[73] Cf. *Sisyphe*, 135: "Kierkegaard supprime ma nostalgie et Husserl rassemble cet univers."
[74] Cf. *Sisyphe*, 135: "Ce n'est pas cela que j'attendais. Il s'agissait de vivre et de penser avec ces déchirements, de savoir s'il fallait accepter ou refuser."
[75] Cf. *Sisyphe*, 135: "Il ne peut être question de masquer l'évidence, de supprimer l'absurde en niant l'un des termes de son équation. Il faut savoir si l'on peut en vivre ou si la logique commande qu'on en meure."
[76] Cf. *Sisyphe*, 135: "Je ne m'intéresse pas au suicide philosophique, mais au suicide tout court. Je veux seulement le purger de son contenu d'émotions et connaître sa logique et son honnêteté. Toute autre position suppose pour l'esprit absurde l'escamotage et le recul de l'esprit devant ce que l'esprit met à jour."
[77] Cf. *Sisyphe*, 135: "Husserl dit obéir au désir d'échapper 'à l'habitude invétérée de vivre et de penser dans certaines conditions d'existence déjà bien connues et commodes', mais le saut final nous restitue chez lui l'éternel et son confort."

never has helplessness inspired such striking harmonies as those of Kierkegaard. But if helplessness has its place in the indifferent landscapes of history, it has none in a reasoning whose exigency is now known."[79] In the end, Camus finds that Husserl's appeal to essences to overcome the absurdity of existence amounts to a relapse into an unphilosophical, nostalgic rationalism that is the intellectual and moral equivalent of philosophical suicide. For Camus, then, Husserl fails to follow the genuine evidence. On the other hand, the question is what evidence there is for the absurd. It would be unphilosophical, after all, to permit Camus to appeal to the absurd as if it were simply supposed to be a "given" of experience. For the supposition that existence is absurd is itself not a fact but an interpretation. As such, it only then makes sense if there is evidence for it.

3. A methodological delimitation of Camus's critique of Husserl's phenomenology

As has already been indicated, there are several crucial points that must be raised here. They pertain especially to the formal and material limitations of Camus's criticisms of Husserl. For the sake of order, it is necessary to take care of these points before moving on to a philosophical response to Camus's critique of Husserl's phenomenology. These points can be organized into six basic groups, namely, general hermeneutics, specific hermeneutics, source availability, source accessibility, potential of eidetic phenomenology, and possibility of existential phenomenology.

1. General hermeneutics. In his review of Camus's *L'Étranger* in *Cahiers du Sud* (1943), Sartre famously, or, depending upon one's viewpoint, infamously, remarks, with direct respect to *The Myth of Sisyphus*, on Camus's seeming lack of full understanding of the philosophers whom he cites, quotes, and criticizes (Sartre 1943/1947, 94): "Camus shows off a bit by quoting passages from Jaspers, from Heidegger, and from Kierkegaard, whom, by the way, he does not always seem to have quite understood."[80] In

---

[78] Cf. *Sisyphe*, 135: "Le saut ne figure pas un extrême danger comme le voudrait Kierkegaard. Le péril au contraire est dans l'instant subtil qui précède le saut. Savoir se maintenir sur cette arête vertigineuse, voilà l'honnêteté, le reste est subterfuge."
[79] Cf. *Sisyphe*, 135: "Je sais aussi que jamais l'impuissance n'a inspiré d'aussi émouvants accords que ceux de Kierkegaard. Mais si l'impuissance a sa place dans les paysages indifférents de l'histoire, elle ne saurait la trouver dans un raisonnement dont on sait maintenant l'exigence."
[80] Cf. "Explication de *L'Étranger*", 94: "M. Camus met quelque coquetterie à citer des textes de Jaspers, de Heidegger, de Kierkegaard, qu'il ne semble d'ailleurs pas toujours bien

corroboration of Sartre's claim, one may note that in his treatment of Heidegger's philosophy, for example, Camus writes without the appropriate nuance of the approach of the author of *Sein und Zeit* (23–24): "Heidegger considers the human condition coldly and announces that that existence is humiliated. [...]"[81] In the paragraph in which he makes this statement, and which is the sole paragraph on Heidegger in *The Myth of Sisyphus* (23–24), Camus repeatedly identifies "le souci", which can only refer to the *Sorge* (care) of *Sein und Zeit*, as "une peur" (fear) or "l'angoisse" (anxiety),[82] when in fact Heidegger in *Sein und Zeit* clearly and distinctly distinguishes between *Furcht* and *Angst* and describes care as the only effective response to fear and anxiety (Heidegger 1927/1977, 140–142, 184–191, 191–196). Thus Camus's interpretation hardly does justice to Heidegger's thinking, and this is to say nothing of the unnecessary headaches that it creates for the English translator of the French text. Also, although it begins with the quotation of a passage from his *Existenzphilosophie* (Jaspers 1938) (9),[83] Camus's treatment of Jaspers is not much better (9–10, 24–25, 32–33). To put it bluntly, he tends to interpret the works of Heidegger (13, 23–24) through those of Georges Gurvitch (cf., e.g., *Les tendances actuelles de la philosophie allemande* [1930]: 210–217), and those of Jaspers (9–10, 24–

---

comprendre."

[81] Cf. *Sisyphe*, 115: "Heidegger considère froidement la condition humaine et annonce que cette existence est humiliée. [...]"

[82] Cf. *Sisyphe*, 115: "La seule réalité, c'est le 'souci' dans toute l'échelle des êtres. Pour l'homme perdu dans le monde et ses divertissements, ce souci est une peur brève et fuyante. Mais que cette peur prenne conscience d'elle-même, et elle devient l'angoisse, climat perpétuel de l'homme lucide 'dans lequel l'existence se retrouve'. Ce professeur de philosophie écrit sans trembler et dans le langage le plus abstrait du monde que 'le caractère fini et limité de l'existence humaine est plus primordial que l'homme lui-même'. Il s'intéresse à Kant mais c'est pour reconnaître le caractère borné de sa 'Raison pure'. C'est pour conclure au terme de ses analyses que 'le monde ne peut plus rien offrir à l'homme angoissé'. Ce souci lui paraît à tel point dépasser en vérité les catégories du raisonnement qu'il ne songe qu'à lui et ne parle que de lui. Il énumère ses visages: d'ennui lorsque l'homme banal cherche à le niveler en lui-même et à l'étourdir; de terreur lorsque l'esprit contemple la mort. Lui non plus ne sépare pas la conscience de l'absurde. La conscience de la mort, c'est l'appel du souci et 'l'existence s'adresse alors un propre appel par l'intermédiaire de la conscience'. Elle est la voix même de l'angoisse et elle adjure l'existence 'de revenir elle-même de sa perte dans l'On anonyme'. Pour lui non plus, il ne faut pas dormir et il faut veiller jusqu'à la consommation. Il se tient dans ce monde absurde, il en accuse le caractère périssable. Il cherche sa voie au milieu des décombres."

[83] Cf. *Sisyphe*, 103–104: "Lorsque Karl Jaspers, révélant l'impossibilité de constituer le monde en unité, s'écrie: 'Cette limitation me conduit à moi-même, là où je ne me retire plus derrière un point de vue objectif que je ne fais que représenter, là où ni moi-même ni l'existence d'autrui ne peut plus devenir objet pour moi', il évoque après bien d'autres ces lieux déserts et sans eau où la pensée arrive à ses confins. Après bien d'autres, oui sans doute, mais combien pressés d'en sortir!"

25) through those of Jeanne Hersch (cf., e.g., *L'Illusion philosophique* [1936]: 157, 190). Hence his results are questionable because they are derivative. On the other hand, Camus's use of Kierkegaard, which is much more extensive than his use of any other philosopher in *The Myth of Sisyphus*, is a topic unto itself and deserves a special examination, one which might mitigate Sartre's harsh judgment. But it is also a different case from Camus's treatment of the phenomenologists and of Husserl.

2. Specific hermeneutics. Although he does not critically comment on Camus's use of Husserl in this regard, it is safe to assume that Sartre means what he says about Camus's treatment of Jaspers, of Heidegger, and of Kierkegaard also to apply to Camus's interpretation of Husserl, perhaps even a fortiori. For the latter is no less complex, and arguably more complex, a thinker than any of the former. As one may imagine, Camus was a bit irritated by what may be interpreted as the condescending remark by Sartre (Camus and Grenier 2003, 66): "I also know that most of his criticisms are fair, but why this acid tone?"[84] Yet Camus's teacher, mentor, and friend, to whom he had expressed his sentiment, was more charitable to Sartre (Camus and Grenier 2003, 67): "Sartre's article was excellent; I did not find the acid tone that you reproach him for. Evidently, he relates you to himself somewhat—that is natural!"[85] The substantive point is that, generally speaking, and specifically with respect to Husserl, Camus's style of philosophizing is not systematic but impressionistic. Sartre, on the other hand, spent many years as an academic philosopher working through the deep and difficult works of Heidegger and Husserl, among those of others, to work out in detail and at length the existential synthesis that yielded his magnum opus *L'Être et le néant* (1943). Yet Sartre's work did not prevent him from grossly oversimplifying the complex relationship between Camus's *The Stranger* and his *The Myth of Sisyphus*.[86] It is particularly striking that in direct connection with his critique of Husserl in *The Myth of Sisyphus* Camus poses the self-probing question (see again 45–46): "Am I to fear having carried too far a theme handled with greater circumspection by its creators?"[87] In context, this is hardly a merely rhetorical question. To be

---

[84] Cf. *Correspondance: Albert Camus–Jean Grenier, 1932–1960*, 88 (March 9, 1943): "Je sais aussi que la plupart de ses critiques sont justes, mais pourquoi ce ton acide?"

[85] Cf. *Correspondance: Albert Camus–Jean Grenier, 1932–1960*, 90 (March 31, 1943): "L'article de Sartre était excellent; je ne lui ai pas trouvé ce ton acide que vous lui reprochez. Évidemment il vous ramène un peu à lui—c'est naturel!"

[86] Cf. "Explication de *L'Étranger*", 93: "M. Camus, dans *Le Mythe de Sisyphe* paru quelques mois plus tard, nous a donné le commentaire exact de son oeuvre [*L'Étranger*] [...]."

[87] Cf. *Sisyphe*, 132: "Dois-je craindre d'avoir mené trop loin un thème manié avec plus de prudence par ses créateurs?"

sure, Camus claims that he does not seek by intent to deliver an examination of the philosophy of Husserl or of anyone else (see again 37, fn.): "But I am not examining the philosophy of Kierkegaard or of Chestov or, later on, of Husserl (this would call for a different place and a different attitude of mind); I am simply borrowing a theme from them and examining whether its consequences can fit the already established rules. It is merely a matter of persistence."[88] None the less, this disclaimer is belied by the simple and obvious fact that in effect Camus does compile a short list of specific points on which he does indeed "examine Husserl's philosophy", however adequately or inadequately.

3. Source availability. The question is whether and to what extent Camus made use of the works of Husserl that were available in his day. In fact, it can be shown that Camus's selection of Husserlian sources to mount his critique of Husserl's phenomenology in *The Myth of Sisyphus* is extremely limited, even given the already very limited resources available to him at the time. For example, aside from a probable allusion to *Cartesian Meditations* (27), the only work of Husserl from which Camus directly quotes in *The Myth of Sisyphus* is the *Logical Investigations*, and not from the *Logical Investigations* proper but from the *Prolegomena to Pure Logic* (46), which are indispensable but preliminary studies to the investigations proper. Yet this text is an energetic exercise in dogmatic absolutism aimed at overcoming the skeptical relativism of logical psychologism that dominated the German intellectual scene before transcendental phenomenology. Whether and to what extent its strong realism is representative of the powerful idealism of Husserl's mature works, is a serious question. In any case, all three passages from the *Prolegomena* are also cited by the Ukrainian-Russian existentialist philosopher Lev Shestov (1866–1938) in his work *Le Pouvoir des clefs* (cf. 329, 346, and 392, respectively).[89] In fact, Camus was apparently reading *The Power of the Keys* (the Russian original appeared in 1923 and a French translation appeared in 1928) during the time in which he was writing *The Myth of Sisyphus* (cf. Camus 1965, 1436, 1439), and he counts Shestov, whom he disapprovingly regards as an existentialist (in his own sense) who proves the absurd only in order to

---

[88] Cf. *Sisyphe*, 126: "On peut penser que je néglige ici le problème essentiel qui est celui de la foi. Mais je n'examine pas la philosophie de Kierkegaard, ou de Chestov ou, plus loin, de Husserl (il y faudrait une autre place et une autre attitude d'esprit), je leur emprunte un thème et j'examine si ses conséquences peuvent convenir aux règles déjà fixées. Il s'agit seulement d'entêtement."

[89] Husserl and Shestov got to know each other in 1928 in Amsterdam. They exchanged correspondence and visits in Freiburg and Paris until 1933. Cf. Husserl 1994, VI, 371–376.

dispel it (23, 25–27, 32–37, 134–135), among those philosophers whom he wants to criticize. It is generally accepted, of course, that in his critique of phenomenological essentialism Camus is obliquely referring to Husserl's second magnum opus, the *Ideas for a Pure Phenomenology and Phenomenological Philosophy, First Book: General Introduction to Pure Phenomenology* (1913), in which Husserl presents transcendental phenomenology, for the first time in full book form (after "Philosophy as Rigorous Science" [1911]), as an eidetic science as distinguished from empirical psychology as a factual science. There is, however, no evidence for this supposition that would convince a conscientious scholar beyond a reasonable doubt. Therefore, even given the potential sources for Camus's critique that were available to him at the time and under the circumstances, the case that he tries to make against Husserl rests from the start on a very shaky textual basis.

4. Source accessibility. There is also a much more severe problem here for Camus's critique of Husserl to overcome. For one must consider, in addition to Husserl's extensive published works, his innumerable unpublished manuscripts, whose length, breadth, and depth can match the corresponding dimensions of the published works. His philosophical corpus comprises both the former and the latter. Thus it is only at one's own risk that one ignores the unpublished writings in favor of the published ones or vice versa. Here as everywhere one must heed Husserl's telling remark (Letter to Adolf Grimme, March 5, 1931): "Indeed, the greatest part of my life's work, and, as I even believe, the most important part, is still stuck in my manuscripts, which due to their extensiveness are hardly any longer to be managed."[90] In fact, only a very small portion of Husserl's life's work was accessible to anyone working in the academy, not to mention to someone writing as a figure in the literary world, in the late 1930s and early 1940s. Even today, after the appearance of more than 40 volumes in the Husserliana series of the *Gesammelte Werke* of Husserl (1950 ff.), almost all of which run to several hundred and a few of which run to a thousand pages or more, many more manuscripts and much more material remains to be managed, organized, and published. Yet the situation is even more complicated than that. On the one hand, it would be unfair to dismiss Camus's critique of Husserl on the basis of an absence of evidence that was not at his disposal. On the other hand, if the case is not merely about the history of ideas but

---

[90] Cf. Husserl 1994, III, 90: "In der That, der größte u. wie ich sogar glaube wichtigste Theil meiner Lebensarbeit steckt noch in meinen, durch ihren Umfang kaum noch zu bewältigenden Manuscripten."

rather also about the material merits and demerits of the philosophical positions involved, then Husserl's arguments should be judged on the basis of all the relevant evidence, including that which had not yet been "discovered" in Camus's time and thus had not yet been "disclosed" to Camus in his role as critic. Yet, and there is no contradiction here, it is also possible and necessary to judge Camus's critique of Husserl's phenomenology based solely on the evidence that he presents in *The Myth of Sisyphus*.

5. Potential of eidetic phenomenology. In fact, not only is the general picture of Husserl's phenomenology hard to bring into focus (it is a very big picture with a great many details, and also a very big puzzle with a great many pieces), but Husserl's phenomenological essentialism, as well as his concept of essence, is also much more complex than Camus or anyone else could ever have imagined. A case in point is that in a recently published collection of Husserl's previously unpublished texts on the doctrine of essences and the method of eidetic variation as a way to achieve essences in their proper evidences (Husserl 2012), the editor divides the selected research manuscripts on these topics into five major phases: (1) provisional considerations on the concept of the universal (1891–1901: pp. 1–28); (2) investigations of the role of insight into essences in the making of judgments and the formation of concepts (1901–1917: pp. 29–118); (3) analyses of lowest essences as distinguished from specific and generic essences as well as of the function of phantasy in eidetic variation (1917–1918: pp. 119–200); (4) studies of the intuition of essences as pure thinking and of the delimitation of typical essences and exact essences (1918–1925: pp. 201–260); and (5) exemplary analyses of essences of physical and morphological realities and treatments of the problems of the eidos "I" and of the eidos "world" (1926–1935: pp. 261–394). Abstracting from the issue of the intrinsic rightness or wrongness of the editorial division of these texts into thematic areas, it is clear that interpretations of other texts of Husserl on eidetic questions would be incomplete, indeterminate, and uncertain without appropriate attention to these texts. Again, one should not eliminate essences before all the evidence is in. Rather, one should adjust one's judgments to the evidence as it comes in. In this regard, Camus's passing and dismissive reference to the distinction between "formal essences" and "material essences" is, of course, interesting (see again 47).[91] This allusion

---

[91] Cf. *Sisyphe*, 132: "Me dire que toutes les essences ne sont pas formelles, mais qu'il en est de matérielles, que les premières sont l'objet de la logique et les secondes des sciences, ce n'est qu'une question de définition."

to what Husserl eventually describes as the distinction between "exact essences" and "morphological essences" is, however, by no means dispositive. It is, after all, Husserl himself who, in a critique of Brentano's demand for a scientific classification of "psychic experiences" (*psychische Erlebnisse*) in terms of mathematical categories, argues that such phenomena and their contents can only be described in terms of morphological concepts (see Husserl 1976, 135–158, as well as the anticipation of this significant difference already in Husserl 1984a, 248–252).

6. Possibility of existential phenomenology. Yet these formal points pale in comparison with and in contrast to the material differences between phenomenology and existentialism as philosophical approaches to their proper areas of study. The real philosophical problems lie with Husserl's lack of appreciation for existentialism and with Camus's lack of appreciation for phenomenology. At a time when philosophy of existence contemned phenomenology because the latter could not figure out how to apply its own established methods to the former's concrete, particular concerns (cf. Camus, *The Myth of Sisyphus*), and when phenomenology disdained philosophy of existence because it also could not see what the new approach could contribute to its perennial questions (cf. Husserl, "Philosophy as Rigorous Science"), there seemed to be, at least for a long time, no third way to synthesize these two philosophical approaches (cf. Heffernan, "Phenomenology Is A Humanism"). Given the vast gap of misunderstanding between philosophy of essence and philosophy of existence, phenomenological existentialism or existential phenomenology would indeed have to wait a long time for its own time. Yet that time would eventually come (cf., e.g., Spiegelberg 1971², 1/271 ff., and 2, passim). In any case, Camus does not do justice to Husserl by interpreting phenomenology as a kind of existentialism of the escapist variety. In fact, Camus's own philosophy in *The Myth of Sisyphus*, which no one would misunderstand as existentialism in the sense in which he understands it in the work, is itself a kind of philosophy of existence. Therefore there must be a real distinction between philosophy of existence and existentialism. The point is that Husserl's phenomenology too has a legitimate application to the classic topics of philosophy of existence. Later there will be more to say about the positive connection between phenomenology and philosophy of existence.

To conclude, one should note that there is a certain imbalance in Camus's use of literary sources versus philosophical resources in *The Myth of*

Sisyphus. On the one hand, his employment of philosophical texts to substantiate his interpretations of thinkers such as Jaspers, Heidegger, and Husserl appears extremely selective and strikingly sporadic. On the other hand, his deployment of literary texts to support his readings of writers such as Shakespeare (80–82), Dostoevsky (104–112), and Kafka (124–138) seems more substantial and even systematic. Yet there may be a third way here, since Kierkegaard (who is mentioned by name 28 times) and Nietzsche (who is mentioned by name 9 times) should be regarded as special cases located somewhere between the philosophical thinkers and the literary figures. In this regard, it is not insignificant that Camus characterizes himself not as a philosopher but as an artist (Camus 1966, 113): "Why I am an artist and not a philosopher? Because I think according to words and not according to ideas."[92] In fact, he is emphatic about not being a philosopher (Camus 1965, 1427): "I am not a philosopher. I do not believe sufficiently in reason to believe in a system [...]."[93] Perhaps it is most accurate to describe Camus as "a philosophical novelist" (Camus 1963, 10): "One can think only in images. If you want to be a philosopher, write novels."[94] Indeed, Camus regards even the greatest philosophers as novelists of a sort (100): "The philosopher, even if he is Kant, is a creator. He has his characters, his symbols, and his secret action. He has his plot endings."[95] Finally, he remarks on the inextricable links between novels, philosophies, and images (Camus 1969, 199): "A novel is never anything but a philosophy put into images. And in a good novel the whole of the philosophy has passed into the images."[96]

---

[92] Cf. *Carnets II*, 146 (October, 1945): "Pourquoi suis-je un artiste et non un philosophe? C'est que je pense selon les mots et non selon les idées."
[93] Cf. *Essais*, 1427 ("Interview with *Servir*", December 20, 1945): "Je ne suis pas un philosophe. Je ne crois pas assez à la raison pour croire à un système. Ce qui m'intéresse, c'est de savoir comment il faut se conduire. Et plus précisement comment on peut se conduire quand on ne croit ni en Dieu ni en la raison."
[94] Cf. *Carnets I*, 23 (January, 1936): "On ne pense que par image. Si tu veux être philosophe, écris des romans."
[95] Cf. *Sisyphe*, 177: "Le philosophe, même s'il est Kant, est créateur. Il a ses personnages, ses symboles et son action secrète. Il a ses dénouements."
[96] Cf. *Essais*, 1417 ("Review of *La nausée* by Jean-Paul Sartre", October 20, 1938 [published in *Alger-Républicain*]): "Un roman n'est jamais qu'une philosophie mise en images. Et dans un bon roman, toute la philosophie est passée dans les images."

4. A philosophical response to Camus's critique of Husserl's phenomenology

Yet the question remains whether it is possible to challenge Camus's interpretation of Husserl's phenomenology in *The Myth of Sisyphus* on strictly philosophical grounds. The answer is that it is, indeed, and that there are several different ways in which one can do it. One way would be to attempt to counter Camus's criticisms point-by-point. But this approach would involve a great deal of rebuttal and it seems unnecessarily negative, though it might be fruitful and useful to perform such a counter-critique on some other occasion. Another way would be to examine not what Camus includes in his critique but what he excludes from it. This approach has the advantage that it leaves open the possibility that Camus and Husserl might actually agree on a number of other issues, some of which might even separate them both from the existentialists as Camus describes them, at the same time as it brings out latent strengths in Husserl's phenomenology that Camus neglects. First and foremost, for example, Camus fails to do justice to Husserl's essential, indispensable concept of *constitution*. In the following observations, then, the emphasis is not on a point-by-point refutation of Camus's critique of Husserl's phenomenology, but rather on a special, indeed, unique, strength of Husserl's philosophy that Camus completely overlooks.

In fact, despite his close attention to Husserl's idea of intentionality, Camus does not mention his concept of constitution once in *The Myth of Sisyphus*. The near exceptions prove the strict rule, because the casual references to "consciousness" (13) and "construction" (19) hardly amount to a serious analysis of this foundational concept in phenomenology. This is a remarkable occurrence, or rather non-occurrence, because "constitution" (*Konstitution*) is the technical term in Husserl's philosophy in particular and in phenomenology in general that refers to the creative activity and spontaneous achievement of consciousness that bridges the gap between the human need for meaning and the indifference of the world to provide sense, and that does so without any appeal to anyone or anything transcendent (Sokolowski 1970). Indeed, in its potentially existential application, Husserl's concept of constitution is preeminently suitable for describing and clarifying how, as Camus himself argues, from the fact that human life in general has "no meaning", that is, no determinately preexistent and categorically eternal meaning, it does not follow that a human life in particular is not worth living. For from the supposition that there is no such thing as *the meaning of life* it does not follow that it is not possible to live *a meaningful life*. It is especially telling that Camus himself then engages in a bit of abstract thinking when he repeatedly talks in *The Myth of Sisyphus* of the question about "the meaning of life" (*le sens de la vie*) as being "the most urgent of all questions" (4, 7, 32, 60).[97] Indeed, one can get the impression that he does this disingenuously, that is, so that the position of the absurd, namely, that "life is meaningless" (whatever that means), looks preferable, at least at first sight, to the position of reason, namely, that "life is meaningful" (whatever that means). From a phenomenological perspective, however, life can be "meaningless" in the sense that one cannot passively locate (the) meaning in life, but life can be *meaningful* in the sense that one must actively create (a) meaning in life. The determinacy of the question depends on the definiteness of the articles. Thus meaning is neither "in" the world nor "in" consciousness. Rather, it constitutes itself, that is, presents itself, at those points of contact at which existence and world collaborate to bridge the absurdity gap between the two distinct but inseparable parts of the one whole, that is, in the concrete life of an individual, particular human being (cf. Heidegger's concept of *Jemeinigkeit*: *Sein und Zeit*, 41–43, 187–188, 190–191, 221, 240, 263, 278, 280, 297–298). Therefore phenomenology suggests an answer to the basic question of philosophy of existence, not to say of the "worldview" ("Weltanschauung": Husserl 1987, 41–62) "existentialism", by proposing that individual human beings must make sense of their own concrete lives by performing particular meaning-bestowing acts, and not only cognitive acts with theoretical contents but also axiological acts with practical contents. This is a life-affirming view with which Camus hardly takes issue.[98]

Thus it is not dispositive that for most of his philosophical life Husserl was preoccupied with cognitive, theoretical cases of constitution and only began, toward the end of that life, that is, in his "crisis period" (Moran 2012), to apply the phenomenological concept of constitution in an existential manner, for this fact does not close off but rather opens up creative possibilities to be actualized. The point is that Camus does not stop to consider that in *The Crisis of the European Sciences and Transcendental*

---

[97] Cf. "Preface to the American Edition of *The Myth of Sisyphus and Other Essays*", v: "The fundamental subject of 'The Myth of Sisyphus' is this: it is legitimate and necessary to wonder whether life has a meaning; therefore it is legitimate to meet the problem of suicide face to face. The answer, underlying and appearing through the paradoxes which cover it, is this: even if one does not believe in God, suicide is not legitimate."

[98] Cf. "Preface to the American Edition of *The Myth of Sisyphus and Other Essays*", v: "Although 'The Myth of Sisyphus' poses mortal problems, it sums itself up for me as a lucid invitation to live and to create, in the very midst of the desert."

Phenomenology (Husserl 1976² [originally 1936]), of which he displays no awareness, Husserl expands his philosophical horizon to include the question about the genuine meaning of human existence. Understanding the crisis of the European sciences as a symptom of the crisis of European philosophy and as an expression of the life-crisis of European humanity, and interpreting European science, philosophy, and humanity as representative of their global-historical counterparts, Husserl argues in the *Crisis* that the life-crisis of European humanity is reflective of the critical condition of global-historical humanity. Thus the crisis of "European" life emerges as a crisis of *human* existence, and Husserl's phenomenology unfolds as a creative search for an answer to the question not only about the sense of the life-world but also about the meaning of human life, that is, about the meaning of the whole of human existence, both individually and collectively ("die Fragen nach Sinn oder Sinnlosigkeit dieses ganzen menschlichen Daseins": Husserl 1976², 3–6, 8, 11, 15, 17). Thus phenomenology shares with philosophy of existence the conviction that human beings live in a world not in which life makes sense, but in which they must make sense of life. Accordingly, too, the genuine essence of human existence is not passively "given" but actively "taken", because it involves an entelechy that constitutes itself in an evolutionary achievement, and it is the evidentiary result of an existential struggle for meaning against annihilating forms of meaninglessness, namely, irrationalism, mysticism, positivism, and skepticism (Husserl 1976², 1–17). In this respect, Husserl's hermeneutical-historical approach to the question about the meaning of human existence suggests an understanding of phenomenology as a form of humanism, and perhaps even as a unique kind of philosophy of existence, that is, an ethical philosophy that requires that human beings, individually and collectively, take absolute moral responsibility for the presuppositionless application of reason to life (Heffernan 2014).

Thus it is at his own risk that Camus ignores Husserl's concept of constitution and its potential relevance as a creative resource of phenomenology for clarifying how human beings can make sense of their world(s). Had he not done so, he might have appreciated that from a consistently phenomenological perspective even the concept of "the absurd" itself is a *constituted* one. For there is nothing "given" about it that is not also "taken". In fact, according to Camus, "the absurd spirit" or "the absurd human being" interprets human existence in terms of the category of "the absurd" and arrives at a corresponding interpretation ("l'esprit absurde": 26, 43–44; "l'homme absurde": 66–67, 72, 74, 77, 83, 94, 99, 117, 123). This fact, as well as Camus's own expressly stated commitment to follow the evidence wherever it leads him (49–50), raises the question of what evidence counts for and/or against the absurd interpretation of things as distinguished from the rational one. In no case, however, is "the absurd" an apriori *factum brutum* of human existence, something absolutely, adequately, and apodictically evident in and of itself, that one first identifies and that one then charges other thinkers with not having recognized because they want to "leap" to other aspects of reality, also constituted, that they hold, for other reasons, for equally important or comparably compelling. From a Husserlian perspective, then, Camus is all too insistent on the apriori absurdist outcome of any search for meaning in life and all too diffident about the potential of phenomenology, or of any philosophy or worldview, to make a significant contribution in this regard. Yet it is not only possible but also necessary to understand Camus to be presenting not merely literary interpretations of but also genuinely philosophical arguments for his positions (v–vi), because, in insisting that he follows "absurd reasoning" to its "bitter end" (3–10, esp. 9, 44, 68, 92), he repeatedly—to repeat: *repeatedly*—appeals to "evidence" to support his statements (4, 6, 9, 35, 46, 49–50, 52, 60–61, 78, 83, 115, 135). In no case should one allow this "evidence", accurately calibrated or wildly exaggerated, to go without proper cross-examination. All of this holds even if, and especially when, one takes into account Camus's "necessary" but *questionable* distinction between a "philosophy of evidence" and a "philosophy of preference" (Camus 1966, 62): "One must make up one's mind to introduce into matters of thought the necessary distinction between a philosophy of evidence and a philosophy of preference. In other words, one can end up with a philosophy distasteful to the mind and to the heart *but which commands respect*. Thus my philosophy of evidence is the absurd. But that does not keep me from having (or, more precisely, from knowing) a philosophy of preference […]."[99] Yet this distinction would properly be the topic of a different paper.

5. Conclusion: The common ground between Camus and Husserl

It remains to remark neutrally on Husserl's often and overly sanguine doctrine of essences. It is true, of course, that Camus's critique seems to have some merit in that it is easy to get the impression that phenomenology

---

[99] Cf. *Carnets II*, 82–83 (February 10, 1943): "Il faut se décider à introduire dans les choses de la pensée la distinction nécessaire entre philosophie d'évidence et philosophie de préférence. Autrement dit, on peut aboutir à une philosophie qui répugne à l'esprit et au coeur *mais qui s'impose*. Ainsi ma philosophie d'évidence c'est l'absurde. Mais cela ne m'empêche pas d'avoir (ou plus exactement de *connaître*) une philosophie de préférence […]."

exhibits an unfortunate tendency to look past the empirical facts to gaze at the pure essences, and thus to neglect the concrete individual and to favor the abstract universal—thus Husserl appears to risk missing the trees for the forest. It is also true, however, that in the course of the development of his teaching on eidetic intuition Husserl did seek a solution to the problem of whether there could be such a thing as an eidetic intuition of a particular individual, especially of an embodied human being. Yet his reaction to this prospect can only be described as "skeptical" (Husserl 2012, 366–372). Remarkably, Camus suggests that one of *Plotinus'* "contributions to phenomenology" (*sic!*) was the notion that "there is not only an idea of man but also an idea of Socrates" (48, fn.).[100] Precisely this unique idea would represent the perfect participation of the particular in the universal and vice versa. On the other hand, according to Husserl, even such an individual essence of a particular human being would also have to be constituted by consciousness, as all essences, of abstract universals as well, must constitute themselves in and for consciousness. Therefore it is not only Husserl's doctrine of constitution that Camus overlooks, but also the indispensable role that constitution plays in the eidetic intuitions of pure essences, of whatever kind they may be, as well as in the sensuous intuitions of empirical facts. Camus's critique of Husserl's essentialism could, then, have benefitted from prior analyses of Husserl's theory of the evidence of essences (eidetic evidence)—if only he had consulted them (Hering 1921, Ingarden 1925, Levinas 1930). Yet again, not all essences are exact, for example, as in mathematical and logical disciplines, for some essences are morphological, for example, as in typical and regional investigations, and there can be no doubt as to which kind of essences plays a much more important role in the encompassing descriptive science of all phenomena (Husserl 1976, 135–158).

Here the primary and ultimate philosophical point is that phenomenology, as Husserl conceives of it, is supposed to be an exact science, that is, not an empirical but an eidetic discipline. Thus it does not focus on the individual human being because there can be no science of the particular but rather only of the typical, the general, and the universal. This is an ancient Western notion that it is better not to try to explain here, except to point out that, as Camus perceptively observes, "the Greeks would not have understood

---

[100] Cf. *Sisyphe*, 134, fn.: "A. — À cette époque, il fallait que la raison s'adaptât ou mourût. Elle s'adapte. Avec Plotin, de logique elle devient esthétique. La métaphore remplace le syllogisme. B. — D'ailleurs ce n'est pas la seule contribution de Plotin à la phénoménologie. Toute cette attitude est déjà contenue dans l'idée si chère au penseur alexandrin qu'il n'y a pas seulement une idée de l'homme, mais aussi une idée de Socrate."

anything about existentialism" (Camus 1966, 88).[101] To the contrary, Husserl's critical, even contemptuous, attitude toward what was in his time called "Existenzphilosophie", as well as toward its proponents and practitioners, is well documented, for example, in the "Afterword" (1930) to his *Ideas I* (1913) (Husserl 1952, 138–162).[102] Therefore phenomenology, in Husserl's sense, would never get involved in the question of the meaning of a life, that is, in the particular problem of the sense of an individual human life. The steady focus on the essential and universal is confirmed by his phenomenological ethics (Husserl 1988, 2004). Indeed, even in those later texts in which Husserl repeatedly and pressingly poses the question of the meaning of human existence, his probing never gets beyond the *essentialist* concerns expressed in this and such *universal* queries. Thus, when he thematizes existential or existentialist questions, his investigations then remain in the realm of the universal and aim to yield eidetically valid judgments about reason, freedom, and God (cf. again, e.g., Husserl 1976², 1–17). This is the case despite the fact that Husserl exhorts his hearers and readers to understand the urgency of the situation in which phenomenology finds itself in having to provide a life-saving and culture-salvaging alternative to the various versions of "irrationalism" of his times. In the end, the actual application of phenomenology to existential concerns is left to real human beings living in the world, or rather delegated, in a noteworthy turn of phrase, to philosophers as "functionaries of humanity" ("Funktionäre der Menschheit": Husserl 1976², 15).

Here Camus's literary approach to the particular phenomena of concrete human existence proves most valuable. Due to the seismic shifts in the meanings of the terms involved between the past and the present, it is often overlooked that Camus's critique of "existential(ist) philosophy" is not only an attack on "existentialism" as he understands it but also an assault on "irrationalism" as he perceives it. Famously Camus denies, of course, being an existentialist, using the technical term itself (Camus 1969, 345): "No, I am not an existentialist. [...] Sartre is an existentialist, and the only book of ideas that I have published, *The Myth of Sisyphus*, was directed against the

[101] Cf. *Carnets II*, 116 (November, 1943): "Les Grecs n'auraient rien compris à l'existentialisme [...]."
[102] Cf. *Ideen III*, 140: "Ich möchte nur ausdrücklich sagen, daß ich allen von diesen Seiten her erhobenen Einwänden—des Intellektualismus, des Steckenbleibens meines methodischen Vorgehens in abstrakten Einseitigkeiten, des überhaupt und prinzipiellen Nichtherankommens an die ursprünglich-konkrete, die praktisch-tätige Subjektivität und an die Probleme der sogenannten 'Existenz', desgleichen an die metaphysischen Probleme—keinerlei Berechtigung zuerkennen kann."

philosophers called 'existentialists'."[103] He even insists on this point (Camus 1965, 1427): "[In *The Myth of Sisyphus*] I critique precisely [...] the existentialist philosophy. In fact, very few people know exactly what existentialism is. This explains a lot of things."[104] As he indicates in his "final interview", and as is most relevant to an understanding of *The Myth of Sisyphus*, however, it is more accurate to say that Camus eventually develops a highly nuanced relationship to existentialism and to the existentialists (Camus 1965, 1926–1927): "If the premises of existentialism are found, as I believe they are, in Pascal, Nietzsche, Kierkegaard, or Shestov, then I agree with them [the premises]. If its conclusions are those of our existentialists [e.g., Sartre], then I do not agree, because they [the conclusions] are contradictory to the premises."[105] In fact, existentialism had become, according to Camus, a kind of new religion, one by which he felt oppressed (Camus 1965, 1926): "Existentialism with us [in France] has led to a theology without God and to a scholasticism as a result of which it was inevitable that they finish by justifying the regimes of the inquisition."[106] Above all, it was the dominance of existentialism that led Camus to render a negative judgment on the philosophy of his time (Camus 1966, 117): "Philosophy is the contemporary form of indecency."[107] At one point, Camus did not preclude the possibility that he might study existentialism

---

[103] Cf. *Essais*, 1424 ("Interview with *Les Nouvelles littéraires*", November 15, 1945): "Non, je ne suis pas existentialiste. [...] Sartre est existentialiste, et le seul livre d'idées que j'ai publié: *le Mythe de Sisyphe*, était dirigé contre les philosophes dits existentialistes."

[104] Cf. *Essais*, 1427 ("Interview with *Servir*", December 20, 1945): "Où [dans *le Mythe de Sisyphe*] je critique, précisément [...] la philosophie existentialiste. En vérité très peu de gens savent exactement ce qu'est l'existentialisme. Ainsi s'expliquent bien des choses."

[105] Cf. *Essais*, 1926–1927 ("Last Interview of Albert Camus", December 20, 1959 [published in *Venture*, Spring 1960]): "Si les prémisses de l'existentialisme se trouvent, comme je le crois, chez Pascal, Nietzsche, Kierkegaard ou Chestov, alors je suis d'accord avec elles. Si ses conclusions sont celles de nos existentialistes, je ne suis pas d'accord, car elles sont contradictoires aux prémisses."

[106] Cf. *Essais*, 1926 ("Last Interview of Albert Camus", December 20, 1959 [published in *Venture*, Spring 1960]): "L'existentialisme chez nous aboutit à une théologie sans dieu et à une scolastique dont il était inévitable qu'elles finissent par justifier des régimes d'inquisition."

[107] Cf. *Carnets II*, 151 (October, 1945): "La philosophie est la forme contemporaine de l'impudeur." It is worth noting that Camus composed, at the end of 1946 or in 1947 (thus long before the public break with Sartre and his existentialism in 1952), *L'Impromptu des philosophes*, a satirical theater piece à la Molière. Written under the pseudonym "Antoine Bailly" and never published during Camus's lifetime, it is his most explicit critique of contemporary philosophy, singling out a disingenuous intellectual seducer by the name of "Monsieur Néant" for special treatment. I am grateful to Giovanni Gaetani (Rome) for drawing my attention to this work, which has been included in volume 2 of the new edition of the *Oeuvres complètes* of Camus in the Bibliothèque de la Pléiade (Paris: Gallimard, 2006–2008 [4 vols.]).

(Camus 1969, 348): "And perhaps it is necessary for me to decide to study existentialism …"[108] Yet the point is that Camus's *rational* alternative to *irrational* existentialism is a consistent and logical thinking through of the absurd in all its ineluctability (49): "The theme of the irrational, as it is conceived by the existentials, is reason becoming confused and escaping by negating itself. The absurd is lucid reason noting its limits."[109] Giving a striking example that links *The Myth of Sisyphus* and *The Stranger*, Camus describes the pure despair and utter horror that is experienced by the man who has been sentenced to death and for whom it is mathematically certain that his head will be chopped off (Camus 1963, 116): "Here the absurd is perfectly clear. It is the opposite of the irrational. It has all the signs of evidence."[110] Again, according to Camus, the existentialists try to "leap" over the limits of reason by appealing to someone or something beyond the limits, but this approach is incoherent and this way out of the inescapable human condition is impossible. His alternative approach to the absurd, on the other hand, which eschews all such nostalgia for the transcendent, may perhaps be most accurately described as an "inexistential philosophy" (Camus 1966, 81).[111]

Thus there is common ground here. For some dimensions of Husserl's phenomenology are not only tenable but also consistent with some of the statements that Camus makes in *The Myth of Sisyphus* about "absurd freedom" (51–65), about "the absurd human being" (66–92), about "absurd

---

[108] Cf. *Essais*, 1427 ("Interview with *Les Nouvelles littéraires*", November 15, 1945): "Peut-être faudrait-il aussi que je me décide à étudier l'existentialisme …"

[109] Cf. *Sisyphe*, 134: "Le thème de l'irrationnel, tel qu'il est conçu par les existentiels, c'est la raison qui se brouille et se délivre en se niant. L'absurde, c'est la raison lucide qui constate ses limites."

[110] Cf. *Carnets I*, 141 (December, 1938): "Il n'y a qu'un cas où le désespoir soit pur. C'est celui du condamné à mort (qu'on nous permette une petite évocation). On pourrait demander à un désespéré d'amour s'il veut être guillotiné le lendemain, et il refuserait. À cause de l'horreur du supplice? Oui. Mais l'horreur naît ici de la certitude—plutôt de l'élément mathématique qui compose cette certitude. L'Absurde est ici parfaitement clair. C'est le contraire d'un irrationnel. Il a tous les signes de l'évidence. Ce qui est irrationnel, ce qui le serait, c'est l'espoir passager et moribond que cela va cesser et que cette mort pourra être évitée. Mais non l'absurde. L'évident c'est *qu'on* va lui couper le cou et pendant qu'il est lucide—pendant même que toute sa lucidité se concentre sur ce fait qu'on va lui couper le cou."

[111] Cf. *Carnets II*, 106 (September 1, 1943): "Puisque le mot d'existence recouvre quelque chose, qui est notre nostalgie, mais puisqu'en même temps il ne peut s'empêcher de s'étendre à l'affirmation d'une réalité supérieure, nous ne le garderons que sous une forme convertie—nous dirons philosophie inexistentielle, ce qui ne comporte pas une négation mais prétend seulement rendre compte de l'état de 'l'homme privé de …' La philosophie inexistentielle sera la philosophie de l'exil."

creation" (93–118), and, above all, about "The Myth of Sisyphus" itself (119–123). For what Camus and Husserl, and Sisyphus as well, all share is the grim determination, the heroic-tragic courage, and perhaps even the cheerful resoluteness, to perform "the infinite tasks" that philosophical destiny or spiritual fate has meted out to and demands of them (121—cf. Husserl 1976², 73, 319, 323–324, 326, 336, 338–339, 341, on "die Philosophie als unendliche Aufgabe"). Thus intent and effect can be two different things, and Husserl may emerge, Camus's interpretation of phenomenology as a kind of existentialism notwithstanding, as a modern Sisyphus, or certainly as a philosophical figure deserving of the name "Sisyphus" (123): "The absurd man says 'yes', and his effort will henceforth be unceasing."[112] For his part, Husserl claims to be nothing more than "someone who lived through the fate of a philosophical existence in its entire seriousness" (Husserl 1976², 17).[113] Ironically, Camus, perhaps under the influence of Sartre's recently articulated but quickly questioned distinction between "Christian existentialists" and "atheistic existentialists",[114] once even referred to Husserl as an "existentialist", and as an "atheistic" one at that ("l'existentialisme athée, avec Husserl, Heidegger et bientôt Sartre": Camus 1965, 1427).[115] Here again Camus displays his usual keen impressionistic instinct, because, although he does not deny the existence of God, Husserl methodically and rigorously brackets the divinity out of his phenomenological philosophy (Husserl 1976, 124–125), since, according to him, God too is constituted by the consciousness that intends him (Husserl 1974, 257–258).[116] In this regard, Camus also says paradoxically of himself

---

[112] Cf. *Sisyphe*, 197–198: "L'homme absurde dit oui et son effort n'aura plus de cesse."

[113] Cf. *Krisis*, 17: "Ich versuche zu führen, nicht zu belehren, nur aufzuweisen, zu beschreiben, was ich sehe. Ich erhebe keinen anderen Anspruch als den, in erster Linie mir selbst gegenüber und demgemäß auch vor Anderen nach bestem Wissen und Gewissen sprechen zu dürfen als jemand, der das Schicksal eines philosophischen Daseins in seinem ganzen Ernste durchlebte."

[114] Cf. *L'existentialisme est un humanisme*, 26 (the lecture was originally held by Sartre on October 29, 1945): "Ce qui rend les choses compliquées, c'est qu'il y a deux espèces d'existentialistes: les premiers, qui sont chrétiens, et parmi lesquels je rangerai [Karl] Jaspers et Gabriel Marcel, de confession catholique; et, d'autre part, les existentialistes athées parmi lesquels il faut ranger Heidegger, et aussi les existentialistes français et moi-même."

[115] Cf. *Essais*, 1427–1428 ("Interview with *Servir*", December 20, 1945): "L'existentialisme a deux formes: l'une avec Kierkegaard et Jaspers débouche dans la divinité par la critique de la raison, l'autre, que j'appellerai l'existentialisme athée, avec Husserl, Heidegger et bientôt Sartre, se termine aussi par une divinisation, mais qui est simplement celle de l'histoire, considérée comme le seul absolu. On ne croit plus en Dieu, mais on croit à l'histoire. Pour ma part, je comprends bien l'intérêt de la solution religieuse, et je perçois très particulièrement l'importance de l'histoire. Mais je ne crois ni à l'une ni à l'autre, au sens absolu. Je m'interroge et cela m'ennuierait beaucoup que l'on me force à choisir absolument entre saint Augustin et Hegel. J'ai l'impression qu'il doit y avoir une vérité supportable entre les deux."

(Camus 2008, 112): "I do not believe in God *and* I am not an atheist."[117] Therefore, if it is possible for Camus to call Husserl an "existentialist", then surely it is also permitted to refer to Camus as an "existentialist", albeit as one who is above and beyond the irrationalism, nihilism, and pessimism of the existentialism of his times.[118]

Yet it is surely time to put an end, once and for all, to the (un)philosophical equivalent of name-calling. In fact, both Husserl and Camus are above and beyond existentialism understood as a dismal and depressing worldview portending doom and gloom, because they are both phenomenologists and philosophers of existence in the life-affirming sense that they describe both the phenomenon and the phenomena of human existence in unique ways that defy the usual stereotypes (Barrett 1958) and supply the usable original types (Schacht 2012). In any case, Camus's philosophical argument in *The Myth of Sisyphus* is that there must be a third alternative to the nihilism of existentialism and the essentialism of phenomenology. In the end, the purpose of any genuine philosophy, whether it be phenomenology, existentialism, philosophy of existence, philosophy of the absurd, or any other contemplative way of thinking or reflective way of living, is neither to tell people what *the meaning of life* is nor to tell them that life has *no meaning*. It is, rather, to help each and every person to live *a meaningful life* individually and people together to live *meaningful lives* collectively. Properly understood, then, both Camus's philosophy of existence and Husserl's philosophy of phenomena show that the search for *the meaning of life* can be a major obstacle to living *a meaningful life*.

---

[116] Cf. also Husserl 2014 (Husserliana XLII), Part III—Metaphysics: Monadology, Teleology, and Philosophical Theology.

[117] Cf. *Carnets III*, 128 (November 1, 1954): "Je lis souvent que je suis athée, j'entends parler de mon athéisme. Or ces mots ne me disent rien, ils n'ont pas de sens pour moi. Je ne crois pas à Dieu *et* je ne suis pas athée."

[118] Cf. "Preface to the American Edition of *The Myth of Sisyphus and Other Essays*", v: "[…] this book declares that even within the limits of nihilism it is possible to find the means to proceed beyond nihilism. In all the books I have written since, I have attempted to pursue this direction."

Works Cited/Further Reading

This bibliography is not an attempt to encompass all the philosophical sources of *The Myth of Sisyphus*. Rather, its aim is to convey a provisional but reliable idea of the philosophical horizon of Camus's essay, both with respect to what is present in it and with respect to what is absent from it. Therefore the list includes scholarly (secondary) literature written long after Camus's death. The literary sources of the essay are, of course, another matter altogether. Multiple works of the same author are listed chronologically, except for translations, which are listed immediately under originals.

Aristotle (1984). *Metaphysics*, in *The Complete Works of Aristotle* (2 vols.). Ed. Jonathan Barnes. Princeton: Princeton University Press.

——. (1999²). *Nicomachean Ethics*. Tr. Terence Irwin. Indianapolis/Cambridge: Hackett.

Aronson, Ronald (2012). "Albert Camus", *The Stanford Encyclopedia of Philosophy*. Ed. Edward Zalta, http://plato.stanford.edu/archives/spr2012/entries/camus/.

Barrett, William (1958). *Irrational Man: A Study in Existential Philosophy*. New York: Doubleday.

Bielawka, Maria (1996). "Husserl and Camus: In Search of Time Accomplished", *Analecta Husserliana* 48 (1996), 39–40.

Camus, Albert (1936). *Entre Plotin et Saint Augustin*, in *Essais*, 1220–1313. Ed. Roger Quilliot and Louis Faucon. Paris: Gallimard.

——. (2007). *Christian Metaphysics and Platonism*. Tr. Ronald Srigley. Columbia: University of Missouri Press.

——. (1942/1965). *Le Mythe de Sisyphe: Essai sur l'absurde*, in *Essais*, 89–211. Ed. Roger Quilliot and Louis Faucon. Paris: Gallimard.

———. (1955/1983). *The Myth of Sisyphus and Other Essays*. Tr. Justin O'Brien. New York: Knopf/Vintage (Random House).

———. (1962/1). *Théâtre, récits, nouvelles*. Ed. Roger Quilliot. Paris: Gallimard.

———. (1962/2). *Carnets I: Mars 1935–Février 1942*. Paris: Gallimard.

———. (1963). *Notebooks 1935–1942*. Tr. Philip Thody. New York: Knopf.

———. (1964). *Carnets II: Janvier 1942–Mars 1951*. Paris: Gallimard.

———. (1966). *Notebooks 1942–1951*. Tr. Justin O'Brien. New York: Knopf.

———. (1965). *Essais*. Ed. Roger Quilliot and Louis Faucon. Paris: Gallimard.

———. (1969). *Lyrical and Critical Essays*. Ed. Philip Thody and tr. Ellen Kennedy. New York: Knopf.

Camus, Albert, and Grenier, Jean (1981). *Correspondance: Albert Camus–Jean Grenier, 1932–1960*. Ed. Marguerite Dobrenn. Paris: Gallimard.

———. (2003). *Correspondence, 1932–1960*. Tr. Jan Rigaud. Lincoln: University of Nebraska Press.

Camus, Albert (1989). *Carnets III: Mars 1951–Décembre 1959*. Paris: Gallimard.

———. (2008). *Notebooks 1951–1959*. Tr. Ryan Bloom. Chicago: Dee.

———. (2006–2008). *Oeuvres complètes* (4 vols.). Ed. Jacqueline Lévi-Valensi and Raymond Gay-Crosier. Paris: Gallimard.

Crowell, Steven, ed. (2012). *The Cambridge Companion to Existentialism*. Cambridge: Cambridge University Press.

Fiut, Ignacy (2009). "Albert Camus: Phenomenology and Postmodern Thought", *Analecta Husserliana* 104, 341–354.

Foley, John (2008). *Albert Camus: From the Absurd to Revolt*. Montreal: McGill-Queen's University Press.

Grenier, Jean (1957). *L'Existence malheureuse*. Paris: Gallimard.

Gurvitch, Georges (1930). *Les tendances actuelles de la philosophie allemande: E. Husserl, M. Scheler, E. Lask, N. Hartmann, M. Heidegger (Cours libres faits à la Sorbonne)*. Paris: Vrin.

Hanna, Thomas (1958). *The Thought and Art of Albert Camus*. Chicago: Regnery.

Heffernan, George (2014). "Phenomenology Is A Humanism: Husserl's Hermeneutical-Historical Struggle to Determine the Genuine Meaning of Human Existence in *The Crisis of the European Sciences and Transcendental Phenomenology*", *Analecta Husserliana* 115, forthcoming.

Heidegger, Martin (1927/1977[14]). *Sein und Zeit*. Tübingen: Niemeyer.

——. (1962). *Being and Time*. Tr. John Macquarrie and Edward Robinson. New York: Harper and Row.

Hering, Jean (1921). *Bemerkungen über das Wesen, die Wesenheit und die Idee*, in *Jahrbuch für Philosophie und phänomenologische Forschung* 4, 495–543. Ed. Edmund Husserl. Halle an der Saale: Niemeyer.

Hersch, Jeanne (1936). *L'Illusion philosophique*. Paris: Alcan.

Hughes, Edward, ed. (2007). *The Cambridge Companion to Camus.* Cambridge: Cambridge University Press.

Husserl, Edmund (1950/1973²). *Cartesianische Meditationen und Pariser Vorträge* (Husserliana I). Ed. Stephan Strasser. The Hague: Nijhoff.

——. (1950). *Cartesian Meditations: An Introduction to Phenomenology.* Tr. Dorion Cairns. The Hague: Nijhoff.

——. (1952). *Ideen zu einer reinen Phänomenologie und phänomenologischen Philosophie, Drittes Buch: Die Phänomenologie und die Fundamente der Wissenschaften* (Husserliana V). Ed. Marly Biemel. The Hague: Nijhoff.

——. (1974). *Formale und transzendentale Logik: Versuch einer Kritik der logischen Vernunft* (Husserliana XVII). Ed. Paul Janssen. The Hague: Nijhoff.

——. (1969). *Formal and Transcendental Logic.* Tr. Dorion Carins. The Hague: Nijhoff.

——. (1975). *Logische Untersuchungen, Erster Band: Prolegomena zur reinen Logik* (Husserliana XVIII). Ed. Elmar Holenstein. The Hague: Nijhoff.

——. (1970/2001²). *Logical Investigations.* Tr. J. N. Findlay. Oxford: Routledge.

——. (1976). *Ideen zu einer reinen Phänomenologie und phänomenologischen Philosophie, Erstes Buch: Allgemeine Einführung in die reine Phänomenologie* and *Ergänzende Texte (1912–1929)* (Husserliana III/1–2). Ed. Karl Schuhmann. The Hague: Nijhoff.

——. (2014). *Ideas for a Pure Phenomenology and Phenomenological Philosophy, First Book: General Introduction to Pure Phenomenology.* Tr. Daniel Dahlstrom. Indianapolis: Hackett.

———. (1976²). *Die Krisis der europäischen Wissenschaften und die transzendentale Phänomenologie* (Husserliana VI). Ed. Walter Biemel. The Hague: Nijhoff.

———. (1970). *The Crisis of European Sciences and Transcendental Phenomenology: An Introduction to Phenomenological Philosophy.* Tr. David Carr. Evanston: Northwestern University Press.

———. (1984a). *Logische Untersuchungen, Zweiter Band: Untersuchungen zur Phänomenologie und Theorie der Erkenntnis, Erster Teil* (Husserliana XIX/1). Ed. Ursula Panzer. The Hague: Nijhoff/Kluwer.

———. (1984b). *Logische Untersuchungen, Zweiter Band: Untersuchungen zur Phänomenologie und Theorie der Erkenntnis, Zweiter Teil* (Husserliana XIX/2). Ed. Ursula Panzer. The Hague: Nijhoff/Kluwer.

———. (1987). *Aufsätze und Vorträge (1911–1921)* (Husserliana XXV). Ed. Thomas Nenon and Hans Rainer Sepp. Dordrecht: Nijhoff/Kluwer.

———. (1988). *Vorlesungen über Ethik und Wertlehre 1908–1914* (Husserliana XXVIII). Ed. Ullrich Melle. Dordrecht: Kluwer.

———. (1994). Husserliana Dokumente, *Band III: Briefwechsel* (10 vols.). Ed. Karl Schuhmann with Elisabeth Schuhmann. Dordrecht: Kluwer.

———. (2004). *Einleitung in die Ethik: Vorlesungen Sommersemester 1920 und 1924* (Husserliana XXXVII). Ed. Henning Peucker. Dordrecht: Kluwer.

———. (2008). *Die Lebenswelt: Auslegungen der vorgegebenen Welt und ihrer Konstitution: Texte aus dem Nachlass (1916–1937)* (Husserliana XXXIX). Ed. Rochus Sowa. Dordrecht: Springer.

———. (2012). *Zur Lehre vom Wesen und zur Methode der eidetischen Variation* (Husserliana XLI). Ed. Dirk Fonfara. Dordrecht: Springer.

———. (2014). *Grenzprobleme der Phänomenologie: Analysen des Unbewusstseins und der Instinkte, Metaphysik, Späte Ethik (Texte aus dem Nachlass 1908–1937)* (Husserliana XLII). Ed. Rochus Sowa and Thomas Vongehr. Dordrecht: Springer.

Ingarden, Roman (1925). *Essentiale Fragen: Ein Beitrag zum Wesensproblem*, in *Jahrbuch für Philosophie und phänomenologische Forschung* 7, 125–304. Ed. Edmund Husserl. Halle an der Saale: Niemeyer.

Jaspers, Karl (1931). *Die geistige Situation der Zeit.* Berlin/Leipzig: de Gruyter.

———. (1951/1957). *Man in the Modern Age.* Garden City: Doubleday.

———. (1932). *Philosophie, Zweiter Band: Existenzerhellung.* Berlin: Springer.

———. (1970). *Philosophy, Volume 2.* Tr. E. B. Ashton. Chicago: University of Chicago Press.

———. (1938). *Existenzphilosophie: Drei Vorlesungen gehalten am Freien Deutschen Hochstift in Frankfurt a. M., September 1937.* Berlin/Leipzig: de Gruyter.

———. (1971). *Philosophy of Existence.* Tr. Richard Grabau. Philadelphia: University of Pennsylvania Press.

Kierkegaard, Søren (1844/1935). *Le Concept d'angoisse.* Tr. Paul-Henri Tisseau. Paris: Alcan.

———. (1844/1980). *The Concept of Anxiety.* Tr. Reidar Thomte and Albert Anderson. Princeton: Princeton University Press.

———. (1849/1932). *Traité du désespoir: La Maladie mortelle.* Tr. Knud Ferlov and Jean-Jacques Gateau. Paris: Gallimard.

————. (1849/1983). *The Sickness Unto Death*. Tr. Howard and Edna Hong. Princeton: Princeton University Press.

Lazere, Donald (1973). *The Unique Creation of Albert Camus*. New Haven: Yale University Press.

Levinas, Emmanuel (1930). *Théorie de l'intuition dans la phénoménologie de Husserl*. Paris: Vrin.

————. (1973). *The Theory of Intuition in Husserl's Phenomenology*. Tr. André Orianne. Evanston: Northwestern University Press.

Marcel, Gabriel (1925). "Existence et objectivité", *Revue de métaphysique et de morale* 30, 175–195 (reprinted as an appendix in *Journal métaphysique*, 309–329).

————. (1927). *Journal métaphysique*. Paris: Gallimard.

————. (1933). *Position et approches concrètes du mystère ontologique*. Paris: de Brouwer.

————. (1956/1984). *The Philosophy of Existentialism*. New York: Citadel.

McBride, Joseph (1992). *Albert Camus: Philosopher and Littérateur*. New York: St. Martin's.

McCarthy, Patrick (1982). *Camus*. New York: Random House.

Montaigne, Michel de (1967). *Essais*, in *Oeuvres complètes*. Ed. Robert Barral and Pierre Michel. Paris: Seuil.

————. (1991). *The Complete Essays*. Tr. M. A. Screech. London: Penguin.

Moran, Dermot (2012). *Husserl's "Crisis of the European Sciences and Transcendental Phenomenology": An Introduction*. Cambridge: Cambridge University Press.

Nietzsche, Friedrich (1883–1885/1988). *Also sprach Zarathustra: Ein Buch für Alle und Keinen*, in *Kritische Studienausgabe* 4. Ed. Giorgio Colli and Mazzino Montinari. Deutscher Taschenbuch Verlag/de Gruyter: Munich/Berlin.

———. (2006). *Thus Spoke Zarathustra: A Book for All and None*. Tr. Adrian Del Caro. Cambridge: Cambridge University Press.

Poincaré, Henri (1902). *La Science et l'hypothèse*. Paris: Flammarion.

Sagi, Avi (2002). *Albert Camus and the Philosophy of the Absurd*. Amsterdam: Rodopi.

Sartre, Jean-Paul (1936). *L'Imagination*. Paris: Alcan.

———. (2012). *The Imagination*. Tr. Kenneth Williford and David Rudrauf. London/New York: Routledge.

———. (1939/1947). "Une idée fondamentale de la phénoménologie de Husserl: L'intentionnalité", in *Critiques littéraires (Situations, I)*, 33–35. Paris: Gallimard.

———. (1943/1947). "Explication de *L'Étranger*", in *Critiques littéraires (Situations, I)*, 92–112. Paris: Gallimard.

———. (1943/2007). "A Commentary on *The Stranger*", in *Existentialism Is a Humanism*, 73–98. Tr. Carol Macomber. New Haven: Yale University Press.

———. (1943). *L'Être et le néant: Essai d'ontologie phénoménologique*. Paris: Gallimard.

———. (1956). *Being and Nothingness*. Tr. Hazel Barnes. New York: Gramercy.

———. (1946/1996). *L'existentialisme est un humanisme*. Ed. Arlette Elkaïm-Sartre. Paris: Gallimard.

——. (1946/2007). *Existentialism Is a Humanism*. Tr. Carol Macomber. New Haven: Yale University Press.

Schacht, Richard (2012). "Nietzsche: After the Death of God", in *The Cambridge Companion to Existentialism*, 111–136. Ed. Steven Crowell. Cambridge: Cambridge University Press.

Shestov, Lev (1923/1928). *Le Pouvoir des clefs*. Tr. Boris de Schloezer. Paris: Gallimard.

——. (1923/1968). *Potestas clavium*. Tr. Bernard Martin. Athens: Ohio University Press.

Sokolowski, Robert (1970). *The Formation of Husserl's Concept of Constitution*. The Hague: Nijhoff.

Spiegelberg, Herbert (1971²). *The Phenomenological Tradition: A Historical Introduction* (2 vols.). The Hague: Nijhoff.

Sprintzen, David (1988). *Camus: A Critical Examination*. Philadelphia: Temple University Press.

Todd, Olivier (1996). *Albert Camus: Une vie*. Paris: Gallimard.

——. (1997). *Albert Camus: A Life*. Tr. Benjamin Ivry. New York: Knopf.

Final Note

This paper is the revised version of a paper that was presented at the Seventh Annual Meeting of the Albert Camus Society U.K. / U.S., Swedenborg Society, Bloomsbury, London, November 7, 2013. I wish to express my gratitude to the participating members of the Camus Society for their contributions to the improvement of the paper.

Camus's Killers: Motivations for Murder

by Simon Lea

Murder is a recurring theme in Camus's fiction; in this essay we will be looking at nine of his fictional murderers and their different motivations for killing. Of those surveyed, three are based on real-life killers: Caligula, Kaliayev and the Parisian parricide. However, what we discover is that Camus has very little interest in the real-life phenomena of murder and that murders when they occur are merely plot devices to trigger discussions of other more philosophical topics such as honour and shame, solidarity and loneliness, power and submission. We begin with one of the real-life murderers, Ivan Kaliayev, the inspiration for Camus's play *The Just Assassins*. His belief that he was innocent of murder is compared and contrasted with two of Camus's other characters who also claimed to have killed in the innocence of their hearts: Patrice Mersault[1] of *A Happy Death*, and Martha from *The Misunderstanding*. We return to Kaliayev to explore the role of honour and duty in respect to the killings. From here we move on to the renegade missionary from the short story *The Renegade;* we contrast his motivation for murder with those already mentioned and compare him to the murderous emperor in *Caligula*. Next, we look at Daru's prisoner, an Arab guilty of murdering his cousin, taken from the short story *The Guest* and then Camus's account of a young Parisian man, who murdered his parents with an axe, mentioned in his essay *Reflections on the Guillotine*. Neither this man nor the murder he committed appears in any of Camus's fiction; however, his case is of interest as Camus considers him "a monster" and discusses his attitude to capital punishment regarding the case; Meursault, hero of *The Stranger*, labelled a monster and sentenced to death, is the last of Camus's killers in our discussion.

---

[1] To avoid any confusion between Patrice Mersault and Meursault of *The Stranger,* I will hereafter refer to the former as Patrice.

Innocent murderers

Kaliayev cannot seem to make up his mind about the killing of the Grand Duke. If he is a prisoner of war,[2] as he later claims in gaol, then presumably he thinks of the Duke as an enemy combatant killed in battle. However, he also claims to have carried out a "verdict"[3] and to have carried out "an act of justice"[4] – this would make the Duke a criminal justly executed. At one point he denies killing a man at all: "I threw the bomb at tyranny, not at a man."[5] Although he feels pity for the Duchess, he acknowledges her as his enemy and blames her for forcing him into becoming a murderer: "Look at me! I swear to you I wasn't made to be a murderer."[6] At this point he seems to accept that he *is* a murderer but that he can cease to be one by choosing to die: "Let me prepare myself to die. If I did not die – it's then I'd be a murderer."[7] Dora agrees; after learning of his death she proclaims: "Yanek is a murderer no longer."[8] For Stepan, when they made their choice to be revolutionaries they made their choice to be murderers. When he says this to Kaliayev, the response is indignant: "That's a lie! I have chosen death so as to prevent murder from triumphing in the world. I've chosen to be innocent."[9]

Patrice Mersault's attitude towards his crime, the murder of Zagreus for his money, evolves over the course of the novel. He is initially repulsed by the act of killing; the others kill with their eyes open, "It was Patrice who closed his eyes."[10] The closest he gets to guilt or horror at his actions is during his stay in Prague after discovering a dead man lying in the street with wounds similar to those he inflicted on Zagreus. "The man's head had been lying on the wound, and three or four fingers would have fitted inside that wound. Mersault stared at his hands and fingers, and childish desires rose in his heart."[11] In the following chapter he sits on the train staring at his hands: "He knew them, recognized them, yet they were distinct from himself, as

---

[2] Camus, Albert. *Caligula & Three Other Plays*. Trans. Justin O'Brien. 1st ed. New York: Vintage Books, 1962, 282.

[3] Ibid, 286.

[4] Ibid.

[5] Ibid, 282.

[6] Ibid, 288.

[7] Ibid.

[8] Ibid, 301. Yanek is Kaliayev's real name.

[9] Ibid, 261.

[10] Camus, Albert. *A Happy Death*. Trans. Richard Howard. 1st ed. London: Penguin Books, 1973, 9.

[11] Ibid, 54.

though capable of action in which his will had no part."[12] However, as the other Meursault's mother used to say, "after a while you can get used to anything,"[13] and one day Patrice realizes that:

> not once since Vienna had he thought of Zagreus as the man he had killed with his own hands. He recognized in himself the power to forget which only children have, and geniuses, and the innocent. Innocent, overwhelmed by joy, he understood at last he was made for happiness.[14]

Here, Patrice is confusing the innocence of naivety, guilelessness, possessed by children and some savants with the innocence of those who are blameless of any crime. Later in the novel, after Dr. Bernard tells him he feels contempt for men whose crimes are motivated by the desire for money, Patrice thinks about his motivation for killing Zagreus – was it *simply* for the money? It wasn't greed that led him to kill; he needed the money as "a weapon" to end "the sordid and revolting curse" that is poverty. He now thinks of his crime as a kind of spiritual battle: "opposing hatred with hatred. And out of this beast-to-beast combat, the angel sometimes emerged, intact, wings and halo and all, in the warm breath of the sea."[15] Patrice talks as if it was kill or be killed, that it was either him or Zagreus and he chose himself. Indeed, prior to the killing he saw himself as existing in a kind of living death:

> Things that in other circumstances would have excited him left him unmoved now, for they were simply part of his life, until the moment he was back in his room using all his strength and care to smother the flame of life that burned within him.[16]

He was in danger of becoming like the mother in *The Misunderstanding* who "lived through [her life] by dint of habit, which is not so very different from death."[17] Patrice knew that if he did nothing to escape his situation, he would be condemned to a kind of living death; he therefore kills in order to live. It seems too late for the mother in the play but her daughter Martha is

---

[12] Ibid, 55.
[13] Camus, Albert. *The Stranger*. Trans. Matthew Ward. 1st ed. New York: Vintage International, 1989, 77.
[14] *A Happy Death*, 62.
[15] Ibid, 95.
[16] Ibid, 14.
[17] *Caligula & Three Other Plays*, 121.

still desperately grasping at happiness. Her motivations for murder resemble closely those of Patrice. They both kill in order to acquire the money they believe essential for happiness. She wants to use the money to move south from Czechoslovakia and he uses his money to travel north to Czechoslovakia. Both consider their lives unbearably diminished by their circumstances and see killing (for money) as the only way out. Patrice carefully plans his crime, in order to make Zagreus's death look like suicide; and Martha is careful to select victims that won't be missed and meticulously disposes of their bodies under the cover of darkness in order to make them "vanish from the face of the earth."[18] Curiously, in both cases, it is their victims that, unwittingly, talk them into killing. Zagreus makes it clear to Patrice that in order to be happy one needs time, and in order to have time one must have money. He argues:

> Happiness, too, is a long patience. And in almost every case, we use up our lives making money, when we should be using our money to gain time [...] To have money is to have time. That's my main point. Time can be bought. Everything can be bought. To be or to become rich is to have time to be happy, if you deserve it.[19]

He goes on to tell Patrice that:

> At twenty-five, Mersault, I had already realized that any man with the sense, the will, and the craving for happiness was entitled to be rich. The craving for happiness seemed to me to be the noblest thing in a man's heart. In my eyes, that justified everything. A pure heart was enough... [20]

His final words on the subject are: "Don't take anything seriously except happiness. Think about it, Mersault, you have a pure heart. Think about it."[21] The next time they meet, Patrice shoots him in the head and takes his money. In Martha's case she is almost ready to go along with her mother and allow Jan to live; but, as she explains to her mother:

---

[18] *Caligula & Three Other Plays*, 116.
[19] *A Happy Death*, 34.
[20] Ibid.
[21] Ibid, 37.

> If you must know, it was he who made up my mind for me. You talked me into sharing your reluctance. But then he started telling me about those countries where I've always longed to go, and by working on my feelings hardened my heart against him. Thus innocence is rewarded.[22]

However, there are differences between Martha and Patrice. She kills a brother she fails to recognize; Patrice kills a man whom he ends up seeing as a brother: "He was overcome by a violent and fraternal love for this man from whom he had felt so far, and he realized that by killing him he had consummated a union which bound them together forever."[23] In contrast, the death of Martha's brother brings home to her just how much she hates him: "I hate him, yes, I hate him for having got what he wanted!"[24] It is not just that Jan managed to escape to the south and the sun; his death stirs up a feeling of love from deep within his mother's heart that could never be felt for Martha. The mother spells it out: "love for a daughter can never be the same thing. It strikes less deep. And how could I now live without my son's love?"[25] Martha's killing fails to bring her the happiness she seeks and, further, destroys any possibility of ever being happy. Patrice kills Zagreus and ends up with the happiness he sought:

> So many evenings had promised him happiness that to experience this one as happiness itself made him realize how far he had come, from hope to conquest. In the innocence of his heart, Mersault accepted this green sky and this love-soaked earth with the same thrill of passion and desire as when he killed Zagreus in the innocence of his heart.[26]

Patrice comes to the realization that he killed Zagreus "in the innocence of his heart," whereas Martha never believed that she had done anything wrong by killing Jan (or any of the previous victims for that matter). In fact, she thinks of *herself* as the victim of injustice. After the discovery of Jan's true identity and her mother's unexpected grief, Martha cries out: "oh, the unfairness of it all, the injustice done to innocence!"[27] As far as she is concerned, Martha is innocent of any crime (although she acknowledges

---

[22] *Caligula & Three Other Plays*, 117.
[23] Ibid, 104.
[24] Ibid, 125.
[25] Ibid, 121.
[26] *A Happy Death*, 96.
[27] *Caligula & Three Other Plays*, 124.

others would see her as a criminal); and when her mother abandons her she uses words like "defrauded" and "cheated"[28], words usually used by the *victims* of crime rather than criminals who have been double-crossed by their accomplices. We don't know the mother's motivation for assisting with the killing; it is possible that at one time she shared Martha's desire to escape to the sun but has now forgotten how she came to be a killer. Reluctant through weariness to go through with the murder she asks her daughter, "Are we really obliged to go through with it under these conditions, and to over-ride everything for the sake of a little more money?"[29] But it is not just for a little more money that Martha needs to kill "but for a home beside the sea, and forgetfulness of this hateful country."[30] She feels that her mother has a "duty" to help her because it was she who brought her "into the world in a land of clouds and mist, instead of sunshine."[31] She also feels that she has done her duty towards her mother, and that there must be a reckoning: "Don't forget that it was I who stayed beside you, and *he* went away." Martha is not only loyal to the family but committed to their shared beliefs; she reminds her mother it is she "who had taught me to respect nothing."[32] After learning that she has killed her son, the mother completely abandons the family philosophy. Martha can hardly believe her ears when she hears her mother speaking in "this new, amazing way."[33] Then, when the mother starts referring to herself as a criminal and a murderer, her daughter is scandalized: "I can't bear to hear you talking like that, about crime and punishment; it's ... despicable!"[34] The bond that Martha believed to have with her mother, "And on whom in all the world should I rely, if not the woman who had killed beside me?"[35] resembles the bond shared by Kaliayev and the other revolutionaries in *The Just Assassins*.

Kaliayev and Dora choose to kill because they believe they're "killing so as to build up a world in which there will be no more killing."[36] For them, the deaths they bring about through assassination mean life for others. Their leader, Annenkov, in the final scene reminds Dora: "The path we have chosen, also, leads to life. To life for others. Russia will live, our children's children will live."[37] The group is tied together by a strong honour code;

---

[28] Ibid, 123.
[29] Ibid, 99.
[30] Ibid.
[31] Ibid.
[32] Ibid, 120.
[33] Ibid.
[34] Ibid, 121.
[35] Ibid, 131.
[36] *Caligula & Three Other Plays*, 145.

honour and shame is the topic of most conversations within the play. When Kaliayev refuses to throw his bomb at the Duke's carriage because there are children inside, it is because "killing children is a crime against a man's honour."[38] However, despite this, he is still prepared to go out and kill the children if the group demand it. His failure to carry out the assassination leaves him ashamed; he believes that he has let down the cause and the others. He will honour his commitment to them, even if this means the murder of children, but he will kill himself afterwards. The difference, for him, between this suicide and allowing himself to be killed after assassinating the Duke is that if the children die, *he* will die a murderer and without honour.

Kaliayev chooses to kill because he wants a better future for the people of Russia, but he also wants to be loved by his fellow terrorists. When Stepan displays open hostility towards him, Kaliayev is hurt and saddened. When Dora tries to lift his spirits, telling him not to be sad because Stepan doesn't like him, he replies: "I *am* sad. I want you all to love me. When I joined the group I cut adrift from everything, and if my brothers turn against me, how can I bear it?"[39] We have also seen that Martha sought the same kind of bond with her mother (and presumably her father too before he died). She killed not just for a better future but out of a sense of duty towards her family.

The assassins, Patrice, Martha and her mother are all aware that others see them as criminals. However, they all, for different reasons, manage to convince themselves that they are innocent of murder. The terrorists consider that they absolve themselves through their consent to die (Dora even makes a case that they give more than they take because "throwing the bomb and then climbing the scaffold – that's giving one's life *twice*. Thus we pay more than we owe."[40] Patrice believes that he killed Zagreus in some kind of self-defence, and that the lack of any feelings of guilt is the same thing as a lack of any kind of guilt (he doesn't feel guilty therefore is is not guilty). Martha believes in nothing except an honour commitment to her family (and the family philosophy) and the duty her mother has towards her as a member of the honour group; since killing in order to acquire the money needed for Martha's happiness does not violate the code *and* helps

---

[37] Ibid, 295.
[38] Ibid, 260.
[39] Ibid, 245.
[40] Ibid, 247.

her mother do her duty towards her daughter, as far as Martha is concerned there is nothing wrong with murder. While Martha believes up until the end that she is innocent, her Mother, upon the realization that the man she helped kill is her son, accepts that she is a murderer. However, she takes her own life not because she believes murderers ought to be killed but because she can no longer live after being reminded of her son's love. She considers murderers "good for nothing,"[41] and understands why society gets rid of them.

Perhaps our killers have a hard time seeing themselves as murderers because none of their killings are personal. Patrice killed Zagreus not because he hated him or wanted the man dead but because murder was the only means to the man's money. Likewise, Jan dies not because of any animosity his mother or sister feel towards him, he was merely in the wrong place and the wrong time and saying the wrong things. The Grand Duke is targeted because he is the duke not because of any of his personal qualities; if another another man was duke then it would be him blown to smithereens. Before throwing the bomb, Dora even cautions Kaliayev to be on his guard, not to see the duke as a man: "Perhaps the Grand Duke has gentle eyes, perhaps you'll see him smiling to himself, scratching his ear. Perhaps – who knows? – you'll see a little scar on his cheek where he cut himself shaving. And if he looks at you, at that moment..."[42] The reply comes: "It's not he I'm killing. I'm killing despotism."[43] Next, we are going to look at a killer who positively delights in dispatching his victim: The missionary from Camus's short story *The Renegade*.

The Renegade

The missionary creeps out of the House of the Fetish, his legs still restricted by a length of cord attached to his ankles, to collect a rifle he knows is left unguarded. Then he makes his way to a position hidden in a pile of rocks and waits for the arrival of his replacement, a missionary named Father Beffort. When he shoots at Beffort he does so in the name of his new god, the Fetish. He prays: "may your power be preserved, may the offence be multiplied, may hate rule pitilessly over a world of the damned, may the wicked forever be masters, may the kingdom come, where in a single city of salt and iron black tyrants will enslave and possess without pity!"[44] The face

---

[41] Ibid, 121.
[42] Ibid, 248.
[43] Ibid.

of the man he has just killed appears to smile and this is too much for him; with the butt of his rifle he smashes in his enemy's face and the sound of wood on flesh is pleasant to him. What once was a man is left in the desert as carrion, a feast for hungry jackals.

The renegade missionary was a prisoner in the city of salt; he has been kept tied up like an animal and fed the way chickens are, grain scattered before him on the ground. He is beaten and mutilated, shaved and forced to watch ritual ceremonies in which women are beaten and raped before an idol he calls the Fetish. On one occasion he attempts to seize and rape one of the women beneath the Fetish. On her face is tattooed a mask of the god worshipped by her people; by raping and defiling her body, the missionary would be desecrating the god in whose house he has been confined and humiliated. But before he can succeed in his plan, the sorcerer and his men burst in and pull him away. They beat him, "dreadfully on the sinful place,"[45] and cut out his tongue. From this moment onwards he is converted.

His new god is the master who "could be destroyed but not converted."[46] In his previous life, the missionary would purposely seek out offences; he wanted to be acknowledged by those attempting to offend him and then revered by these same people when they fail. Mocked and tormented, he would take the abuse until his abusers, appalled at his resilience, would throw themselves on their knees to worship the God that had made this man so strong. The more powerful the adversary, the greater his victory when they submitted to God. This was his motivation for seeking out the city of salt, to "get the upper hand of those savages."[47] Stories of the savage treatment meted out to the previous missionary, who barely escaped with his life, only serve to excite the renegade further. However, the faith of the "black Eskimos" living in their igloos of salt is too powerful for him to overcome. The ripping out of his tongue finally defeats the man who sought "to rule in short by the sheer force of words over an army of the wicked."[48] His dreams of power evaporated, the void is filled with a new love for the dark god: "For the first time, as a result of offences, my whole body crying out in a single pain, I surrendered to him and his maleficent order, I adored in him the evil principle of the world."[49] His new god could not be converted

---

[44] Camus, Albert. *Exile And The Kingdom.* Trans. Justin O'Brien. 1st ed. London: Penguin, 2002, 46.
[45] Ibid, 42.
[46] Ibid, 43.
[47] Ibid, 35.
[48] Ibid, 34.

but he can be destroyed and the imminent arrival of Father Beffort accompanied by a French garrison (to ensure the natives don't cut off his "you know what"[50]) threatens his destruction. Thus the renegade sneaks away with a stolen rifle to kill the man that threatens his god.

It is not only to prevent the arrival of Beffort that the renegade kills; the murder is designed to incite a reprisal by the French troops. The 'masters' will be forced to defend the city and, after defeating the soldiers, the renegade believes they will be inspired to venture out and conquer the world. "[They will] sow their salt on the continent, all vegetation, all youth will die out, and dumb crowds with shackled feet will plod beside me in the world-wide desert under the cruel sun of the true faith."[51] After the remains of the missionary have been discovered, the renegade is crucified by his masters and left in the desert to die. Somewhere in the distance he can hear what sounds like the soldiers sacking the city. An inverted Christ, he calls out to the Fetish, "why hast thou forsaken me?"[52] A voice from nowhere says: "If you consent to die for hate and power, who will forgive us?"[53] He discovers at his feet the beaten and bloody sorcerer, presumably cast out from the city. The renegade realizes that he was wrong and wants to return home and rebuild the city – but of mercy this time. He asks his former master for help and instead a handful of salt is shoved in his mouth.[54] The renegade's decision to kill is a result of his quest for power. He is seduced by power and switches allegiances, Protestantism to Catholicism to Fetish worship, following whoever is the strongest. With each change, his position within the group changes and he is given a little more power; he left the congregation of the protestant church to join the Catholic seminary and left the seminary to end up as the self-appointed messiah of the Fetish religion. When things don't work out as he expected, he wants to return back to the beginning, building a city of mercy rather than one based on hate. If return were ever possible we know that he would move along the same path and simply repeat the same mistake.

In one way, the renegade is similar to Kaliayev and his assassins because he believes that the taking of a life will inspire others to act. Unlike the revolutionary terrorists of the play, the renegade wants a world in which

---

[49] Ibid, 43.
[50] Ibid, 45.
[51] Ibid, 47.
[52] Ibid, 48.
[53] Ibid.
[54] Not literally, he cannot form actual words after his tongue has been removed.

children are born slaves rather than free. In addition, the killing of Father Beffort is also personal; the renegade smashes his victim's head into ground meat because he thought he detected a smile on the man's lips; whereas Kaliayev hoped his hatred for tyranny would blind him, preventing him from seeing the man behind the Duke's title. He wants to kill his victim "with joy!"[55] but will be unavailable to if he sees a man instead of a Duke. The killer we turn to next delights in killing, and unlike the others who kill only once each, has many victims. Taking a life, for Caligula, is more than simply a means to an end; he doesn't kill in order to bring about something else that will make him happy, he kills because that is how he enjoys his freedom. Patrice stopped killing, and had no desire to do so, once he had the money he needed, and the same would apply for Martha had her mother not abandoned her. The revolutionary terrorists killed so that one day there would be no more killing. The renegade missionary killed in order to force his masters into enslaving the world. Caligula kills because it gives him a peculiar kind of happiness.

Caligula

Unlike the others discussed so far, Caligula is the only one who kills *downwards* in the social scale. Patrice and Martha killed the rich, in order to steal their money and make possible a new life for themselves. Kaliayev, and his comrades, assassinated the Grand Duke, a noble and a tyrant. Even the renegade killed a man who had managed to rise further than he in the Catholic Church; Father Beffort was an authorized and sanctioned missionary, unlike his murderer who was not deemed ready. Caligula is the top man in Rome and so can only kill beneath him; however, it must be said that he selects his victims from a pool of nobles. When he kills it is all part of a grand performance; as the curtains open, so to speak, he "invites" his mistress Caesonia, "to the most gorgeous of shows, a sight for gods to gloat on, a whole world called to judgement."[56]

Camus makes it clear that over the three years that pass during the play, Caligula kills many times. On stage we see or hear of six killings. He kills Scipio's father and Lepidus's son; executes a knight called Rufius and forces poison down the throat of Meriea. When one of the patricians, Cassius, hears that Caligula is gravely ill, he rashly calls out, "O Jupiter,

---

[55] *Caligula & Three Other Plays*, 249.
[56] Ibid, 17.

take my life in place of his!"[57] A fit and healthy Caligula enters the room and thanks Cassius for his sacrifice – since he is fit and well Jupiter must have accepted the trade – Cassius is dragged away screaming. The final murder we see Caligula commit is the strangulation of Caesonia; as he pulls his forearm tight across her throat, he comments, "Well, Caesonia, you have seen out the most unusual drama. It's time the curtain fell for you."[58] She was there at the beginning of his "show" and dies as the curtains fall. These killings were designed to teach a lesson: the death of Cassius illustrates Caligula's method; Cassius's empty words, intended to put on display of grief he certainly did not feel, are taken literally and his life is forfeited. For Caligula, these words prove that Cassius failed to take seriously the life he possessed. To hammer home the point, perhaps more to himself that the others, Caligula mutters the following as the man is led away screaming:

> Soon the sea roads will be golden with mimosas. The women will wear their lightest dresses. And the sky! Ah Cassius, what a blaze of clean, swift sunshine! The smiles of life. Life my friend is something to be cherished. Had you cherished it enough, you wouldn't have gambled it away so rashly. The loser must pay. There's no alternative.[59]

Caligula tells Caesonia that there must be two kinds of happiness "and I've chosen the murderous kind."[60] He exercises "the rapturous power of a destroyer," and *"this* is happiness."[61] In this he appears similar to the renegade for whom evil became the path to happiness; and, like the renegade, Caligula realises at the end that he has made a mistake. "I have chosen the wrong path, a path that leads to nothing. My freedom isn't the right one."[62] Patrice manages to discover the right freedom, whereas Caligula fails; to see why Caligula's freedom is not the right one we can look to Camus's discussion of Sade in *The Rebel*.

Caligula kills with absolute freedom, his impossible dream: to kill the world and win "the god-like enlightenment of the solitary."[63] His last victim, his mistress, must die because her existence keeps alive in him the last vestige

---

[57] Ibid, 60.
[58] Ibid, 71.
[59] Ibid, 61.
[60] Ibid, 71.
[61] Ibid, 72.
[62] Ibid, 73.
[63] Ibid, 72.

of sentiment that would taint "the utter loneliness that is [his] heart's desire."[64] However, once completely alone and awaiting death from the approaching mob, he feels nothing but fear. This is quite unlike Patrice, who finds happiness in harmony with the universe and dies a happy death; Caligula finds only himself. Instead of holding the world in his hands (or the moon), he stands in front of a mirror screaming, "I stretch out my hands, but it's always you I find, you only, confronting me, and I've come to hate you."[65] He ends up very much like Sade's killers, discussed in *The Rebel*. They, like him, realise that the heart is "the weak spot of the intellect" and "must be exterminated."[66] They also only enjoy the effects they crave from killing *during* the act, "then another object must be brought under subjection and killed, then another, and so on to an infinity of all possible objects."[67] Caligula's freedom and happiness comes from "the ineffable joy of the unpunished murderer; the ruthless logic that crushes out human lives."[68] When Sade's murderers run out of victims they turn on each other until only one remains:

> The most powerful, the one who will survive, is the solitary, the unique, whose glorification Sade has undertaken – in other words himself. At last he reigns supreme, master and God. But at the moment of his greatest victory, the dream vanishes. The Unique turns back towards the prisoner whose unbounded imagination gave birth to him and they become one. In fact he is alone, imprisoned in a blood-stained Bastille, entirely constructed around a still unsatisfied, and henceforth undirected, desire for pleasure.[69]

When Caligula runs out of victims he awaits the moment when he stands supreme as master and God, but this moment does not arrive. He is alone, imprisoned in his blood-stained palace. It is clear that Caligula is bent on some kind of suicide by mob; he provokes those around him beyond the point of tolerance and, when plots against his life are discovered, he chooses to do nothing. However, when the time comes he realises that "after despising others," he finds himself, "as cowardly as they."[70]

---

[64] Ibid.
[65] Ibid, 73.
[66] Camus, Albert. *The Rebel*. Trans. Anthony Bower. 1st ed. London: Penguin Books in association with Hamish Hamilton, 2000, 38.
[67] Ibid, 40.
[68] *Caligula & Three Other Plays*, 72.
[69] *The Rebel*, 41.
[70] *Caligula & Three Other Plays*, 73.

Caligula's *performance* has been some kind of experiment conducted in public; his aim was the same as Sade's dream: "the demand for total freedom and dehumanization coldly planned by the intelligence. The reduction of man to the object of experiment."[71] However, total freedom did not bring Caligula the happiness he craved; the experiment was a failure. Why does Patrice's experiment succeed? Patrice is wholly singled-minded in his pursuit of happiness; but it is not until the end of the novel that he discovers the conditions required for "the singular happiness he sought."[72] From the murder of Zagreus until this moment, he has been stumbling along trying different things and hoping he'll find happiness; in effect, it is through experimentation that he discovers the "humiliating yet priceless truth" he was seeking. Going back to *The Rebel*, we read:

> It helps to anticipate everything so that no unexpected tenderness or pity occurs to upset the plans for complete enjoyment [...] But enjoyment must be prevented from degenerating into attachment, it must be put in parentheses and tempered. Objects of enjoyment must also never be allowed to appear as persons. If a man is an 'absolutely material species of plant', he can only be treated as an object and as an object for experiment.[73]

Even before murdering Zagreus, Patrice admits that, "Other people's feelings have no hold over me,"[74] he is in no danger from feelings of tenderness or pity creeping up on him unexpectedly. However, in the beginning of the novel, Patrice suffers terribly from jealously; he cannot stand the idea of another man having ever had sex with his girlfriend Marthe even if it occurred *prior* to their relationship. Catching the eye of a man in the cinema who he believes might have been a former lover of Marthe sends him into a whirlpool of delirious jealousy. He later forces her to tell him the names of all the men she'd ever slept with and promise that if they pass one in the street that she'll point him out. This jealousy is humiliating for Patrice, it is a weakness that he now thinks Marthe will exploit (and she does). His reaction is not brought about by feelings of tenderness for Marthe but from wounded pride. When he makes love to a woman, what turns him on is that by allowing him to enter her body she has, in his mind, *surrendered herself* to him.[75] His pleasure comes not solely from his

---

[71] *The Rebel*, 42, 43.
[72] *A Happy Death*, 84.
[73] *The Rebel*, 38, 39.
[74] *A Happy Death*, 33.
[75] Ibid, 25.

conquests but from being seen by others as a *conqueror*. He seeks out the most desirable women – as in, the women desired by the most number of men – ones like Marthe, a "painted goddess,"[76] who "display[ed] in public, at his side, the beauty she offered him day after day like some delicate intoxication."[77] Then, after parading her around in front of his peers, he takes her home to revel in the joys of "possessing a lovely body, at mastering it and humiliating it."[78] What Patrice once mistook for love, was in fact this desire for power. He would look for women who were 'goddesses' in order to prove his power by mastering and humiliating them.[79] However, one cannot defile a goddess[80] if she has already been defiled, hence his inability to stand the idea of another man having been with Marthe before him. When, halfway through the book, Patrice realizes that his 'love' for Marthe was "nothing more than the delighted astonishment of a power acknowledged and awakened by conquest,"[81] he accepts that what attached him to her was his vanity and pride. Whereas Caligula had to overcome feelings of tenderness and pity that attached him to others, Patrice had to overcome his pride. In this respect, Patrice is similar to the renegade missionary who, as we have seen, continually sought conquest and power, and is taught a humiliating lesson that allows him to overcome his pride. Patrice saw Marthe as a goddess, an animal divinity, and wanted to exert his power over her through sex; the renegade attempted to rape a woman with a mask of the fetish god tattooed to her face (she literally resembled the dark god). The missionary finally accepts the fetish as his god from whom he wants nothing but to be permitted to serve; Patrice accepts that what he mistook for love was in fact vanity and "knew he was not made for such a love, but for the innocent and terrible love of the dark god he would

---

[76] Ibid, 22.

[77] Ibid, 20.

[78] Ibid, 61.

[79] Other characters created by Camus raise women up in their minds only to go on to humiliated them. Raymond in *The Stranger* pays all his mistress' bills and refers to her as "your highness". When he discovers that she has betrayed him his answer is to sexually humiliate her. Clamence in *The Fall* tells his interlocutor that he would often put women on a pedestal in order to knock them off again: "Nevertheless, setting them so high, I made use of them more often that I served them. How can one make that out?" (*The Fall*, 43)

[80] One can defile her with other men as part of a group acting in unison. In his essay *Love of Life*, Camus describes a female exotic dancer ("seizing her breasts with both hands and opening her red, moist mouth") entertaining a crowded bar filled exclusively by men. "Like an unclean goddess rising from the waves, her eyes hollow, her forehead low and stupid [...] she was like an ignoble and exalting image of life, with despair in her empty eyes and thick sweat on her belly..." (*Lyrical And Critical Essays*, 54) For Camus, along with the other men, the spectacle of humiliated goddess fills them with a lust for life.

[81] *A Happy Death*, 61.

henceforth serve."[82] Both men learn that they were looking for 'god' in the wrong place; however, only Patrice realizes that attempts to conquer god are futile.[83]

Although Patrice gives up his desire to 'conquer' goddesses, he still uses women as "objects of enjoyment," and is careful to make sure that, to him, they remain objects.[84] Reminding ourselves of the extract from *The Rebel* quoted above, Camus says: "Objects of enjoyment must also never be allowed to appear as persons." Patrice is very careful with his next girlfriend Lucienne to treat her only as an object. The terms of marriage he offers her are humiliating (although he attempts to convince both her and himself that they are not): they are to live apart with her only calling on him when he summons her for sex. After a brutal scene in which he explains that he never loved her (and never said that he did), Lucienne tells him that she thinks he is not happy. His reply makes clear her status as object; tightening his grip on her neck he replies violently: "I will be [...] I have to be. With this night, this sea, and *this flesh* under my fingers."[85] (my emphasis) Lucienne is treated by Patrice as if she were no more than a feature of the natural world, a piece of flesh to be used by him at will. Whereas to have sex with Marthe was to force submission from a goddess, to have sex with Lucienne was to consummate a love for the world. *A Happy Death* ends with the lines: "He looked at Lucienne's swollen lips and, behind her, the smile of the earth. He looked at them with the same eyes, the same desire."[86] Murder, for Patrice, may have been a one-off but he continues, to the end, in treating others merely as objects to be used as part of his experiment. So why does his experiment succeed whereas Caligula's fails? He appears to be following the same rules – criticized by Camus in *The Rebel* – as Caligula and so one would expect that he too would discover at the end of the road that he'd taken the wrong path. But there is, in fact, a crucial difference between Patrice and Caligula. Patrice seeks harmony with the world whereas Caligula is filled with scorn at the idea. Patrice, would sometimes walk out to the ruins at Tipasa, "Then he would lie down among the wormwood bushes, and with his hands on the warm stone would open his eyes and his heart to the intolerable grandeur of that seething sky. He would match the

---

[82] Ibid.

[83] 'God' in this sense is not the God of Christianity, although the renegade experiments with Christianity.

[84] Talking about his sexual conquests, Clamence in *The Fall* says: "I looked merely for objects of pleasure and conquest." (44)

[85] *A Happy Death*, 81.

[86] Ibid, 106.

pounding of his blood with the violent pulsation of the sun at two o'clock..."[87]
In Act II of the play, Caligula mocks Scipio's ideas of a "certain harmony"
between man and nature. He pretends to agree with his former friend,
displaying an understanding of the subject that shows he once genuinely
shared these ideas, waiting until the moment Scipio embraces him in the
belief that they share a common love before scornfully disabusing him of
the notion. The renegade differed from Patrice in that he never gave up his
lust for power and conquest, he accepted no limit in attaining his end,
whether that be to build an eternal city of good or of evil. In this, he is a
reflection of the ideas expressed in *The Rebel*. Caligula, on the other hand,
differs from Patrice in that he sought to create his own values out of
nothing; believing that the world had no meaning, he set out to destroy
everything and create for himself a happiness *ex nihilo*. In this, he is a
reflection of the ideas expressed in *The Myth of Sisyphus*. Unlike Patrice
(and the just assassins, and Martha) Caligula and renegade kill others not in
order to live but in order to die; they are committing what Camus terms a
superior suicide. Speaking of Caligula:

> But if his truth is to rebel against fate, his error lies in negating
> what binds him to mankind. One cannot destroy everything
> without destroying oneself. This is why Caligula depopulates the
> world around him and, faithful to his logic, does what is necessary
> to arm against him those who will eventually kill him. *Caligula* is
> the story of a superior suicide.[88]

Camus says that Caligula learns in the end that "no-one can save himself all
alone and that no-one can be free at the expense of others."[89] Now, it must
be said that Patrice *does* save himself and that other people are treated
merely as objects to be used as a means to his end. However, Camus
recognised that this book was flawed and chose not to seek publication;
instead he wrote *The Stranger* which we'll be discussing in this essay. But
first, we are going to look at one of Camus's killers that might not instantly
spring to mind in a discussion of murder in Camus's literature; Daru's Arab
prisoner.

---

[87] Ibid, 85. We see the same idea in *Nuptials in Tipasa*, "I open my eyes and heart to the
unbearable grandeur of this heat-soaked sky." (67) And in *Summer in Algiers*, "But to be pure
means to rediscover that country of soul where one's kinship with the world can be felt,
where the throbbing of one's blood mingles with the violent pulsations of the afternoon sun."
(90)
[88] *Caligula & Three Other Plays*, vi.
[89] Ibid.

Daru's prisoner

The Arab prisoner, in the short story *The Guest*, murders his cousin; it's not clear exactly what happened and what led up to the crime but the gist of the matter is that during a dispute over a debt the man killed his cousin with a billhook. The only thing the man himself says on the matter is that "He ran away. I ran after him."[90] When Daru, the school-teacher tasked with keeping the Arab overnight and then handing him over to the police at a nearby village the next day, asks him if he is sorry for his crime, the man does not understand. It is ambiguous whether the misunderstanding is due to a language or a cultural problem. Camus is more interested in matters of honour rather than justice in this story. The focus is on Daru's decision to let his prisoner go instead of handing him over to the police, rather than on the correct attitude to the Arab's crime. When Balducci, the old gendarme who brings the prisoner to the school house, tells him what the Arab has done, "Daru felt a sudden wrath against the man, against all men with their rotten spite, their tireless hates, their blood lust."[91] He is disgusted by the crime but also by having imposed upon him the duty of prison-warder and the task of handing the man over to the police. The conversation Daru has with Balducci is more about the distinction and tension between the group of European settlers, to which the two men belong, and the native Arab population of which the prisoner is, obviously, a member. Before allowing the gendarme time to speak after asking about the Arab's crime, Daru wants to know whether the man can speak French; when the answer comes, "No, not a word," the school-teacher wants to know "Is he against us?"[92] Knowing on whose side the prisoner belongs is of greater importance to Daru than the crime he committed and why he did it. The gendarme wants to arm Daru with a revolver and tie the prisoner's hands but Daru refuses. Conversation turns to the possibility of a coming uprising and the need for their group to defend itself; Daru assures the old man that this he is prepared to do. Clearly, for Daru, killing in self-defence is acceptable but to bind a man and lead him at gunpoint to the police (and quite probably the guillotine) is not. The gendarme admits that putting a rope on a man makes him feel ashamed but he does so because it is necessary: "But you can't let *them* have their way."[93] (my emphasis). Between shame at having dishonoured himself as a man and dishonouring himself by letting down the other members of his group, the gendarme has a greater aversion of the

---

[90] *Exile And The Kingdom*, 75.
[91] Ibid, 70.
[92] Ibid.
[93] Ibid, 72.

latter. In this respect he is similar to Kaliayev who is prepared to overcome his aversion to murdering children and do so if his fellow terrorists demand it. Daru's membership of the honour group is explicitly mentioned by the gendarme when he reminds him: "You're from hereabouts and you are a man."[94]

Dishonour, shame, within an honour group is felt keenly by its members; to be shamed is to feel diminished, less of a man. The reference to being a man is intended as a reminder that Daru, despite threatening to betray the group, is at this moment still whole. Another feature characteristic of honour groups is the importance of insult. To suggest that a member has betrayed the group, has dishonoured themselves, is an insult that must be acknowledged and answered. In the same way, to choose to betray the group and go against the honour code is an insult to other members. Daru's refusal to follow orders is to Balducci an insult that must be acted upon. However, after some consideration he says to Daru, "If you want to drop us, go ahead; I'll not denounce you."[95] In the end, the old man seems more hurt than offended by Daru; he says good-bye but refuses to allow Daru to see him out and walks away without looking back.

The decision not to hand the Arab over to the police is not made out of any sympathy for the man's plight or for the group to which he belongs. Indeed, Daru resents even having to spend the night with him; sleeping in the same room "bothered him [...] by imposing on him a sort of brotherhood he knew well but refused to accept in the present circumstance."[96] It is what the Arab has done that makes impossible any alliance between the two men. "That man's stupid crime revolted him, but to hand him over was contrary to honour. Merely thinking about it made him smart with humiliation."[97]

Daru's solution to his moral dilemma is to put the decision into the hands of the guilty man. In the morning, he leads him out to where the village of Tinguit (where the police station is) can be made out in the distance. Giving the man food and money he tells him that he's leaving and that the choice is his: to walk to the village and hand himself in or head in the other direction and find shelter with the nomads. When the Arab walked towards Tinguit, Daru watched, "with a heavy heart."[98] But why the heavy heart? This is a

---

[94] Ibid.
[95] Ibid.
[96] Ibid, 77.
[97] Ibid, 79.

question I'll leave unanswered. When Daru gets back to the school house he finds, scrawled on the blackboard: "You handed over our brother. You will pay for this."[99] Daru ends up isolated, hated by two groups, "In this vast landscape he had loved so much, he was alone."[100]

The short story is an examination of honour and loyalty rather than murder; the reader wonders what Daru ought to have done to balance his competing loyalties and sense of honour rather than judge what action and/or attitude to take against a murderer. Indeed, whilst the conflict of loyalties seems realistic – similar but different to the conflict in the story *The Silent Men*, between the loyalty and solidarity of the striking workers and their sense of solidarity with a man, their boss, who faces a sudden threat to his child – the account of the murderer and his fellow "brothers" seems contrived. Why did these men not simply liberate their brother during the night, or follow Daru and their unshackled brother down into the valley the following day? There were so many chances for these men to act that the reader must ask why they were more concerned with revenge than with securing the freedom of one of their own. The only reason the Arab has committed murder is to give Daru a dilemma; Camus has no interest in tackling how murderers ought be be treated. In fact, with none of Camus's killers, discussed above, has there been a need to worry about how to deal with the problem of murderers in our midst. In *The Misunderstanding* there is no need to trouble ourselves over how the murderers ought to be treated; Camus kills the father off before the play begins, the mother drowns herself when she discovers that it is her son who she has helped kill, and Martha hangs herself after being abandoned by her mother. In *A Happy Death*, Patrice dies of sickness and the terrorists in *The Just Assassins* consent to be hanged. Caligula needed to be be stopped and is assassinated by Cherea and the others; however he accepted from the start that an early and violent death would be his inevitable end if he went down his chosen path. In this respect he is every bit as suicidal as Kaliayev and Dora. The question of what to do about Caligula has only one answer and that is death by assassination; allowing him to continue is not an option and there can be no question of life imprisonment or exile. Camus deals with the subject of how society ought to deal with murderers in his essay *Reflections on the Guillotine.*

---

[98] Ibid, 81.
[99] Ibid, 82.
[100] Ibid.

Parisian parricide

We are interested here not so much in Camus's arguments against capital punishment but in his thoughts on murder. In the essay Camus deals with two types of murder: unpremeditated killing carried out in the heat of the moment under the influence of rage and/or intoxicating substances; and those types of murder that can be considered *heinous*. Referring to the murder of children, Camus writes, "Men who commit such a heinous crime are, I believe, classified among the irremediable."[101] He is concerned with discussing these killers because they are the ones most often judged deserving of the death penalty. "To be sure, the killer of children is a particularly vile creature who scarcely arouses pity."[102] Anticipating the reader is sensing a ...*but*, Camus assures us that he doesn't want to reduce the culpability of "certain monsters" however goes on to suggest that, while it is probable that none of his readers, were they forced to live in squalid conditions, would ever "go as far as to kill children," had the child-killers lived in better conditions (and without access to alcohol) they "would perhaps have had no occasion to go so far."[103] He then goes on to cite a statistic, without offering any satisfactory evidence to support it, that, "95 per cent of the killers of children are alcoholics." It does seem that Camus is trying to reduce the culpability of these monsters; however, he is attempting – not to excuse those who commit heinous crimes – to undermine the idea that the real responsibility of an offender can ever be precisely measured. For him, "there never exists any total responsibility or, consequently, any absolute punishment or reward [..] no-one should be punished absolutely if he is thought guilty, and certainly not if there is a chance of his being innocent."[104]

Heinous crimes are not limited to child murder; killing one's own father, for example, is generally considered to be a more terrible crime than killing the father of someone else. Without attempting to come up with a definition of what makes a crime *heinous* or to draw up a definitive list of heinous murders, it's possible to think up some examples that would be generally accepted as belonging to this category of crime: killing for the pure enjoyment of killing, especially if the murder involves a sexual element;

---

[101] Camus, Albert. *Resistance, Rebellion, And Death.* Trans. Justin O'Brien. 1st ed. New York: Vintage International, 1995, 211.
[102] Ibid, 207.
[103] Ibid.
[104] Ibid, 210.

killing purely out of expediency; killing through extreme negligence, allowing children, the elderly or infirm to perish through sheer indifference to their needs; the deliberate targeting of civilians during a military, or some such, action; deaths resulting from the systematic humiliation of a group of people through extreme poverty, slavery, displacement from their land, and so on. When Camus writes, "that each of us, however honourable he may be, can foresee the possibility of being someday condemned to death,"[105] he did not mean that each of us can imagine one day being executed for any of the crimes listed above, nor any crimes like them. Rather, he believes that we can imagine a day when the State decides that our deaths are necessary for political reasons. Most people have, Camus argues, more to worry about from the violence of the State rather than that of their fellow citizens. If today, this seems a little far-fetched, he does allow that "It may be that the proportions be reversed in another thirty years."[106] To allow the death penalty is to give the State a justification for killing its citizens and this, for Camus, is more to be feared than allowing child-murderers to live. But capital punishment doesn't just threaten the lives of heinous murderers but also:

> the man who doesn't know that he is going to kill, who makes up his mind to do it in a flash and commits his crime in a state of frenzy or obsession, nor the man who, going to an appointment to have it out with someone, takes along a weapon to frighten the faithless one or the opponent and uses it although he didn't want to or didn't think he wanted to.[107]

Camus would much rather focus on this type of killer because it is the only kind of killing the majority of his readers could ever imagine possibly carrying out themselves. It is far easier to convince someone that capital punishment is wrong if you can get them to think from the condemned man's point of view. However, what we are interested in are those "certain men [that] are irremediable in society that they constitute a permanent danger for every citizen and for the social order, and therefore, before anything else, they must be suppressed."[108] Camus tells the story of one of these men. A young Parisian man, a kind and affectionate man devoted to his family, who one day after becoming annoyed by a remark made by his father killed both his parents with an axe in a frenzied attack. After the

---

[105] Ibid, 227.
[106] Ibid.
[107] Ibid, 188.
[108] Ibid, 211.

murders, he calmly washed and changed his clothes before stepping out to visit the family of his fiancée. There he spent a pleasant visit without giving any clue to his murderous activities carried out just hours previously. Once back at home, the killer telephoned the police and told them he had just discovered his parents murdered. His blood-stained trousers were discovered at the scene and, without much prompting, the young man confessed to the murders. Apart from his unusually calm and unaffected demeanour, and some odd comments such as taking pride in the number of people who attended his parents' funeral, he was judged sane and condemned to death. Camus says:

> Many "monsters" offer equally impenetrable exteriors. They are eliminated on the mere consideration of the facts. Apparently the nature or the magnitude of their crimes allows no room for imagining that they can ever repent or reform. They must merely be kept from doing it again, and there is no other solution but to eliminate them. On this frontier, and on it alone, discussion about the death penalty is legitimate.[109]

This brings us, finally, to Camus's most infamous killer: the "monster" Meursault.

The Stranger

Meursault, hero of *The Stranger*, is Camus's most puzzling killer. He has almost nothing in common with any of the others mentioned above. Unlike Patrice Mersault, Martha and her mother, Kaliayev and Dora, Caligula, the renegade missionary, Daru's Arab prisoner, or the Parisian parricide, all of whom make a choice to kill, Meursault appears to kill by accident. Indeed, it is debatable whether he is actually guilty of murder. If the killing was an accident, and this will be discussed below, then Meursault has no reason for killing his victim; however, he could still *benefit* from the man's death even if he didn't plan it. But unlike with the others the Arab's death brings no benefit to his killer; at least Daru's prisoner and the parricide could claim that the murder gave them some sort of satisfaction. Meursault actually expresses annoyance at the Arab's death; asked if he feels sorry for what he'd done, he says: "I thought about it for a minute and said more than sorry I felt kind of annoyed."[110] Camus explains in his 1955 preface to *The*

---

[109] Ibid, 219.
[110] *The Stranger*, 70.

Stranger: "[Meursault] is asked, for example, to say that he regrets his crime, in the approved manner. He replies that what he feels is annoyance rather than real regret."[111] Finally, unlike the others, Meursault offers no explanation or justification for taking a man's life. All of Camus's killers offer some kind of justification for killing except the parricide whom Camus accepts is a "monster."

Meursault excepted, Camus's killers can be sorted into two groups: those for whom killing is both enjoyable and essential to their plans; and those who kill only because it is necessary to achieve their ends. As we have already seen, Caligula needs to kill, he cannot carry out his experiment without murder. When he takes a life it is with "the rapturous power of the destroyer [...] And this, *this* is happiness."[112] The renegade, likewise, needs to kill the incoming missionary; there is no acceptable scenario for him in which Father Beffort can live. And he enjoys smashing the man's face in with the butt of his rifle. Kaliayev needs to kill the Duke; the man must die for there to be a spectacle of terror to inspire the people. When he goes out to kill it is, "With joy!"[113] In these stories Camus is interested in killing in the pursuit or defense of an ideal. The focus is on the *killing* and the audience is intended to reflect on their attitude to politically and religiously motivated murder.

In the other group: Martha and her mother kill because they need to steal their victims' money; neither of them enjoy the act of killing and in fact choose not take the men's lives directly. Instead, they put the men to sleep and throw them still alive into the water. If it were possible to take the money without killing the man then they would take it. Looking over Jan's sleeping body, they reassure and comfort themselves with the idea that, "From now on, everything will be easy for him. He will pass from a dreamful sleep into dreamless sleep. And what for others is a cruel wrench will be for him no more than a protracted rest." Martha adds that she is "glad he is being spared any pain."[114] If Patrice woke one morning to discover he'd inherited a fortune from a distant aunt, we cannot imagine him stopping off to kill Zagreus before leaving for Prague. When he does kill him it is efficiently and without enjoyment; and because it is the only way to get the money he needs in order to stand a chance of living a happy life. The

---

[111] *Lyrical And Critical Essay*, 336.
[112] *Caligula & Three Other Plays,* 72.
[113] Ibid, 249.
[114] Ibid, 114.

murders in these two stories are, in a way, more like the 'cosy murders' of popular fiction. In fact, the killing of Zagreus in the opening chapter of *A Happy Death* is very similar to the murders seen in the opening scenes of the television programme *Columbo*.[115] The killings discussed in *The Misunderstanding* are more like something seen in a cheap horror film.[116] The murders of Zagreus and Jan are plot devices used to heighten the tension. Camus does not intend the audience to reflect on the act of murder and it's consequences. Instead, Camus is concerned with the role played by others in a single individual's pursuit of happiness; of the conflict between indifference to, and need for, the company of others.[117]

Absent from these two groups are Daru's prisoner and the Parisian parricide. These two men cannot really be considered members of *Camus's killers*. Both men are examples of the two types of murder discussed by Camus in *Reflections on the Guillotine* – in the case of the parricide, he is not even a literary creation but a real-life example of what Camus considers to be "a monster." The murder committed by the Arab, the slaying of his cousin in the midst of a family dispute over money, is the most true-to-life murder to be found in Camus's literature. Meursault is also an exception; his case is very similar to the Parisian parricide in that we can understand neither his motivation for killing nor his reaction to killing.

Meursault's crime

The prosecutor at Meursault's trial invites the jury to consider the murder of the Arab as a vicious act of underworld violence. He suggests that Meursault and Raymond were working together and that the Arab got in the way of business; presumably as warning to others not to mess with them, Meursault shot and killed the Arab before mutilating his corpse. The reader, of course, knows that this is not what happened. The Arab was the brother of

---

[115] The comparison *may* not be as far-fetched as it first appears; the TV series was actually inspired by Dostoevsky's *Crime and Punishment*. Lt. Columbo was intended to be a detective in the style of Petrovich, employing psychological games to entrap intellectually arrogant killers who believe they have committed the perfect murder. Patrice, in the novel, does get away with murder, and unlike Raskolnikov is not plagued with guilt.

[116] Although there have been similar real-life cases. In the 1980s in California, Dorothea Puente, dubbed *the death house landlady*, drugged and killed her tenants in order to cash and keep their social security cheques. Puente would put her victims to sleep with sleeping pills before suffocating them and burying the bodies.

[117] Caligula can actually fall into both camps, which is its strength and probably why of all his plays it is widely considered to be the best.

Raymond's mistress and he and Raymond had already had run-ins in the past. A few days prior to the killing, Raymond had telephoned Meursault at work to warn him that the Arab and his friends might be hanging around outside the apartment. On the Sunday morning, as Meursault, Marie and Raymond head off to the beach, the Arabs are waiting and watching from across the street. Later, Meursault guesses that the bags they were carrying must have revealed to the Arabs where the three were going. After lunch, Meursault, Raymond and his friend Masson go for a walk on the beach and are attacked by the Arab and his friend. The fight would have been won by Raymond and Masson (Meursault hangs back, to fight three-on-two would be dirty) but for Raymond's pride; he turns to show off in front of Meursault and the Arab uses this lapse in concentration to slash Raymond in the face with his knife. Humiliated and angry, Raymond is taken to have his face bandaged and later storms off on his own down the beach. Meursault follows after him and the pair have another run-in with the two Arabs. This time, Raymond pulls a gun and Meursault, very skilfully, convinces his friend not to fire and disarms him. Satisfied that his honour has been restored, Raymond returns to Masson's beach chalet but Meursault goes back out and down the beach. After a long walk in the hot sun, he bumps into the Arab who is on his own this time. The man is sitting in the sand and Meursault is standing; they are about 10 metres apart. Meursault grips the handle of the gun which is still in his jacket pocket. The two men stare at each other and Meursault, sweating and burning under the sun, takes an involuntary step forward; the Arab draws his knife and points it at Meursault.

> All I could feel were the cymbals of sunlight crashing on my forehead and, indistinctly, the dazzling spear flying up from the knife in front of me. The scorching blade slashed at my eyelashes and stabbed by stinging eyes. That's when everything began to reel. The sea carried up a thick, fiery breath. It seemed to me as if the sky split open from one end to the other to rain fire. My whole being tensed and I squeezed my hand around the revolver. The trigger gave; I felt the smooth underside of the butt; and there, in that noise, sharp and deafening at the same time, is where it all started.[118]

The killing itself reads like an improbable accident. The men are ten metres apart, Meursault can barely see the Arab and he talks of the trigger giving way rather than him squeezing the trigger. There is no mention of him even

---

[118] *The Stranger*, 59.

drawing the weapon; we are told that he grips the handle of the gun while it is still in his jacket. The Arab is killed stone dead, with a single-shot, fired without aiming from ten metres away. From his account of events, it appears not that Meursault wasn't thinking straight but that he wasn't thinking at all. Later, he tells us that, "at the police station, nobody seemed very interested in my case."[119] The examining magistrate who interrogates him is also not very interested in the killing, "What interests me is you."[120] After getting Meursault to go over the events that led up to the shooting he simply repeats "Fine, Fine," until they reached the part in the story where Meursault is standing over the body; at this point the magistrate stops him by saying "Good."[121] What really interests the man is what Mersault did next; and why. Meursault tells him what he did but refuses to say why. Continuing from exactly where we left off in the excerpt from chapter 6, we can see what happened:

> I shook off the sweat and the sun. I knew that I had shattered the harmony of the day, the exceptional silence of a beach where I'd been happy. Then I fired four more times at the motionless body where the bullets lodged without leaving a trace.[122]

Meursault shakes off the delirium brought about by a combination of excessive alcohol consumption and walking bareheaded under the midday Algerian sun, "I shook off the sweat and the sun," and then has a realization about what he had done, "I knew that I had..." Then, after pulling himself together and pausing for thought, he desecrates the corpse of the man he has just killed. Camus makes it absolutely clear that *this* is what is troubling the magistrate. Three times he asks Meursault to provide an explanation. One: "Why did you pause between the first and second shot?"[123] Two: "Why, why did you shoot at a body that was on the ground?"[124] Three: "Why? You must tell me. Why?"[125] Meursault understands that for the magistrate, who is now brandishing a crucifix and talking about repentence, "there was one thing that wasn't clear in my confession, that fact that I had hesitated before I fired my second shot. *The rest was fine*, but that part he couldn't understand."[126] (my emphasis)

---

[119] Ibid, 63.
[120] Ibid, 66.
[121] Ibid, 67.
[122] Ibid, 59.
[123] Ibid, 67.
[124] Ibid, 68.
[125] Ibid.

Meursault doesn't earn the nickname, "Mr. Antichrist," because he killed a knife-wielding Arab on the beach but because he fails to understand that there is something wrong with desecrating a corpse. When the case goes to trial, the prosecutor argues for the death penalty on the grounds that Meursault is "a monster".

> "Tomorrow, gentlemen, this same court is to sit in judgement of the most monstrous of crimes: the murder of a father." According to him, the imagination recoiled before such an odious offense. He went as far as to hope that human justice would mete out punishment unflinchingly. But he wasn't afraid to say it: my callousness inspired in him a horror nearly greater than that which he felt at the parricide. And also according to him, a man who is morally guilty of killing his mother severs himself from society in the same way that the man who raises a murderous hand against the father who begat him.[127]

The day before, when challenged by the defence for spending too much time focusing on the funeral, the prosecutor dramatically accuses Meursault "of burying his mother with crime in his heart!"[128] He wants to use Meursault's attitude towards his mother's death to show his lack of humanity: his lack of tears or visible emotion, his smoking and allowing others to smoke around the coffin, his failure to pay his respects at the grave; as well as his behaviour the next day: picking up a woman on the beach and taking her to see a comedy film. This treatment of his mother's remains and memory after her death is, the prosecutor argues, just as bad *morally* as if he had murdered the woman. The fact that Meursault can see nothing wrong in mutilating the corpse of the man he killed or show any remorse for the fact that he took a man's life (even if it was an accident, as he claims) is simply further proof of the his callousness. It is interesting to note here that Meursault is being treated by the court as equal and opposite to the Parisian parricide mentioned in *Reflections on the Guillotine* – he murdered his parents but was glad to see that they had a large and well-attended funeral, Meursault did not actually kill his mother but appears to care nothing about respect paid to her after her death. What outrages the examining magistrate and the prosecutor (and later the jury and the judge) is that Meursault shows absolutely no respect for the dead. In his essay on the death penalty Camus claims that in the past there was some justification for the death penalty on

---

[126] Ibid.
[127] Ibid, 101, 102.
[128] Ibid, 96.

the grounds that although it was considered the supreme punishment, people did not believe it took the form of an absolute judgement:

> In fact, the supreme punishment has always been, throughout the ages, a religious penalty. Inflicted in the name of the king, God's representative on earth, or by priests or in the name of society considered as a sacred body, it denies, not human solidarity, but the guilty man's membership in the divine community, the only thing that can give him life. Life on earth is taken from him, to be sure, but his chance of making amends is left him. The real judgement is not pronounced; it will be in the other world.[129]

Meursault is considered a monster, and his death sentence justified in the eyes of his society, not because he killed a man, but because he *desecrated* the bodies of his mother and his victim. However, as Camus will later ask: "But what is the value of such a justification in the society we live in, which in its institutions and its customs has lost all contact with the sacred?"[130]

If we try to find a motivation for the killing of the Arab by Meursault we won't find one because he didn't have one. Unlike all killings discussed above, the death was from the result of an accident. This is not to suggest that Meursault is blameless; he was guilty of recklessly endangering the man's life as soon as he put his finger on the trigger of the gun. What was his motivation for desecrating the body after he'd killed the man? Camus appears to have included mutilation in order to depict a society that has lost all contact with the sacred hypocritically condemn a man for acts of desecration. Meursault, our narrator, cannot offer us any enlightenment on the matter because he doesn't fully understand what has happened. The response from his society to his crimes is so baffling to Meursault that he cannot follow the arguments laid out in court; he is still confused at the end of the novel when he demands the prison chaplain tell him, " What would it matter if he were accused of murder and then executed because he didn't cry at his mother's funeral?"[131] Meursault was accused and executed because he failed to treat the lifeless bodies of his mother and the man he killed as sacred objects.

---

[129] *Resistance, Rebellion, And Death*, 222.
[130] Ibid, 225.
[131] *The Stranger*, 121.

Both Meursault and Patrice discover happiness through harmony with the world before they die. The murder of Zagreus gave Patrice the means to find his happiness and when he achieves it, the murder is just a memory that brings with it no feelings of horror, shame or guilt. Meursault realizes that he is happy in his prison cell awaiting his death by guillotine. Opening himself up to "the gentle indifference of the world," he finds it like himself: "so like a brother, really – I felt that I had been happy and that I was happy again."[132] The only part the Arab's death plays in Meursault reaching this point is that it is his death and mutilation that set in motion the sequence of events that led to Meursault receiving the death penalty. Without the enormous fear he experienced waiting for the dreaded moment his cell door would be opened by the executioner, he never would have begun his prison meditations. The meditation took the following form: first he focused solely on the fact he was going to die, accepting that he was always going to die along with everyone else and that twenty more years would make no difference; only then did he allow himself to imagine that he would be pardoned and have twenty more years of life. If he managed to accept that the latter ought to be accepted with same level-headedness as the former, he "gained an hour of calm."[133] It is during one of his hard-earned moments of calm that the chaplain enters his cell uninvited. An angry outburst from Meursault ensues and after waking up from an exhausted sleep he achieves his enlightenment. If, like Camus, we consider the death penalty to be a kind of legally sanctioned murder, Meursault achieves his happiness not from murdering someone else but under the threat of being murdered himself.

---

[132] Ibid, 123.
[133] Ibid, 115.

Works Cited

Camus, Albert. *Caligula & Three Other Plays*. Trans. Justin O'Brien. 1st ed. New York: Vintage Books, 1962.

——. *Exile And The Kingdom*. Trans. Justin O'Brien. 1st ed. London: Penguin, 2002.

——. *The Fall*. Trans. Justin O'Brien. 1st ed. London: Penguin, 2000.

——. *A Happy Death*. Trans. Richard Howard. 1st ed. London: Penguin Books, 1973.

——. *Lyrical And Critical Essays*. Trans. Ellen Conroy Kennedy. Ed. Philip Thody. 1st ed. New York: Vintage Books, 1970.

——. *The Rebel*. Trans. Anthony Bower. 1st ed. London: Penguin Books in association with Hamish Hamilton, 2000.

——. *Resistance, Rebellion, And Death*. Trans. Justin O'Brien. 1st ed. New York: Vintage International, 1995.

——. *The Stranger*. Trans. Matthew Ward. 1st ed. New York: Vintage International, 1989.

L'Exil et le royaume (Exile and the Kingdom): Giving Voice to Voicelessness

by Benedict O'Donohoe

It is well-known that Camus's quarrel with Sartre and the coterie of *Les Temps Modernes* (*Modern Times*), over their critical reception of *L'Homme révolté* (*The Rebel*, 1951), left him depressed and despondent about his ability to pursue his projected "triptych" of works on the theme of Don Juan and love.[1] Indeed, he lost confidence in himself as a thinker and writer and entered a period of virtual sterility for five years, publishing only two collections of (mostly) pre-1951 essays—*Actuelles II* and *L'Été*—before the appearance of the masterly, but self-accusatory, *La Chute* in 1956.[2] That novella had initially been intended for inclusion in the collection of short stories, *L'Exil et le royaume*, which Camus envisaged as a way of restoring his confidence and credibility as a writer. These would be what the French call *exercices de style*—as Camus himself put it, treating the theme of exile "in six different ways [...] ranging from the internal monologue to the realistic narrative".[3] These would re-establish him as a literary figure of the first rank, a writer of range and sensibility: neither a "one-hit-wonder"— with the extraordinarily successful *L'Étranger* (*The Outsider*), 1942—nor a pale imitator of Sartre (and his critical punch-bag). In short, *Exile and the Kingdom* is above all an exercise in Camus re-finding his voice as a writer.

---

[1] See Roger Quilliot in Albert Camus, *Théâtre, récits, nouvelles* (henceforth cited TRN), 2037.

[2] Specifically, Camus's output from *The Rebel* to the posthumous publication of his last unfinished novel, *The First Man*, is as follows: *L'Homme révolté* (1951), *Actuelles II* (1953), *L'Eté* (1954), *La Chute* (1956), *Réflexions sur la guillotine* (1957), *L'Exil et le royaume* (1957), *Actuelles III* (1958), *La Postérité du soleil* (1965), *La Mort heureuse* (1971), *Le Premier Homme* (1994). See : http://www.etudes-camusiennes.fr/wordpress/category/camus/sonoeuvre/, accessed 12/06/13.

[3] See Camus's *Prière d'insérer* for the first edition: "Un seul thème, pourtant, celui de l'exil, y est traité de six façons différentes, depuis le monologue intérieur jusqu'au récit réaliste" (TRN, 2039). All translations from French are my own.

In this paper, I propose to explore the paradox that Camus's six short stories in *Exile and the Kingdom* are obsessed with loss of voice and the impossibility of communication. "La Femme adultère" (The Adulterous Woman) presents a protagonist "surrounded by a language she does not understand" and trapped in a loveless marriage to a dull man with whom she cannot begin to communicate. "Le Renégat" (The Renegade) consists entirely of the rambling inner monologue of a man whose tongue has been torn out and whose stream of consciousness makes little more sense than the guttural grunts he persistently interjects. "Les Muets" (The Silent Men) announces by its very title—literally, "the mutes"—that loss of voice, or failure to communicate, lies at the heart of the unhappy misunderstanding that inexorably unfolds between the employer and his men. "L'Hôte" (The Host, or The Guest) exploits the ambiguity of its French title to destabilise meaning from the outset, propelling the reader along with its three characters into a confusion of miscommunication. "Jonas, ou l'artiste au travail" (Jonas, or the Artist at Work) ironically and comically dramatizes the situation of Camus himself, that of a famous artist who is running out, simultaneously, of living space and creative ideas, until his "inspirational star" is all but snuffed out. Finally, "La Pierre qui pousse" (The Growing Stone) follows an exiled protagonist caught up in an esoteric rite, acted out in a foreign language in a strange country, an "outsider" isolated by the ineffable. Through analyses of the first four shorter stories only, I will argue that their composition over a four-year period acted as a kind of homeopathic therapy: writing about loss of voice enabled Camus to re-discover his voice as a writer, to publish the consummate *La Chute* (*The Fall*) in 1956—a by-product of *Exile and the Kingdom*—and to resume the project of *Le Premier Homme* (*The First Man*) which, sadly, would never be brought to fruition.

I will not rehearse here the notorious quarrel with Sartre, except to note that—although Camus gave a good account of himself in his "Lettre au Directeur des *Temps Modernes*" (i.e. Sartre), responding to Francis Jeanson's initial critique of *L'Homme révolté*—Sartre's scathing and brutal reply (published in the same issue of the journal) left him deeply wounded.[4] Camus's friend and critic Roger Quilliot[5]—who edited the first scholarly edition of the complete works in two volumes of the Pléiade collection—records that Camus began to plan *Exile and the Kingdom* only *after* this

---

[4] *Les Temps Modernes*, no. 82, August 1952 (see Contat and Rybalka, *Les Écrits de Sartre*, 250). Camus's letter to Sartre is reproduced in *Essais* as "Révolte et servitude", 754-74. Sartre's harsh reply is reproduced in *Situations, IV* as "Réponse à Albert Camus", 90-125.

[5] Author of, *inter alia*, *La Mer et les prison : Essai sur Albert Camus*, 1956.

bruising polemic. This was a time when he was filled with a feeling of "tragic solitude"—Camus's own phrase, writing in his *Carnets* (*Notebooks*)—when he was plagued by doubts about the value and meaning of his work, and did not know why he was "envied and contested". Quilliot argues that "La Femme adultère", specifically, paved the way for *La Chute*, with the same air of "betrayal, duplicity, shadows and anxieties."[6]

David Walker—one of the foremost British experts on Camus in the post-war generation—confirms that "the stories were outlined after the break with Sartre" and that the "sense of exile which is the basic theme thus derives added force from [Camus's] personal situation [...]." And he goes on to clarify that: "During the next few years—a period when Camus was dogged by ill-health and self-doubt—the project was to become the sometimes tenuous thread by which hung Camus's hopes of a creative renewal."[7] This testimony is supported in turn by Roger Quilliot who, in 1954, was preparing his monograph on Camus. Quilliot notes that in July of that year, Camus told him that he had not worked for six months and that his wife Francine's illness and the needs of his children combined to make him indifferent to the reception of his book of essays, *L'Été*, published earlier in the year. Quilliot records that this "long pause was making him anxious", that he felt his "work was drying up now he had reached the age of forty", and that he was afraid of being "buried" by academic studies.[8] The comparison with the situation of Jonas is all too clear. And Quilliot expands upon the autobiographical infrastructure of the stories as follows:

> Parisian exile, the solitude of the writer, grown too famous and at the same time burdened with tiresome chores, often the object of jealousy; the painful sense of being a prisoner of his own work, of his own vocabulary, of a misleading image that the critics and the public have constructed of him. No doubt all of this lies at the origin of the *Nouvelles de l'exil* that he planned from 1952.[9]

Camus was apparently tired also of his reputation for moralism and virtue, which was for him a logical consequence of the Resistance, "an explosion of virtue". He wanted to move away from Manichaeism and towards a more complex, nuanced view of empirical experience.[10] But why, in particular,

---

[6] See Roger Quilliot in TRN, 2040.
[7] David H. Walker, "Introduction" to his critical edition of Albert Camus, *L'Exil et le royaume*, xiv.
[8] See Roger Quilliot in TRN, 2037.
[9] Ib., 2038.

would he attempt to do so through the medium of the short story? Here too, I will quote Roger Quilliot:

> In fact, Camus had a crisis of confidence, for numerous reasons, and felt temporarily incapable of undertaking the three panels of his triptych: theatre, essay, novel; so he strove to fill the gap with short stories and adaptations. This was a way of maintaining a certain rhythm of work, and also (if I may say so) of keeping his hand in. All these stories, with their varied techniques ("The Renegade", a monologue; "Jonas", a satire; "The Silent Men", a realist text; and "The Adulterous Woman", "The Guest" and "The Growing Stone", three semi-realist, semi-symbolic stories), were for Camus like musical scales, a renewal of forms.[11]

As I have already noted, Camus's own brief preview (*Prière d"insérer*) supports Quilliot's interpretation of his purpose in these stories, so I shall now turn to the texts themselves in order to illustrate this thesis.

La Femme adultère (The Adulterous Woman)

In the first of these *nouvelles* the protagonist, Janine, is also in effect the narrator because everything is seen and told from her point of view, albeit in the third person. This enables Camus to depict her sense of alienation without much explicit evocation and rather by repeated implication. Very soon we learn that she finds her forename "ridiculous" because she is "tall and well-built", whereas Janine is of course a diminutive form of the name Jeanne.[12] In her very body, therefore, she is "ill-at-ease [...] would have liked to take up less space" [21], and although when men look at her—like the French soldier on the bus—she can tell she is still desirable, and "blushes" [14], this does not make her feel any more at home either in herself or in her marriage, by which she is "bored" [15]. She had not wanted to accompany Marcel on this trip, selling direct to the Arab merchants, and her outsider status is emphasised by every use of the Arabic tongue: "The driver rattled off a few words in this language she had heard all her life, without ever understanding it" [16].

---

[10] Ib.

[11] Ib., 2039.

[12] Albert Camus, *L'Exil et le royaume* (Folio edition), 12-13. All page references in the text are to this edition of the work.

By the time the Arab shepherds appear outside the bus, mysteriously and silently—"*Muets*" [17]—Janine has not yet spoken a single word to Marcel, and it is a feature of their relationship that they scarcely exchange any dialogue. Rather, Marcel mutters his prejudices to himself and Janine generally keeps her own counsel: "Janine followed without replying" [23]. When she first speaks—to concur that the best way to do business is to "deal with each other face to face" [ib.]—Janine both excludes herself linguistically and draws our attention obliquely to the fact that this is precisely what she and Marcel are incapable of doing: communicating in person. Janine is triply alienated: in her language, in her marriage and in the exotic context of this patriarchal society: "[The Arab men] turned their faces towards this '*étrangère*' [stranger, foreigner, outsider: i.e. Janine], yet did not see her, and then—lightly and silently—they began to walk past her [...]" [25].

This oppressive, almost deafening silence on all sides is broken only by the vastness of desert and sky that she beholds from the ramparts of the fort: "It seemed to Janine that the whole sky reverberated with a single short bursting note, whose echoes [...] died away suddenly leaving her silent before the limitless expanse [of desert]" [ib.]. Fittingly, perhaps, she is unable to find the voice to reply to this silence: "Above the desert, the silence was as vast as space itself. // Janine, leaning full length on the parapet, was without voice, incapable of tearing herself away from the void that opened out before her" [26].[13] Likewise, later on, when she awakes in the middle of the night and feels drawn back to the ramparts: "The silence around her was total. [...] She was speaking but her mouth uttered no sound. She was speaking but she hardly even heard [or understood] herself" [29]. Again, the ambiguity of the French verb *entendre*—which, in an English misborrowing, we could call a *double-entendre*—leaves us guessing whether her speech cannot be heard or merely cannot be understood. But the effect is much the same: she "strained her ears for a call which seemed to her to be close by. [...] a mute call which she could, after all, hear or silence at will, but the meaning of which she would never know unless she responded to it at once" [31].

Janine's response is to return to the ramparts, where "Not a breath, not a sound [...] came to disturb the solitude and the silence that surrounded

---

[13] Again: "She only knew that this kingdom [...] would never be hers, save at this fleeting moment perhaps, when she opened her eyes to the suddenly static sky [...] whilst the voices rising from the Arab town abruptly fell silent" [27].

[her]" [33]. What she seeks, therefore, is a kind of communion of quietude, an ecstasy that can only come from her sharing the all-enveloping silence in a way that is almost carnal:

> Leaning her whole upper body against the parapet, [...] she waited only for her still overwhelmed heart to be at peace again and for silence to settle within her. [...] the water of the night began to fill Janine [...] rose gradually from the obscure centre of her being and spilled over in uninterrupted waves in her mouth full of groans. [33-34]

This sensual consummation not only represents, but is also, in fact, the act of the adulterous woman: filled up with nature's fertilising fluid, crying out loudly in orgasmic satisfaction, rediscovering her voice. This explains in large part why she cannot divulge her secret to Marcel:

> [Marcel] sat up suddenly. He spoke and she didn't understand what he was saying. [...] he looked at her, without understanding. She was weeping, copiously uncontrollably: "It's nothing, my dear", she said, "it's nothing." [34]

For, although Janine has found her voice again, it is not one that a man of Marcel's straitened sensibility could possibly hear or understand. For her, this experience is something so momentous that she could not begin to articulate it to Marcel. And so, for him, it must remain literally nothing. Although Janine re-finds her voice, the gulf of mutual misunderstanding between Marcel and herself remains as deep as ever.

Le Renégat, ou Un Esprit confus (The Renegade, or A Confused Mind)

Roger Quilliot finds this short story "mysterious in the reading and even after critical study [because] the *Carnets* are practically devoid of references to this text."[14] He manages to find two such references, nevertheless, the first indicating that "a progressive missionary goes to civilise the barbarians, who cut off his ears and his tongue, and reduce him to slavery. He awaits the next missionary and kills him, in hatred."[15] So, the protagonist and narrator of this story—the man whose stream of consciousness it relates—has had

---

[14] TRN, 2043.
[15] Camus, cited by Quilliot in TRN, 2044.

his tongue torn out. He is therefore clinically without articulation, as the ghastly gargling sounds of "raa-raa", which punctuate his externalised inner monologue, remind us intermittently. Like Janine, he is voiceless, yet also like her, he hears other voices in his head:

> Since they cut my tongue out, another tongue [...] works non-stop in my head, something speaks, or someone who is suddenly silent and then everything begins again oh I hear too many things that I am not even saying, what a mess, and if I open my mouth, it's like the noise of gravel being shaken. [37]

These are the very opening lines of the story, which go on to tell us that the internal tongue is saying "order" (amongst other things), which, we are told, the protagonist had "always desired". The conflict of these inner voices presumably explains the story's sub-title and possibly also articulates Camus's own confusion at the time of writing (that crisis of confidence evoked in his notebooks, as we have seen). "Order" is what the protagonist imagined he would impose upon these "savages", exercising an "absolute power" that he both "dreamt of" and, as he puts it, "rolled around incessantly on [his] tongue" [41]. The tongue, therefore, like the word of God itself, will be the source and seat of power for this young missionary— just as it is, of course, for the writer. This being so, it is perhaps inevitable that when he is first tortured in a ritual of the Fetish, his ordeal begins by having his lips twisted until they bleed [46]. For the mouth is the primary organ of dissent and revolt, uttering cries of protest, revolution and conversion. As he witnesses for the first time the Sorcerer's rape of a handmaiden, the protagonist "cries out loud and screams in terror" [48]. These, as it turns out, are the last meaningful sounds he will ever make with his now "tongue-less mouth" [ib.].

The trope of the mutilated mouth reaches its apogee when the renegade recalls "the day they cut out [his] tongue and [he] learned to adore the immortal soul of hate", all the time still hearing "that tongue within [him] speaking" [50]. That fateful day, when "madness seized [him] by the tongue" [ib.], his last scream was that of a "beast" and an "almost cool and cutting caress sliced across [his] tongue" [51]. He awakes from this terrifying torture to find his mouth "uninhabited", as Camus chillingly puts it, and his dehumanisation is complete: henceforth he is confined to bestial grunting. By assuming the mantle of a convert to his "masters' wicked kingdom", he claims to be "no longer a slave despite [his] mute mouth" [53]. Conflating his sufferings with those of Christ, he imagines that the

Lord's tongue was severed too, "in order to prevent his word from deceiving the whole world" [ib.]. Now, all power resides in the Fetish, "whose only commandment is hatred, the source of all life, cool water like mint chilling the mouth" [ib.]. This conversion from Christian charity to pagan hatred is threatened by the arrival of a garrison of French soldiers, to whom the renegade is alerted, ironically, by "voices speaking a language that I took a while to recognise, because it was my own" [54]. So complete now is his alienation, or exile, that he resolves to murder his successor, for fear, precisely, that *he* will not be silenced in his turn:

> They [the Fetishists] were mad, mad, allowing the town to be invaded, their invincible power and true god to be threatened, and the new man, the one coming, they would not cut out his tongue, he would show off his insolent goodness with impunity, without suffering insult. [54]

He imagines, therefore, that if he intercepts the new missionary and kills him before he reaches the town and the protection of the French garrison, he will thereby save the pagan cult and "his masters" will subsequently "defeat the soldiers and the word of love" [56]. This ultimate act of apostasy—or of loyalty to the Fetish, if we prefer—culminates in a scene of ultimate confusion for the voiced inner consciousness of this voiceless and disordered mind:

> Who is speaking, nobody, the heavens do not sunder, no, no, God is not speaking in the desert, so where is that voice coming from, saying: "If you consent to die for hatred and power, who will redeem us?" Is it another tongue inside me, or the man still lying at my feet, refusing to die and repeating: "Courage, courage, courage!"? [57]

As David Walker rightly observes, it does not matter what the answer to this question is.[16] The key point for my present theme is that the conflict of the inner dialogue continues, and it remains very much a contest of voices—or, more exactly, of expression against its suppression, of articulation contra the inarticulate, of the voiced versus the voiceless. The devastating last line—reminiscent of the servant's blunt "No" at the end of *Le Malentendu* (*The Misunderstanding*, or *Cross Purposes*) seems to suggest that, in any event,

---

[16] See Walker, op. cit., 202.

these voices finally fall silent: "A handful of salt fills the mouth of the chattering slave." [58]

The deliberate paradox of describing the tongue-less renegade as "chattering" reminds us that the same fate—of falling silent—awaits us all. In this dark prognostication, Camus draws our attention not only to a fundamental and defining feature of our Absurd condition—that "men die and are not happy", as his anti-hero Caligula puts it—but also to his own implicit and impressive achievement: namely, to have used his own, supposedly failing, writer's voice to enable his reader to hear the voice of a supposedly voiceless man.

Les Muets (The Silent Men)

We are bound to be struck by the autobiographical traits that we find in this third story. The action is set in a cooperage in Algiers, which is where Camus's maternal uncle, Étienne Sintès, worked and the young Camus used to visit as a child. Étienne was a deaf mute, so the very title of the story evokes his memory. The protagonist, Yvars, is neither deaf nor mute, but he might almost as well be, given the number of occasions on which he fails to speak, or to respond when spoken to. Like his creator, Yvars is forty years old and beginning to feel his age:

> He was getting old too. At forty [...] the muscles do not warm up so quickly. [...] when they called an athlete a "veteran" at thirty, he would shrug and say to Fernande: "If he's a veteran, then I'm already dead." [61-62]

This surely reminds us how Camus was feeling about himself at that time: his sense of having reached a watershed, possibly of having passed his peak in his profession. Like Yvars, Camus felt he had "nothing else to do but wait, quietly, without really knowing what for" [63]. This impression is reinforced when Yvars reflects on the future prospects for his expertise, in the event of its becoming redundant:

> To change your profession is nothing much, but to give up what you know, your own mastery, that's not easy. Having a fine but futile profession, you're stuck, you have to be resigned to it. But resignation isn't easy either. It was difficult to keep your mouth shut, to be unable to argue properly [...]. [64]

In this meditation, we clearly hear echoes of Camus's journal entries around the same date: his fine profession as a creative writer seemed to him threatened with redundancy so long as he remained unable to open his mouth again, to engage with his critics and his reading public. Like Yvars, he felt the need to resist the temptation of resignation, and was conscious of the imperative to rediscover his voice.

The morning on which Yvars returns to work, after the fruitless strike of the workers has been called off, his wife, Fernande, asks him what he and his workmates will say to the boss: "Nothing", replies Yvars in the first of numerous allusions to the refusal of speech, which of course gives the story its title. The paradox here is that the denial of language is enlisted as a potent form of communication: it bespeaks the men's resentment of the manner in which they have been treated, and it will become an eloquent, but ultimately ineffectual, articulation of their revolt against the high-handedness (as they see it) of the boss. In short, as for Camus himself in the early 1950s, silence will serve as self-expression.

Once Yvars arrives at the workplace, mentions of the wilful closure of communication begin to pile up. Ballester, the foreman, had "remained silent" about the strike [67]; the men "keep quiet" as they return to work, yet they are "furious at their own silence, but less and less capable of breaking it, the longer it goes on" [ib.]. When Yvars catches Ballester's eye, the latter nods at him, "without saying anything" [*sans rien dire*, ib.]. The workshop itself is quiet, where the "great mechanical saws [are] strong and silent" [68]. The men take up their work stations "*sans rien dire*" [ib.]; when Ballester issues instructions to each of the men about the work they have in hand, "Nobody replies" [ib.]; the men "all work in silence" [69]. Above all, when the boss, Monsieur Lassalle, enters the workshop and bids the men "*Bonjour*", albeit "less sonorously than usual", "nobody replies" [ib.]. This sullen freezing out of the hitherto respected *patron* is then hammered home—an apposite pun in the circumstances—on the next page: Valery works on, "saying nothing" [*sans rien dire*, 70] and "without replying" when spoken to by the boss; Marcou, the strike leader, likewise "does not reply" and even turns his back on Lassalle, "maintaining his silence" [*toujours silencieux*, ib.]. Lassalle's reaction is to order that Ballester become their mouthpiece as and when they have "got over it". This is a clever tactic on his part for it both implies that he is unmoved by the men's childish gesture of sulking in silence, and reaffirms the hierarchy, atop which he sits, by reminding them they are subordinate to the foreman—who had not approved of the strike [67] and is still prepared to communicate with the boss.

This determination to stand their ground by refusing to communicate becomes, inevitably, a self-defeating strategy on the men's part. In particular, Yvars, we are told, "wanted to speak, but was unable to" [72], when he accompanies Marcou to see Lassalle. The former dismisses the boss's conciliatory overtures as "wind", and Yvars answers his comrades' enquiries by admitting that they "made no reply" [ib.]. When Ballester reprimands them for sulking like children [73], they insist that they have "had their mouths shut" for them, that "anger and impotence sometimes hurt so much that one cannot even cry out—so long as one is a man" [ib.]. With the crisis brought on by the sudden collapse of Lassalle's daughter, Ballester himself begins to fall silent (save for the merest few words [75]), compounding the men's isolation, and especially Yvars's:

> The rest of the afternoon dragged on. Now Yvars could feel only his fatigue and his hardened heart. He would have liked to speak. But he had nothing to say, and nor did the others. On their taciturn faces you could read only sorrow and a sort of obstinacy. [76]

Again, when the boss appears briefly at the end of the day, dishevelled and bidding the men "Good evening" [77] in a "hollow voice", Yvars first thinks it is up to Marcou to say something; and when that does not happen, "Yvars thought that he should call Lasssalle, but the door was already closing behind him" [ib.]. By contrast, Yvars exchanges a warm farewell with his comrades as he heads "quickly" for home, keen to sit on the terrace of the old house in the late afternoon sun: "But, the little girl accompanied him too, and he could not stop thinking about her" [ib.]. When he reaches home and Fernande asks whether "everything had gone alright", Yvars at first "says nothing". Later, however, as they sit outside drinking anisette and looking out to sea, he tells her everything, concluding with the despairing and self-exonerating exclamation: "Ah, it's his own fault!" [78]. His final wish—that they might "both be young again and travel to the far horizon"—betrays a sort of resignation which he had, earlier in the day, felt able to resist.

Roger Quilliot remarks that this story is "almost free of any symbolic intention",[17] and no doubt with good reason. Nevertheless, I would suggest

---

[17] TRN, 2045.

that the modicum of symbolic intention it *does* contain is connected with its central theme of human silence. Like Janine's final inability to communicate with Marcel, or the renegade's amputated tongue and mouth full of salt, Yvars has virtually lost his voice for the expression of human sympathy, by a culpable refusal to make use of it when the occasion demanded. An escape to the far horizon would indeed be no more than an escape: effectively, a confirmation of his muteness.

L'Hôte (The Guest)

Roger Quilliot points out that there are implicit autobiographical elements also in this fourth story.[18] Camus used to say that, if he had not become a writer, "he would have liked to be a doctor or a teacher". And it is immediately obvious, of course, that the name "Daru" bears the same number of syllables and the same vowel sounds as the name "Camus". Quilliot also speculates that the profession of the protagonist might have been chosen "in memory of those teachers who were among the first victims of the uprisings of All Saints' Day 1954". And he traces an influence back to the report of a similar event—namely, the arrest of an indigenous Algerian and his brutal treatment by the police—which Camus read at the age of about twenty, and which had left a deep impression on him. Be that as it may, the question for our present purpose is to ascertain to what extent, if any, these autobiographical threads are woven into the fabric of the author's anxiety about his faltering talent.

Daru, we learn, feels "like a lord" in his domain, and "exiled everywhere else" [83]. But his solitude in this remote place is "monastic" and his default mode is, therefore, "silence" [90]. When the advancing policeman, astride his donkey and with the Arab prisoner in tow on foot, first calls out to him, "Daru does not reply" [84]. This is a familiar refrain from the preceding story, and indeed the paucity and the poverty of communication between the three characters quickly establish a direct rapport with our present theme. For example, Balducci, the gendarme, speaks only short, sharp orders to his prisoner in Arabic, believing (erroneously, as it later appears) that he speaks no French. The latter, squatting by the stove as Daru unties his hands, looks on mutely, "*sans rien dire*" [85]—once again, using that telling little phrase which had punctuated "Les Muets" like a leitmotiv. Daru and Balducci are able to engage in conversation, having first established that the prisoner, the

---

[18] For citations in this paragraph, see TRN, 2048-49.

eponymous "guest", apparently speaks "not a word of French" [87]. However, their conversation rapidly turns into a dialogue of the deaf, with Daru refusing to accept "orders" [86] and insisting categorically that he "will not deliver" the prisoner [88]. He demurs also when required to sign the official paper that Balducci has to submit to his seniors, attesting that his work is done. Consequently, Balducci takes his leave feeling angry and insulted by Daru. Despite their shared condition as *pieds-noirs* and their mutual mother tongue of French, they have failed signally to connect, divided, as it were, by a common language (to paraphrase Oscar Wilde's quip about the Americans and the British).[19]

It is ambiguous whether that language is shared, at all, by the Arab prisoner, referred to only once as Daru's "guest" [91]. The teacher's first word to his nameless guest is spoken in Arabic [90], then followed by a lengthy silence, to which Daru listens:

> It was this silence that had seemed to him painful in the early days of his arrival, after the war. [...] At first, the solitude and the silence had been hard for him in this ungrateful country, inhabited only by stones. [...] In this desert, neither he nor his guest [*hôte*] had any being. And yet, outside of this desert, Daru knew, neither of them could really have lived. [90-91]

When Daru next addresses his "guest", we are *not* told that he does so in Arabic, so we assume it is in French. Is this because the question is a simple one—"Are you hungry?"—and the answer too: "Yes" [91]? Or should we rather infer that the Arab prisoner had hidden his competence in French from Balducci, thereby eavesdropping, in effect, on his captors, two men who are, in reality, *uninvited guests in his country*? This interesting question remains unanswered, even when their somewhat stilted conversation, still presumably in French, reaches a point at which the Arab apparently no longer understands:

> "Are you the judge?"

---

[19] It is possible, of course, that Balducci's "mother tongue" is Italian, just as Camus's mother's tongue was Spanish (or, to be exact, more likely Catalan than Castilian, given that her family hailed from Minorca). Among immigrants of lower social class to Algeria, there were at least as many southern Europeans as there were French, and Camus has clearly chosen this name to suggest that the policeman, of Italian descent but representing French colonial authority, is as much an intruder in Algeria as is Daru.

> "No, I'm keeping you till tomorrow."
> "Why are you eating with me?"
> "I'm hungry. [...] Why did you kill him? [...]."
> "He ran away. I ran after him. [...] Now, what are you going to do with me?"
> "Are you afraid? [...] Do you regret what you did?"
> The Arab looked at him, open-mouthed. Visibly, he did not understand. [92-93]

Is it the word "regret" that the Arab does not understand? Or is it the concept itself? To him, there was no doubt a certain justice in taking the life of his thieving cousin, perhaps even a perfectly justifiable revenge. But, for Daru, there is only the repeated frustration of an inconclusive conversation, another dialogue of the deaf in which even their respective capacities, albeit limited, to express themselves in the other's language result again in impasse.

This intractable situation could be resolved, from Daru's perspective, if his guest would take flight in the night. But, alas, that is not to be. The teacher is reduced next morning to the same monosyllabic utterances as the gendarme whom he is so reluctantly obliged to replace: "'Come on [...]. Go on [...]. I'm coming [...]. It's this way [...].' The Arab watched him, without appearing to understand. 'Let's go', said Daru" [97].

Reciprocal incomprehension reigns supreme. When Daru frees his charge, giving him food and money—enabling him to choose whether to hand himself in to the police at Tinguit, two hours away, or to take his chance of reaching the relative safety of Bedouin tribesmen, a day's walk ahead—the Arab successively "watches him without understanding [...] doesn't know what to do with what he has been given [...] and is seized with a sort of panic on his face" [98]. His last word to his "host" is the supplication: "Listen"; and Daru's last words to his "guest" are this refusal: "No, be quiet. I'm leaving you now."

If only it were so easy to silence the incipient Arab insurgency with an abrupt "Be quiet!". For, as Balducci had warned, "things are beginning to happen" [*Ça bouge*, 86]. Mutual misunderstanding reaches its height—or its depth, if we prefer—when Daru finds scrawled on his blackboard, in an "unskilful" hand, the legend: "You've given up our brother. You'll pay for that" [99]. This message is, we suppose, in French (since we are not told otherwise), and it is ironically framed by the meandering rivers of France, drawn on there by Daru in one of his Geography lessons. This is in itself emblematic of uprising: the invasion of the metropolitan Hexagon, the defacement of its territory, the clear implication that the "brother" is the child of another language, the one also used undoubtedly by the possessor of the uncertain hand spelling out his threatening message in French. And the traitor is the Frenchman, the uninvited guest in the Arabs' land, whose humanitarian gesture of liberating his captive has been radically and fatally misconstrued: "In this vast country that he had loved so much, he was alone" [99].

This poignant last line, with its stress on solitude, exile, disappointment and—perhaps, above all—misunderstanding, points us backward again to the despairing destinations of Janine, the Renegade, and Yvars. But it also points us forward: to the more hopeful solitude, conflated with solidarity, of the unmistakably autobiographical "Jonas", the ironically sub-titled "Artist at Work"; and to the curiously communitarian d'Arrast, hero of "The Growing Stone", whose bizarre adventure in a remote and profoundly foreign culture nevertheless culminates with a sort of integration into it, and his access to a "renewed life" [185]. Space does not permit me to analyse here these last two, much longer, *nouvelles* from my chosen thematic perspective. Nevertheless, I trust the foregoing discussion of the first four novellas substantiates the claim that, in *Exile and the Kingdom*, Camus used the short story form, in its various modes, to explore, to test and ultimately to remedy, his loss of voice as a writer. And that he did so precisely by taking loss of voice as his focal and dominant theme.

Works Cited

Camus, Albert. *Essais* (ed. Roger Quilliot). Paris: Gallimard, " Bibliothèque de la Pléiade ", 1965 (abbreviated below as ESS).

———. *Théâtre, récits, nouvelles* (ed. Roger Quilliot). Paris: Gallimard, " Bibliothèque de la Pléiade ", 1962 (abbreviated below as TRN).

———. *Actuelles II* [1953], in ESS.

———. *Caligula* [1944], in TRN.

———. *La Chute* [1956], in TRN.

———. *L'Été* [1954], in ESS.

———. *L'Étranger* [1942], in TRN.

———. *L'Exil et le royaume*. Paris: Gallimard, 1957. (Also published in TRN, and in the " Collection Folio ", 1972: page references in my text refer to the 1993 Folio edition.)

———. *L'Exil et le royaume* (ed. David H. Walker). Walton-on-Thames: Nelson Harrap, 1981.

———. *Le Malentendu* [1944], in TRN.

Contat, Michel, and Michel Rybalka (eds.). *Les Écrits de Sartre*. Paris: Gallimard, 1970.

Quilliot, Roger. *La Mer et les prisons: Essai sur Albert Camus*. Paris : Gallimard, 1956.

Sartre, Jean-Paul. *Situations, IV*. Paris : Gallimard, 1964.

Sartre, Jean-Paul, and Simone de Beauvoir, et al. (eds.). *Les Temps Modernes*, no. 82, August 1952.

Prolegomena to a Reconsideration of Albert Camus's Philosophical Achievement

by Ron Srigley

For almost sixty years it has been common scholarly practice to interpret Albert Camus as a writer who accepted the premises of the modern project and was committed to developing a morality in accord with them. According to the interpretation, what Camus considered truest about modernity was its insight concerning the absence of a natural order of values and its corresponding claim that meaning is a human construction. This is the insight of Camus's first cycles of books (*The Stranger*, *The Myth of Sisyphus*, and *Caligula*) devoted to the experience of the absurd. However, although Camus never repudiated this insight he was unwilling to accept the conclusion that human morality was therefore illusory. As evidence of this unwillingness he wrote a second cycle of books (*The Plague*, *The Rebel*, and *The Just Assassins*) about the experience of rebellion and the human effort to create meaning without appeal either to God or to nature. Though essentially successful, so the interpretation goes, the analysis was hampered by a reactionary element in Camus's thought that prevented him from accepting the revolutionary violence necessary to create values historically. This reticence was the cause both of his falling out with Jean-Paul Sartre and his subsequent literary paralysis. Unable to follow Sartre in his historicization of value, but unable to retreat to the comforts of nature, the project stalled. From the mid-1950s onward Camus vacillated awkwardly between bitter cynicism (*The Fall*) and empty nostalgia (*The First Man*) without ever managing to overcome the opposition between them or to escape the lingering absurdism that underlay the entire project.[1]

---

[1] Though there are significant differences in detail between them, the analyses offered in the following works are typical of the style of interpretation I am describing. Germain Brée, *Camus*; John Cruickshank, *Albert Camus and the Literature of Revolt*; Jeffery C. Isaac, *Arendt, Camus, and Rebellion*; Thomas Merton, "Camus: Journals of *The Plague* Years"; Bernard Murchland, "The Dark Night before the Coming of Grace"; Jean Onimus, *Albert Camus and Christianity*; David Sprintzen, *Camus: A Critical Examination*.

This style of interpretation was initiated by Sartre himself in 1943 in his essay "An Explication of *The Stranger*" in which he interprets the absurdism of *The Stranger* and *The Myth of Sisyphus* in a distinctively modern way. "In *The Myth of Sisyphus*, which appeared a few months ... [after *The Stranger*], Camus provided us with a precise commentary upon his work. His hero was neither good nor bad, neither moral nor immoral. These categories do not apply to him. He belongs to a very particular species for which the author reserves the word 'absurd.' But in Camus's work this term takes on two very different meanings. The absurd is both a state of fact and the lucid awareness that some people acquire of this state of fact. The 'absurd' man is the man who does not hesitate to draw the inevitable conclusions from a fundamental absurdity."[2]

Camus never speaks about the absurd in this way. For him the absurd is neither a "fact" nor "metaphysic" (*métaphysique*) but an "intellectual malady" (*mal de l'esprit*) from which the absurd man suffers and which he seeks to understand and overcome.[3] Sartre interpretation obscures this aspect of Camus's account, thereby eclipsing its explicit critical content. The effective truth of the procedure is to draw Camus firmly into the modern camp while also reasserting the primacy of Sartre's interpretation of modernity's founding experience.[4]

When Sartre first began writing about Camus's books their meaning was not yet settled and no canonical interpretation had established itself. Nowadays discussions of Camus's modernism are as plentiful as they are predictable and unenlightening. They persuade us principally because we have acquired their habit of not seeing in Camus's books anything other than our own reflection. However, to break the habit all we need do is look again. Were we to do so, even a quick reading of *The Myth of Sisyphus* and *The Stranger* would teach us that for Camus the absurd is not a "fact" of existence but a

---

[2] In *Albert Camus's* The Stranger, ed. Harold Bloom (New York: Infobase Publishing, 2001), 3-18.
[3] Albert Camus, *The Myth of Sisyphus*. Trans. Justin O'Brien (London: Penguin Books, 1988), 10; Albert Camus, *Essais* (Paris: Gallimard, 1965), 97.
[4] Already in a review of Sartre's *La Nausée* in *Alger républicain* in 1938, Camus attempted to distinguish his own understanding of the absurd from the account offered by Sartre. "Life can be magnificent and overwhelming – that is its whole tragedy. Without beauty, love, or danger it would be almost easy to live. And M. Sartre's hero does not perhaps give us the real meaning of his anguish when he insists on those aspects of man he finds repugnant, instead of basing his despair on certain signs of man's greatness." Albert Camus, "On Jean-Paul Sartre's *La Nausée*" in *Lyrical and Critical Essays* ed. Philip Thody. Trans. Ellen Conroy Kennedy (New York: Vintage Books, 1970), 201-202.

tragic condition the experiential source of which is a very ancient wisdom. And from *The Rebel* we would learn that rebellion is not an act of "self-creation through time"[5] but the expression of our "human nature...as the Greeks believed."[6]

It is time to revisit the question of Camus's modernism. In the pages that follow I sketch the outlines of an alternative to the standard interpretation. Contrary to its central claim, I suggest that Camus's first two cycles of books (the absurd and rebellion) provide us with perhaps the most profound and comprehensive critique of modernity since Nietzsche. The depth and comprehensiveness of that critique have been eclipsed by the style of interpretation I have described above, it is true. However, by revisiting briefly the break between Camus and Sartre, and more important, by re-examining the trajectory of Camus's thought, it might be possible for us to recover a sense of the significance of Camus's achievement and the originality of his insight. Camus spent the better part of twenty years both exploring and being uneasily influenced by two primary traditions in the West – Christianity and modernity. *The Rebel* is the book in which the problem of their influence and the question of the relationship between them became so acute that the traditional explanations on which Camus had relied in the past proved no longer viable.[7] The resulting analysis of this complex of problems and influences is by no means flawless, but it gives us the opportunity to examine in an unprejudiced way the nature of Camus's achievement and his critical assessment of both traditions.

* * *

The proper philosophical name for the corner of modernity to which Camus has been consigned by his commentators is existentialism. It is a term that has been used to describe Camus's work for the better part of the last sixty years. Pick up any philosophy textbook and turn to the section entitled

---

[5] The phrase is taken from David Sprintzen, *Camus: A Critical Examination* (Philadelphia: Temple University Press, 1988), 277.

[6] Albert Camus, *The Rebel*. Trans. Anthony Bower (New York: Vintage International, 1991), 16.

[7] This mix of critical insight and traditional appropriation is evident even in Camus's earliest work on the subject. See Albert Camus, *Christian Metaphysics and Neoplatonism*. Trans. Ronald D. Srigley (Columbia: University of Missouri Press, 2007). Many of the formulations of *Christian Metaphysics* are repeated almost verbatim in the history of metaphysical rebellion that Camus develops in the early pages of *The Rebel*. Albert Camus, *The Rebel*, 26-35.

existentialism, and there you will find him listed alongside the likes of Kierkegaard, Heidegger, and Sartre. Compared with the other misnomers he might have received, existentialist is in some ways not a terribly damning one. In the hands of a non-ideological twentieth century critic, it usually means simply heroic or non-fanatical nihilist. Given the current state of the debate in North America, one might just as well say liberal. In any event, as harmless as it may be at this journalistic level of analysis, the appellation is highly misleading and robs us of what is most striking and important in Camus's books and of his best insights when we consider his achievement more seriously. The great irony is that this writer, who has become the poster boy for modern existentialism, was one of modernity's most astute critics and one of the very few who genuinely understood and challenged the teachings of existentialism. It does not seem to matter that Camus denied publically and repeatedly that he was or ever had been an existentialist; nor does it seem to matter that the only book-length study he devoted to the subject was explicitly and resolutely critical of all schools of existentialist thought; [8] contemporary scholarship has insisted and continues to insist that Camus's highest achievement was a rather conventional anti-foundationalism coupled with a robust encounter with the world's meaninglessness.[9] There is nothing much new here, and it is difficult to believe that such insights could have won Camus the approbation of writers like Martin Buber, Hannah Arendt, and Eric Voegelin, to say nothing of the thousands of non-academic readers who found in Camus's books something they did not find in those of other contemporary writers.[10]

Despite his alleged existentialism, Camus always comes off unfavourably in comparisons with Sartre, the true gatekeeper of that philosophical school in France and Camus's most famous critic. The common view was that while Camus may have been a sound moralist and a better novelist, Sartre was the

---

[8] Albert Camus, *Lyrical and Critical Essays*, 345. See also Camus's essay "The Enigma" in Ibid., 154-161.

[9] See Jeffrey C. Isaac, *Arendt, Camus, and Rebellion* (New Haven: Yale University Press, 1992). See particularly Chapter 4: "Revolt and the Foundations of Politics," 105-139. See also Ronald Aronson's recent book, *Camus and Sartre: The Story of a Friendship and the Quarrel that Ended It* (Chicago: The University of Chicago Press, 2004). Aronson writes: "Modern secularism moves toward a nihilistic state of mind because it lacks what Camus regarded as the sole saving insight: that life is absurd, and even though we must rebel, nothing can create order or remove death's sting" (120).

[10] On the basis of polls taken at the time and sales data from Gallimard, Germaine Brée has argued that in 1970 Camus was still the most popular writer in France, leading both Sartre and Marx. Germaine Brée, *Camus and Sartre: Crisis and Commitment* (New York: Delta Books, 1972), 43-44.

real philosopher of the two.[11] The view's influence was due largely to Sartre himself. In his response to Camus's letter to *Les Temps modernes* regarding its review of *The Rebel*, Sartre stated publically that Camus's analysis was at best derivative and sophomoric.

> Tell me, Camus, by what mystery may we not discuss your books without depriving humanity of its reasons for living? ... And what if you are wrong? What if your book simply testifies to your philosophical incompetence? What if it consisted of hastily gathered and second-hand knowledge? ... I have at least this in common with Hegel: you haven't read either one of us. But what an odd habit you have of not going to the sources... I dare not refer you back to *Being and Nothingness*, the reading of which would seem unnecessarily arduous to you: you detest difficulties of thought and hastily declare that there is nothing to understand in order to evade the reproach of not having understood.[12]

There is no reason to take Sartre's work or his highly polemical remarks as the measure of Camus's ability to think philosophically, though this is common practice today.[13] Sartre was an extremely capable writer and intellectual, however Camus was an entirely different story.[14] Whatever problems may be apparent in *The Rebel*, they are not due to any philosophical incompetence on his part. Just the opposite is true. They are the normal and perhaps inevitable confusions and hesitations that attend any effort to think about an old problem in a new way or to change the terms of the debate. Camus may have found modernity's this-worldliness helpful as a means of overcoming analytically Christianity's denigration of nature. But even in his earliest books there is evidence that he was not convinced that modernity itself managed to escape that same denigration or even that genuine "worldliness" was one of its primary ambitions. Indeed in these and

---

[11] For an account of this view, see Tony Judt, *The Burden of Responsibility: Blum, Camus, Aron, and the French Twentieth Century* (Chicago: The University of Chicago Press, 1998), 94, 121.

[12] Jean-Paul Sartre, *Situations IV: Portraits* (Paris: Gallimard, 1964), 92, 100-101, 108.

[13] "Unlike Sartre, Camus was not adept at argumentation; it bored and irritated him." Germaine Brée, *Camus and Sartre: Crisis and Commitment.* 35.

[14] Eric Voegelin offered the following comparison of Sartre and Camus: "Excuse my rough words – I don't mean to be disrespectful to the psychological analyses of Sartre (late in *L'Étre et le Néant*, for example) – but he is a vulgarian and an epigone. He's not interesting. He's not to be compared with Camus; *he* was a thinker! Sartre is not on that level. Eric Voegelin, *Conversations*, ed. R. Eric O'Connor (Montreal: Thomas More Institute Papers, 1980), 26.

other works there is a strong sense that modernity had actually continued and perhaps even exacerbated the Christian problematic.

As Camus's thought matured his critique of Christianity and his critique of modernity began to merge to form a single critical insight. The content of that insight took shape slowly in books like *The Myth of Sisyphus* and *The Rebel*, as well as in a series of shorter "lyrical" essays. As it did so the terms of Camus's analysis also began to change. His earlier distinction between this world and the other world as his principal analytic tool shifted in order better to account for the similarities between the two traditions.[15] *The Rebel* is something like a mid-way point in this development. The this world/other world formulation or immanentization argument of *The Myth* is still apparent in the analysis, but it now exists uneasily alongside a new formulation that Camus introduces in order to capture the totalizing character of both traditions. The "All or Nothing" analysis of *The Rebel* does not simply repeat Camus's earlier argument.[16] The All is not God and the Nothing is not the world, though they have been read that way by some commentators.[17] Rather these terms denote a human aspiration to totality that Camus argues can be found just as well in the transcendent historiography of Joseph de Maistre as in the immanent historiography of Marx or Lenin.[18] This is the analysis that would gradually take shape in the early and middle fifties. Though it is more compelling than the one that preceded it, in *The Rebel* its significance and consequences are only partially worked out and are rendered ambiguous by the fact that they have to compete awkwardly with elements of the earlier analysis that Camus still had not abandoned entirely.

In his "Reply to Albert Camus" Sartre exploited these confusions and hesitations to his own advantage while ignoring the central thrust of the analysis: namely, the apocalyptic character of all modern revolutionary movements, their affinity with certain Christian teachings, and Camus's

---

[15] Albert Camus, *The Myth of Sisyphus*. Trans. Justin O'Brien (London: Penguin Books, 1975), 110.

[16] The term "immanentization" is taken from Eric Voegelin, but it is perfectly consistent with Camus's argument. For an explanation of Voegelin's argument, see Eric Voegelin, *The New Science of Politics* (Chicago: The University of Chicago Press, 1952). See particularly the chapter "Gnosticism – The Nature of Modernity."

[17] William Hamilton, "The Christian, the Saint, and the Rebel: Albert Camus," in *Forms of Extremity in the Modern Novel*, ed. Nathan A. Scott Jr. (Richmond: John Knox Press, 1965), 68-69.

[18] Albert Camus, *The Rebel*, 191-193.

attempt to articulate an alternative free of the excesses of both accounts. He argued that although Camus had understood the illusory character of all forms of meaning, whether metaphysical or religious, he continued to grapple with their absence as a fundamental feature of his thinking.[19] This was particularly true in the case of religion. God may be a fiction, but he was still real enough for Camus to lament his disappearance and to protest against his silence. Nature for its part became a sort of refuge from the madness and violence of history. But this was both reactionary and inconsistent with Camus's own absurdism and his critique of Christianity. With God dead nature died too. For Sartre there was therefore no going back:

> It seems to you that the world offers the same riches as in the past and that it is men who do not want to see them; well then, reach out your hand and see whether it does not all vanish: Nature itself has changed its meaning because the relationships men maintain with it have changed.[20]

The remainder of Sartre's reply is straightforward Marxist critique. With God and nature dead, all that remains is history and the human effort to "give" it meaning.[21] But Camus refused to participate in that effort. To the real struggles of history, which were ugly and more violent because they were directed against human beings who impede history's progress, Sartre argued that Camus preferred his illusory struggles against a non-existent god and a silent nature.[22]

> You refused the Soul and the Idea. But since, according to your own terms, injustice is eternal – that is to say, since the absence of God is constant through the changes of history – the immediate and always renewed relationship of the man who demands to have a meaning (that is to say that one be given to him) to this God who remains eternally silent, itself transcends History. The tension through which man realizes himself – which is, at the same time, an intuitive joy of being – is therefore a veritable conversion which he snatches from his everyday 'agitation' and 'history' in order to make it coincide finally with his condition. One cannot go

---

[19] Sartre, *Situations IV*, 113.
[20] Ibid., 121.
[21] Ibid., 124.
[22] Sartre says, "man's number one enemy is man." Ibid., 120.

> any further; no progress can be found in this instantaneous tragedy.[23]

Sartre's reply to Camus was as effective as it was disingenuous. It is extremely illuminating of the intellectual climate of opinion in France at the time that Sartre was considered almost unanimously to have won the debate, the uncharitable nature of his arguments notwithstanding. Even Camus's friends were of the opinion that Sartre had bested him.[24]

Ronald Aronson has recently offered a more even-handed assessment. He argues that both men's arguments have "the ring of one-sided truth" and that the legitimate insights of what might otherwise have been a private and fruitful exchange between friends were lost in the violence of a public debate that was essentially political and therefore concerned with victory far more than truth.[25] As to the substance of their disagreement, one thing Aronson argues is that rather than answer the specific objections Camus had raised in his letter, particularly his central argument about the violence and immoralism of the modern revolutionary movements Sartre was recommending and supporting, Sartre merely *"changed the subject"* all the better to destroy Camus publically.[26] There is much good sense in Aronson's analysis and a very helpful account of the history of the relationship between the two men. But I think we can go even further in the analysis of Sartre's reply to Camus and in explaining what it was about Camus's account that Sartre seems to have resisted or failed to understand.

Sartre did not merely change the subject of his debate with Camus; he also changed the subject of Camus's book, in much the same way the Jeanson did in his initial review of *The Rebel* for *Les Temps modernes*. One of the complaints that Camus makes repeatedly in his letter to Sartre is that Jeanson grossly misrepresents his argument all the better to dismiss it. Here is one example:

> Your collaborator has preferred to suppress history in my reasoning the better to be able to accuse me of suppressing it in

[23] Ibid., 113.
[24] Oliver Todd, *Albert Camus: A Life*. Trans. Benjamin Ivry (New York: Alfred A. Knopf, 1997), 312.
[25] Ronald Aronson, *Camus and Sartre: The Story of a Friendship and the Quarrel that Ended It*, 153-154.
[26] Ibid., 151.

> reality... Your article, here as in the entire work, replaces historicism with history, which, in effect, suffices to transform the book into its opposite and its author into an unrepentant idealist.[27]

Nothing really changes in Sartre's response. The distinction between history and ideals to which Camus refers is a derivation of the distinction between this world and God and perhaps also of the distinction between history and nature that Sartre uses to interpret his analysis. Sartre's first move is essentially the same as Jeanson's: quietly and without argument he equates history with Marx's brand of revolutionary historicism.[28] As Camus says in his letter, since he is critical of all forms of historicism, the practice has the effect of denying to him any meaningful sense of history at all. And when this assertion is coupled with the assumption that history and nature or history and God are antithetical realities between which one must choose, it requires only a short step to place Camus in the latter camp and to dismiss him altogether as an idealist, a reactionary, or even a reluctant believer.[29]

Sartre misrepresents Camus's argument even more skilfully than does Jeanson. Apart from a few scattered exceptions, the extraordinary thing is that in doing so he set the interpretive parameters that would guide Camus scholarship for the next fifty years. To a contemporary non-partisan reader the scope and influence of the misrepresentation is staggering. Although Camus does at times falter in *The Rebel* and occasionally resorts to the kinds of antitheses and assumptions apparent in Sartre's analysis, try to escape those assumptions he most certainly does. No sensitive reader of *The Rebel* can deny that it is precisely these sorts of antitheses – between nature and history, history and God, the real and the ideal – that Camus is seeking to overcome. Christians may speak about God in a way that Camus could not accept. But the modern negation of all transcendence and any sense of the sacred seemed equally implausible to him.[30] And how could one offer a compelling account of the basic character of life if one was forced from the

---

[27] Albert Camus, *Essais* (Paris: Gallimard, 1965), 763.

[28] Sartre, *Situations IV*, 123-125. Sartre softens the more virulent aspects of Marx historicism in order to make the argument seem that much more obvious and persuasive: "And Marx has never said that History would have an end. How could he say that? One might as well say that one day man would be without goals. He spoke only of an end to prehistory, that is to say, a goal that would be attained within History itself and surpassed as all goals are" (125).

[29] Ibid., 121, 122-123, 113.

[30] "You once wrote: 'Secret of my universe: imagine God without the immortality of the soul.' Can you define more exactly what you meant?" "Yes. I have a sense of the sacred and I don't believe in a future life, that's all. Albert Camus, "Replies to Jean-Claude Brisville," *Lyrical and Critical Essays*, 364.

outset to abandon or ignore things that do not move or change (nature) in favour of things that do (history), or the reverse? The Marxist and existentialist notion that meaning is something human beings simply *make* through historical action was for Camus too proud and too naive to explain experientially both the wonder of human life and its heartbreaking and tragic nature.[31]

What Camus was attempting to articulate in *The Rebel* was an account that did not seek to answer the Christian/modern problematic on its own terms but to reveal the inadequacies of both traditions and to encourage a new exploration of human experience that did not labour under the distorting influence of either tradition's assumptions. This was an ambitious undertaking that in *The Rebel* Camus only partially succeeds in completing.[32] But it was an undertaking for which Sartre apparently did not have the inclination. For all his anti-authoritarian rhetoric and his avowed atheism, Sartre was the one who remained firmly within the orbit of the Christian understanding while Camus bravely and unpopularly forged ahead to free himself from it completely.

Though this renewed exploration of human experience could be undertaken just as well through an examination of the works of other gifted modern writers – Melville, Nietzsche, Faulkner, Char – for Camus the best way to accomplish it was to return once again and wholeheartedly to the real source

---

[31] This idea can be found expressed throughout *The Rebel*. Camus articulated a similar account in a lecture on tragedy he delivered in Athens in 1955, later published in *Lyrical and Critical Essays* under the title "On the Future of Tragedy." "No tragedies, therefore, will spring from romanticism, but only dramas, and among them, only Kleist's or Schiller's reach true greatness. Man is alone, and thus confronted with nothing but himself. He ceases to be a tragic figure and becomes an adventurer" (306). There is an even earlier expression of the same idea in an essay from 1937, "The New Mediterranean Culture": "There are, before our eyes, realities stronger than we ourselves are. Our ideas will bend and become adapted to them." Ibid., 195. Here Camus links this awareness of a greater or stronger reality with tragedy explicitly. In an even earlier essay from *The Wrong Side and the Right Side* Camus writes: "For what struck me then was not a world made to man's measure, but one that closed in upon him. If the language of these countries harmonized with what echoed deeply within me, it was not because it answered my questions but because it made them superfluous." Ibid., 56.

[32] As I argue below, this partiality was in a sense both intentional and unwitting. *The Rebel* was to be followed by a third essay, *The Myth of Nemesis*, which would have completed the historical analysis Camus had begun with *The Myth of Sisyphus*. Because they were parts of a greater structure and a larger project, Camus set very clear limits to the scope of each of his philosophical essays. However, he sometimes fails to achieve his goals even within the terms set by those limitations.

of what is truest and best in us: the Greeks.[33] They represent the only living tradition in the West that is entirely free of Christian and modern prejudices. Getting back to them, however, would not be easy. For Camus it meant first passing through and understanding those things that separated us from them. His sober assessment of the difficulty of that task is apparent in the iconography he employed to describe it:

> The year the war began, I was to board a ship and follow the voyage of Ulysses... But I did what everyone else did at the time. I did not get on that ship. I took my place in the queue shuffling toward the open mouth of hell. Little by little, we entered. At the first cry of murdered innocence, the door slammed shut behind us. We were in hell, and we have not left it since. For six long years we have been trying to come to terms with it. Now we glimpse the warm ghosts of fortunate islands only at the end of long, cold, sunless years that lie ahead.[34]

* * *

What was it for Camus that made modernity hell? And what was it about the modern project that made it so difficult to overcome, both practically and analytically? To reduce something as complex as modernity to a single leading idea would no doubt be to oversimplify matters; yet if such a reduction were permitted, then I would say that the utopian or apocalyptic character of modernity is what best defines it. Camus does his best to investigate all the elements of the contemporary world, from its political structures to its literature to its pragmatic organization and ambitions. Yet he always comes back to this single explanatory idea when trying to understand what modernity is essentially. What does it mean?

The feature that is common to all apocalyptic movements, whether revolutionary or Christian, ancient or modern, is the notion that our present world is radically imperfect and therefore must be superseded by a new and perfect world. The appeal of these movements lies herein: it is their promise of another world that is free of the pain and suffering of this one. Each

---

[33] Frantz Favre's recent book explores the manner in which Nietzsche helped Camus to overcome the pressures of modernity. He claims that what Camus takes from Nietzsche is less his immoralism than his tragic sensibility and his "besoin de noblesse, le courage et la lucidité." Frantz Favre, *Montherlant et Camus: une lignée nietzschéene* (Paris: Lettres modernes minard, 2000), 20.

[34] Albert Camus, "Prometheus in the Underworld" in *Lyrical and Critical Essays*, 139.

apocalypse has its own account of the origin of that pain and suffering and therefore its own particular account of how it might be overcome. But their shared hope for such an overcoming unites them in a common aspiration. As Camus says, apocalyptic thinkers do not aim to understand the world but to transform it.[35] All their efforts are directed toward the achievement of this end. So ingrained is this idea that even some of modernity's most effective critics sometimes concede its claim to absolute novelty, if only to dismiss its achievements as deformative.

The psychology behind this apocalyptic aspiration that Nietzsche examined so carefully in *On the Genealogy of Morals* and *The Anti-Christ* is something that Camus tackles only partially in his cyclical books.[36] A fuller and more direct treatment does not come until *The Fall*, though there are intimations of it elsewhere. What Camus spends most of the middle part of his career doing is sorting out and explaining the consequences of this type of apocalyptic thinking. The first consequence is the most important and the one from which the others follow. If you want to give the world a meaning other than the one it has, or to make its movement toward another, perfect world seem plausible, you first have to remove the original meaning and the limits it places on such aspirations. Existentialism certainly cooperated in that project, though its own apocalyptic ambitions are often either muted or made to appear as later accretions not properly a part of the original account. Nevertheless, like all modern philosophies it sought to rescue humanity from religious, philosophical, and political oppression by undermining the notion of a natural order on which those forms of oppression relied for their legitimacy. Nature means limits, and limits limit the freedom or liberation that is the principal aim of all modern philosophies, including existentialism. They must therefore be removed.

In *The Rebel* Camus says that the real consequence of that desire for liberation was to "empty the world of its substance."[37] Though the immediate object of this critical remark is Christian providentialism, it applies equally well to all modern apocalyptic movements.[38] The complete freedom promised by apocalyptic thinkers requires the absence of any kind

---

[35] Albert Camus, *The Rebel*, 190.

[36] Here the term cyclical refers to those books that belong thematically to one or the other cycle of Camus's works. I explain the significance of these books and their role in Camus work as a whole below.

[37] Albert Camus, *The Rebel*, 190.

[38] "In contrast to the ancient world, the unity of the Christian and Marxist world is astonishing." Ibid., 189.

of restraint. The removal of the world's substance is therefore a condition of that freedom, not an accidental or unintended consequence of its achievement. The providentialism that characterizes these movements is no objection here and does not contradict the desire for liberation. The providential movement *is* the liberation the apocalyptic thinker seeks. It is reality rewritten according to the dictates of his desire and without the constraints of the old world he wishes to leave behind.

In *The Myth of Sisyphus* Camus claims that the consequence of this loss of the world's substance is a corresponding loss of human substance. This is a precise description. The world's meaninglessness does not free Camus's absurd man for heroic acts of self-creation; it is a mirror image of his own emptiness and tempts him to match it through an act of self-destruction. If nothing has any meaning, then neither do I, and suicide is a matter of indifference at best. What saves him from this fateful conclusion is a reconsideration of his initial assertion. He discovers that the sense of meaninglessness from which he suffers is neither in the world nor in him, but in the misrelation between them.[39] Could we say the same thing about meaning? At any rate, once he gains this insight he is no longer tempted by suicide or by Christian and existentialist hopes. He comes to understand that the flat denial of meaning is as empty as the extravagant hopes that people have of attaining it. Both are fictions, and both relieve him of the "weight of [his] life," his substance.[40] It is not surprising that only after escaping them both does he begin to hear the "myriad wondering little voices of the earth rise up."[41]

In *The Rebel* Camus's concern about this loss of substance and the apocalyptic character of modernity shifts from private matters to public ones. Apocalyptic aspirations also have political consequences. These consequences are the focus of Camus's post-war books, particularly *The Plague* and *The Rebel*. The perfection sought by modern revolutionaries proved deadly for those deemed unworthy or unwilling to participate in their project. Take any modern revolution you please, the French, the Russian, the Chinese, or even one of the more recent efforts in Cambodia or Rwanda. In each case political dissent of any kind, and often not even dissent but merely membership in the wrong social or racial group, meant either the concentration camp or summary execution. Freedom from nature meant

---

[39] Albert Camus, *The Myth of Sisyphus*, 33-34.
[40] Ibid, 54.
[41] Ibid., 110.

freedom from the constraints of human nature, too. Camus describes the camps as experiments designed to test the extent of that freedom by determining the malleability of human nature.[42] Without nature to guide them, human beings become raw material in the same sense as the metals we take from the ground or the trees we cut from the forest. They are simply neutral matter, completely open to any form of manipulation deemed necessary by the latest political program.

In the absence of natural limits the scope of human action was greatly expanded because there was virtually nothing to stand in its way, no objective reality and no subjective one either. The modern loss of substance was pre-eminently a loss of moral substance, though we need not explain that loss moralistically. It may be true that at some basic level modern people long ago simply decided in favour of themselves and their own satisfactions in preference to the fateful and terrible encounter with the world that was the teaching of the ancients. Yet there have also been changes in modernity that have encouraged this disposition to occupy a greater portion of the human psyche than one might otherwise expect. A substanceless world on the objective side encourages a substanceless response on the subjective side. It is arguable that the better part of human virtue is achieved and cultivated through an encounter with the hard though purposeful movements of a world not of our own making. This world is beautiful, often joyous, but always tragic. The cardinal virtues of the ancients – wisdom, courage, moderation, and justice – are not moral rules in the narrow sense but insights culled from the history of our relationship to that world and of the human effort be to equal to or to cope with it.

Now what good are such virtues in a world that has no purpose or substance? What is the use of courage when there is nothing left to fear? What is the use of moderation when one is told daily that there are no longer any boundaries or limits and this is proven practically in a hundred different ways? The entire moral edifice of the ancient world begins to collapse from neglect and misuse on a massive social scale. The suggestion that there may be forms of satisfaction this side of a desire's complete exhaustion is met with incredulity. There simply do not appear to be any good reasons to stop.

---

[42] "If there is no human nature, then the malleability of man is, in fact, infinite... Guided by a determinist hypothesis that calculates the weak points and the degree of elasticity of the soul, these new techniques have once again thrust aside one of man's limits and have attempted to demonstrate that no individual psychology is original and that the common measure of all human character is matter." Albert Camus, *The Rebel*, 237-239.

Yet in essays like *The Rebel*, "Helen's Exile," "Prometheus in the Underworld," and the Preface to his Algerian reports in *Actuelles III*, Camus repeatedly does just that. Ultimately to no avail. In "Helen's Exile" he writes:

> In our madness we push back the eternal limits, and at once dark Furies swoop down upon us to destroy. Nemesis, goddess of moderation, not of vengeance, is watching. She chastises, ruthlessly, all those who go beyond the limit... We, who have thrown both the universe and mind out of orbit, find such threats amusing. In a drunken sky we ignite the suns that suit us."[43]

Apocalyptic accounts are total accounts; and total accounts are total precisely because they do not permit the existence of anything that would cause a "fissure in the totality."[44] Anything that transcends or exceeds the apocalyptic dream world must be either distorted to fit the narrative or destroyed. Because all apocalyptic accounts are also utopian, the feature that is always missing from them is the tragic in existence. We do not see the hard and tragic things because we do not want to see them. But since tragic things do happen, they have to be reinterpreted in order to confirm the narrative and ensure a happy outcome. This does not mean that the perfection of these utopian accounts entails the complete absence of evil. In the final apocalyptic kingdom, perhaps. But in this type of literature evil enemies and powers abound and are usually far fiercer and more demonic than anything we find in the literature of the ancient world.[45] Their exaggerated malevolence should not mislead us into thinking that they make for tragedy in the sense that Camus understands it, however. In the apocalypse evil serves the good just as surely as do its supporters. There is never any true breach, never a real failure or success, and the hard edge of reality is never encountered. Even the worst things that happen are somehow part of the providential plan, and that plan is fixed, like the outcome of a prime-time sitcom or the average political debate.[46] In this world not only do things miraculously become their opposite,[47] nothing ever really happens,

---

[43] Albert Camus, "Helen's Exile" in *Lyrical and Critical Essays*, 149.

[44] Albert Camus, *The Rebel*, 238.

[45] Ibid., 27.

[46] As Jean Baudrillard says, "No event is 'real' any longer. Terror attacks, trials, wars, corruption, opinion polls – there's nothing now that isn't rigged or undecidable." Jean Baudrillard, *The Spirit of Terrorism*. Trans. Chris Turner (London: Verso, 2003), 80.

[47] Albert Camus, *The Rebel*, 236. Camus gives the example of *Pravda*, but he also cites the *Spiritual Exercises* of Saint Ignatius: "'We should always be prepared, so as never to err, to believe that what I see as white is black, if the hierarchic Church defines it thus'." Ibid., 242.

which explains the profound boredom that underlies even modernity's most violent and excessive enthusiasms.[48]

* * *

A common way of responding critically to the totalitarian character of modernity is to offer a non-totalizing account that emphasizes difference, promotes uncertainty, and deconstructs hegemonies. Broadly speaking that is the postmodern critique of modernity. It is a critique that has certain resonances with aspects of Camus's own analysis, particularly with the methodology of the cyclical books.[49] In *The Myth of Sisyphus* Camus critiques the excessive eschatological hopes of Christians and existentialists not by trying to formulate the right kind of eschatological hope, but by recommending something akin to hopelessness – the absurd. It is, of course, Camus's absurd – not meaninglessness *per se* but a divorce from a greater reality. But there is little or nothing to be hoped for here by way of reconciliation, and there is a strong suggestion that the modern obsession with meanings of that order is itself the real problem. "I understand now why the doctrines that explain everything to me also debilitate me at the same time. They relieve me of the weight of my own life and yet I must carry it alone."[50] Total meanings – "doctrines that explain everything" – may somehow satisfy, but they have their price. They rob our lives of meaning – "weight," to use Camus's word. And since total meaning provokes feelings of meaninglessness, total meaningless seems preferable: "It was previously a question of finding out whether or not life had to have a meaning to be lived. It now becomes clear that it will be lived all the better

---

[48] "The whole world absentmindedly turns its back on these crimes; the victims have reached the extremity of their disgrace: they are a bore. In ancient times the blood of murder at least produced a religious horror and in this sanctified the value of life. The real condemnation of the period we live in is, on the contrary, that it leads us to think that it is not bloodthirsty enough." Ibid., 279-280.

[49] Jeffrey Isaac explores some of the similarities and dissimilarities between Camus and postmodern thought. Jeffrey Isaac, *Arendt, Camus, and Modern Rebellion*, 227-235. Isaac argues that Camus's critical appropriation of the modern project might have made him a better postmodern than the post-moderns. Though there are, as I have said, such impulses in Camus's books, they are excesses and not the main thrust of the analysis. In order to create the impression that they are, Isaac, like Sprintzen, dismisses Camus's Hellenism and his concern with nature, human and otherwise, as an "unreflective" aspect of his writing. That strategy simultaneously distorts Camus's achievement and takes the Greeks off the table in order to confine the debate to an essentially in-house quarrel between moderns and postmoderns that neither party can ultimately lose.

[50] Albert Camus, *The Myth of Sisyphus*, 54.

if it has no meaning."[51] This is not nihilism, despite its excessive formulation. But it is close. It is something like tough or honourable pessimism offered as an antidote for our penchant for dishonest and extravagant hopes and meanings.

Camus employs a similar strategy in *The Rebel*. He does not try to supersede the alleged perfection of modern revolutionary movements by offering a superior account of order, but by exposing that perfection as fraudulent through the example of his own and others' rebellion and by arguing that there is no justification, historical or otherwise, to think that the need for such acts will ever be eliminated. Not perfection then but an insuperable struggle with imperfection and injustice; not the right kind of meaning or hope but a world without meaning and hope. To modernity's excesses – its totalities – Camus responds by creating as many fissures as he can and by showing us that less really is more.

This is not Camus's best response to modernity. I think there are two reasons why it is inadequate. The first reason is substantial. It is true that indeterminacy, uncertainty, and meaninglessness are constant features of human life. But they are not the only features. There are many things about which most of us are fairly certain, and there are events in life that are so pregnant with meaning that we usually do what we can to avoid them. To consider these post-modern offerings in abstraction from the full range of human experience distorts whatever sense they do have and creates an image of life that is unbalanced and thus unfaithful to the original. It is no doubt true that playful nihilism of this sort is less violent and menacing than the totalitarian nihilism it seeks to replace. But its playfulness is not the same thing as wisdom in the ancient sense and seems ill-equipped to deal with those nihilists who are not playful or with the normal host of violent aggressors with whom we are confronted daily in the contemporary world.

The second reason that such "postmodern" responses to the excesses of modernity are inadequate is evident in a peculiar pattern that emerges in Camus's cyclical books, and that might also characterize a good deal of post-modernity itself. To make the point simply, the complete denial of meaning is just as much a totality as the total meanings it claims to deconstruct, appearances to the contrary notwithstanding. And because one good totality deserves another, the broken or deconstructed version

---

[51] Ibid., 53.

inevitably leads back to its antithesis as the necessary solution to its total denial of meaning. Not immediately, of course. Playful nihilism is often very enjoyable, and can be experienced as liberating and fulfilling in comparison to the totalitarian nihilism that has been left behind. But because this shift does not entail any real change of disposition, a totality is still what one really wants – something extreme, something apocalyptic, something intense. The only difference nowadays is that this totality also has to be safe (and preferably virtual) in accordance with the dictates of our postmodern utopian sensibilities.[52]

In Camus's case this movement or pattern is manifest in a number of ways. Although most of these ways employ explicitly Christian language, they illuminate the character of all forms of totalitarian thinking. In *The Rebel* Camus says that because God is the source of the injustice in the world, he is the antithesis of the movement of rebellion;[53] but he also argues that because it is impossible to imagine any meaningful sense of justice apart from some divine source, rebellion cannot get along without one, and God turns out to be necessary after all.[54] The same type of contradiction occurs in the case of values. Camus claims that transcendent or formal values are oppressive or totalizing because they do not account for the concrete movements of history.[55] But he also says that once such values are rejected, all that remains are these movements, which in the absence of any form of transcendence are both valueless and total.[56]

---

[52] Jean Baudrillard is one of the best observers of these contemporary manifestations of the modern project. Cf. Jean Baudrillard, *The Transparency of Evil: Essays on Extreme Phenomena*. Trans. James Benedict (London: Verso, 1993) and *The Perfect Crime*. Trans. Chris Turner (London: Verso, 1996).

[53] "It would be possible to demonstrate in this manner that only two possible worlds can exist for the human mind: the sacred (or, to speak in Christian terms, the world of grace) and the world of rebellion. The disappearance of one is equivalent to the appearance of the other, despite the fact that this appearance can take place in disconcerting forms." Albert Camus, *The Rebel*, 21.

[54] "That God should, in fact, be exiled from this historical universe and German ideology be born where action is no longer a process of perfection but of pure conquest, is an expression of tyranny." Ibid., 299-300.

[55] "There is, in fact, no conciliation possible between a god who is totally separated from history and a history purged of all transcendence. Their representatives on earth are, indeed, the yogi and the commissar." Ibid., 288. For an account of the terms "yogi and commissar" in their original context and Camus's source, see Arthur Koestler, *The Yogi and the Commissar and Other Essays* (New York: The MacMillan Company, 1967).

[56] "If, in fact, the solitary mind must be explained by something outside man, then man is on the road to some type of transcendence. On the other hand, society has only man as its source of origin; if, in addition, it can be affirmed that society is the creator of man, it would seem as though one had achieved a total explanation that would allow the final banishment of

The reason for these contradictions lies in the antithetical structure itself. Each pole of the antithesis is inherently unstable because it lacks things the other pole claims to possess exclusively but which are essential aspects of human nature. Moreover, the habit of thinking in terms of such totalities leads us to believe that any answer that does not share their totalizing structure must be inadequate. All of these factors conspire to send Camus shuttling awkwardly back and forth between the various antithetical pairs that form so much of the argument of *The Rebel*: God or the world, formal values or creative values, nature or history, and even the absurd or rebellion. They are all false problems and intellectual dead ends. Yet they had for Camus a measure of credibility because they were part of the climate of opinion in France at the time and because they reflected accurately the self-understanding of many of the participants in the debate, both past and present. How tempting to frame the moral crisis of the twentieth century in terms of the transcendence/immanence distinction when almost everyone who was party to the argument, whether for or against, understood it in that way.

As early as 1946 Camus understood that this "postmodern" response to modernity was insufficient and he was willing to say so publically. In his notebooks there is a report of a conversation with Sartre, Sperber, Koestler, and Malraux in which Camus abandons the kinds of concessions described above and states his criticism of modernity and his own positive recommendations simply and straightforwardly. In response to Koestler's proposal to formulate a "minimum political code of ethics" and to abandon "false scruples" like "soul-searching" and worrying about who might misuse your words and for what purpose, Camus offers the following reply: "'Don't you believe that we are all responsible for the absence of values? And that if all of us who come from Nietzscheism, from nihilism, or from historical realism said in public that we were wrong and that there are moral values and that in the future we shall do the necessary to establish and illuminate them, don't you believe this would be the beginning of a hope?'"[57] This is a remarkable statement. In the present company it did not receive much support. But it was an extraordinarily honest and frank thing to say nonetheless, and it is typical of a sentiment or idea that runs throughout Camus's books and that also forms part of his corpus. Camus has moments of utter clarity about the nature of the modern predicament that are almost

transcendence." Albert Camus, *The Rebel*, 200.
[57] Albert Camus, *Notebooks 1942-1951*. Trans. Justin O'Brien (New York: Paragon House, 1991), 145-146.

entirely free of both modern and Christian assumptions. But in the books belonging to the cycles such insights are less frequent than one might otherwise expect and are often overshadowed by competing formulations that lack their analytic clarity. This is due in part to the project of the cyclical books themselves.

* * *

The books that comprise the cycles of the absurd and rebellion were written in order to offer a critical examination of the nature and origin of modernity. As Camus originally conceived it, that project required him to set aside his best insights into the human condition in order to explore the modern world on its own terms.[58] These are the famous "starting point" arguments of *The Myth of Sisyphus* and *The Rebel* in which Camus restricts his analysis of modernity to a narrow range of experiences that he takes as his primary concern. The following passage from *The Rebel* is typical in this regard. "The first and only evidence that is supplied me, within the terms of the absurdist experience, is rebellion. Deprived of all knowledge, incited to murder or to consent to murder, all I have at my disposal is this single piece of evidence, which is only reaffirmed by the anguish I suffer."[59] To claim that rebellion is the *first* piece of evidence one has to go on in an analysis of modernity is perhaps understandable given the historical circumstances, though it is overstated nonetheless; but to claim that such an experience is the *only* evidence one has at one's disposal is highly problematic and unnecessarily restrictive, particularly given that Camus's subsequent analysis makes it amply clear that rebellion by no means exhausts the range of human experience of reality.

Behind this rather odd methodological restriction lies a much more understandable motivation for the project: Camus wanted to face frankly the reality of his own time and considered it cowardly and dishonourable to do otherwise. A noble ambition, certainly, but not without its dangers. By the mid-1950s there appeared a new refrain in Camus's notebooks, letters, and

---

[58] The following remark from article entitled "Pessimism and Courage" that first appeared in *Combat* in 1946 is a clear statement of the procedure: "No, everything is not summed up in negation and absurdity. We know this. But we must first posit negation and absurdity because they are what our generation has encountered and what we must take into account." Albert Camus, "Pessimism and Courage" in *Resistance, Rebellion, and Death*. Trans. Justin O'Brien (New York: Vintage Books, 1974), 59.
[59] Albert Camus, *The Rebel*, 10.

published writings. It ranged from a quiet lament that he was losing his own voice in his effort to depict the nature of his time to an awareness of the failure of the project of the cyclical books as a whole to a wholesale rejection of all that is modern and the need to find a "new language." A few remarks from letters and the notebooks will help to convey the complexity of these sentiments. In 1952 Camus wrote: "My future books won't turn away from the problems of the hour. But I would like them to subjugate it rather than be subjugated by it. In other words, I dream of a freer creation..."[60] In 1958 the tone of the refrain changes: "I have taken the path of the era – with its frustrations – so as not to cheat and affirm after having shared in suffering and denial, just as I had actually felt it. Now we must transfigure, and this is what distresses me in the face of this book [*The First Man*] that I must make and that binds me. Perhaps the painting of a certain distress has completely exhausted the men of my age and we will no longer be able to speak our true faith."[61] By 1959 Camus states his disaffection with the contemporary world openly and expresses the need for a completely new orientation: "To be honest, I'm absolutely disgusted with what is being said and written, with what is 'modern' or 'of our time,' as we say, including my old books. And if I cannot find a new language, I prefer to remain silent."[62]

Though the analysis of modernity that Camus developed in the cyclical books was by no means negligible, neither was it complete. By the time he had reached the end of the second cycle, the project had effectively collapsed under the weight of its own methodological and substantial limitations. After a period of uncertainty lasting several years, Camus wrote *The Fall*. The analysis of *The Fall* was the point at which Camus broke with the project of the cyclical books completely in order to state the critique of modernity unequivocally.[63] That analysis was almost entirely negative, a portrait of the "aggregate of vices of our whole generation in their fullest expression," but also offered glimpses of what still might be possible for us.[64] What remained to be done was to articulate a genuine alternative to modernity, positively stated and free of the lingering contradictions of the cyclical books. That was the task of *The First Man*. It was also the task of

---

[60] Albert Camus, *Notebooks 1951-1959*. Trans. Ryan Bloom (Chicago: Ivan R. Dee, 2008), 35.
[61] Albert Camus, *Notebooks 1951-1959*, 232.
[62] Albert Camus, Jean Grenier, *Correspondence, 1932-1960*. Trans. Jan Rigaud (Lincoln: University of Nebraska Press, 2003), 191.
[63] For a more complete analysis of the project of the cyclical books and the manner in which Camus finally broke with that project in *The Fall*, see my *Albert Camus' Critique of Modernity* (Columbia: University of Missouri Press, 2011).
[64] Albert Camus, *The Fall*. Trans. Justin O'Brien (New York: Vintage International, 1991).

Camus's proposed essay "The Myth of Nemesis."[65] The latter work was to entail both a return to the Greeks and a completion of Camus's historical inquiry into the origins of modernity by tracing its inception back to "the passage from Hellenism to Christianity...the true and only turning point in history."[66]

Of *The First Man* we have only an unedited and posthumously published fragment; of "The Myth of Nemesis" we have even less – only a number of scattered notebook entries written over the course of a decade. An analysis of those works and of the position they would have entailed cannot be completed for the simple reason that the works themselves were not completed. However, there is an avenue of inquiry that might shed light on the direction of Camus's thought and give us an idea of what he had learned and perhaps also unlearned through the analyses of the cyclical books.

In the 1958 Preface to *The Wrong Side and the Right Side,* Camus wrote that though he had learned a many things since the original publication of that work, about "life itself" he knew "no more than what is said so clumsily" there.[67] He went on to write something even more striking: "If, in spite of so many efforts to create a language and bring myths to life, I never manage to rewrite *The Wrong Side and the Right Side*, I shall have achieved nothing. I feel this in my bones."[68] For Camus this ambition was both a decision and an impulse native to artists and perhaps to all people: "at least I know this, with sure and certain knowledge: a man's work is nothing but this slow trek to rediscover, through the detours of art, those two or three great and simple images in whose presence his heart first opened."[69]

The project of the cyclical books required Camus to set aside an exploration of life closer to the insights of his own best understanding at the time in order to undertake a critical analysis of the age and its ambitions. After completing that analysis to the extent that was possible given its premises and methodology, Camus claimed explicitly and often that he now wished to return to the "ancient path (*ancient chemin*)" he first began to explore in *The Wrong Side and the Right Side*.[70] From the extant text of *The First Man* it is

---

[65] Albert Camus, *Notebooks 1951-1959*, 172, 192.
[66] Albert Camus, *Notebooks 1942-1951*, 183.
[67] Albert Camus, *Lyrical and Critical Essays*, 13.
[68] Ibid., 16.
[69] Ibid., 16-17.
[70] Albert Camus, *Essais* (Paris: Gallimard, 1965), 12.

clear that this work was intended to fulfill Camus's ambition, at least in part. Like *The Wrong Side and the Right Side* and *Nuptials*, *The First Man* offers a vivid image of the world of his youth and of the lives of those who surrounded him – the poor, the forgotten, the violent, the silent.

What is remarkable about this return is the extent to which Camus succeeded in completing it, at least as far as the existing documents allow us to judge. *The First Man* is, of course, even in its unfinished and unedited form, better written and more artfully constructed than either *The Wrong Side and the Right Side* or *Nuptials*. But in terms of its content, orientation, and mood, what is most outstanding about it is how closely it resembles those early works. Gone are the strain of the cyclical books and the background of modern despair with which these books were contending. Camus's voice is more assured, like that of one who speaks about things he knows. And what does he know? As we learn from the religious iconography of the cyclical books (absurdity, rebellion, fall) and its relationship to that of *The First Man*, Camus's ambition in the latter work was to describe the nature of human life "before the fall," that is, without the Christian presumption of a definitive fall or change in human nature requiring a final redemption in the after life.[71] In other words, *The First Man*, as Camus promised in his 1959 Preface to *The Wrong Side and the Right Side*, was an attempt to describe "life itself."

This was an extremely interesting and promising project. It was nothing short of an attempt to explore the full amplitude of human experience without the distorting influence of two traditions – Christianity and modernity – that had occupied so much of Camus's talent and energy through the middle years of his career. However, there is one feature of "life itself" and the full amplitude of human experience that Camus seems to have learned through the writing of the cyclical books, perhaps most vividly expressed in *The Fall*, that appears to be missing from his new Eden – humour.

The nature of the human condition described in *The Fall* is definitive for Camus, even if the dark and menacing manner in which Clamence responds to it is not. According to that description, human beings are by nature "double," inescapably divided between their love of the good and their self-love. According to the analysis, so deeply troubled by their duplicity are

---

[71] For a fuller discussion of this matter, see my *Albert Camus' Critique of Modernity*.

human beings that they spend much of their lives attempting to escape it or hide it from themselves and others. Such efforts may assume many forms, some more pernicious than others, but they all revolve around the need to feel innocent and therefore free of the judgement that attends their lack of innocence or self-love. These efforts reach all the way to the various apocalypses with which we are acquainted in which the good and evil are separated and unity restored, at least for some.

Contrary to these ambitions, *The Fall* offers a tragic conception of life in which duplicity can be ameliorated but never overcome. This includes human mortality and the lack of resolution it entails. That final incompleteness is hard to bear, which is perhaps why people have invented so many artful devices to escape it. Yet Camus believed not only that facing that truth frankly was salutary for human life but also that life itself engenders its own, more honest forms of relief from its darkest truths. This is apparent in *The Fall*. Not only is the book funny; what is says about humour and comedy more generally is true. For instance, in a very lucid moment Jean-Baptiste Clamence makes a declaration that is essentially the same as the one Socrates makes in book 10 of the *Republic*: "I have never been really able to believe that human affairs were serious matters. I had no idea where the seriousness might lie, except that it was not in all this I saw around me – which seemed to me merely an amusing game, or tiresome."[72] The over-emphasis on human importance was for Camus the fundamental impulse of modernity's attempt to bring about a permanent improvement of the human affairs and Christianity's desire for a final redemption. In both cases this over-emphasis tended toward humourlessness. What could be so funny when human salvation is at stake?

For Camus in *The Fall* as for Socrates in the *Republic* limiting seriousness encourages both humour and playfulness and allows us better to judge the significance of our lives and their meaning. Humour in this regard is its own form of transcendence and an experience that eases suffering by restoring proportion. *The First Man* in the form it has come down to us is brimming with insight into human longing and the mystery of our condition. Jacques Cormery, the book's protagonist, even claims to have first encountered that

---

[72] Albert Camus, *The Fall*, 86-87. "The law presumably says that it is finest to keep as quiet as possible in misfortunes and not to be irritated, since the good and bad in such things aren't plain, nor does taking it hard get one anywhere, nor are any of the human things worthy of great seriousness." Plato, *Republic*. Trans. Allan Bloom (New York: Basic Books, 1968), 604bc.

"nameless mystery" during a Catholic Mass, though not in the Mass's symbols and divine personages.[73] What is less apparent in the book is that complex and beautiful human disposition described by Socrates as Er observes the souls being ushered before the seat of Necessity to choose their lives for the next round of mortal existence: "He said that this was a sight surely worth seeing: how each of the several souls chose a life. For it was pitiful, laughable, and strange (ἐλεινήν ... καὶ γελοίαν καὶ θαυμασίαν)."[74]

[73] Albert Camus, *The First Man*, 170-171.
[74] Plato, *Republic*, 620a.

Works Cited

American Journals. Trans. Hugh Levick. New York: Paragon House, 1987.
Carnets III: Mars 1951–Décembre 1959. Paris: Gallimard, 1989.

Christian Metaphysics and Neoplatonism. Trans. Ron Srigley. Columbia: University of Missouri Press, 2007.

Correspondence, 1932–1960. With Jean Grenier. Trans. Jan Rigaud. Lincoln: University of Nebraska Press, 2003.

Essais. Paris: Éditions Gallimard, 1965.

Exile and the Kingdom. Trans. Justin O'Brien. New York: Vintage International, 1991.

The Fall. Trans. Justin O'Brien. New York: Vintage International, 1991.

The First Man. Trans. David Hapgood. New York: Alfred A. Knopf Canada, 1995.

Lyrical and Critical Essays. Trans. Ellen Conroy Kennedy. Ed. Philip Thody. New York: Vintage Books, 1970.

The Myth of Sisyphus. Trans. Justin O'Brien. London: Penguin Books, 1988.

Notebooks, 1935–1942. Trans. Philip Thody. NewYork: Paragon House, 1991.

Notebooks, 1942–1951. Trans. Justin O'Brien. New York: Paragon House, 1991.

Notebooks, 1951–1959. Trans. Ryan Bloom. Chicago: Ivan R. Dee, 2008.

The Outsider. Trans. Joseph Laredo. London: Penguin Books, 1983.

The Plague. Trans. Stuart Gilbert. London: Penguin Books, 1960.

Le premier homme. Paris: Gallimard, 1994.

The Rebel. Trans. Anthony Bower. New York: Vintage Books, 1991.

Resistance, Rebellion, and Death. Trans. Justin O'Brien. New York: Vintage Books, 1974.

Théâtre, récits, nouvelles. Paris: Gallimard, 1962.

Youthful Writings. Trans. Ellen Conroy Kennedy. New York: Alfred A. Knopf, 1976.

Other Works Cited

Aronson, Ronald. *Camus and Sartre: The Story of a Friendship and the Quarrel That Ended It.* Chicago: University of Chicago Press, 2004.

Baudrillard, Jean. *The Spirit of Terrorism.* Trans. Chris Turner. London: Verso, 2003.

Brée, Germaine. *Camus.* Rev. Ed. New York: Harcourt, Brace, and World, 1964.

——. *Camus: A Collection of Critical Essays.* Ed. Germaine Brée. Englewood Cliffs, N.J.: Prentice-Hall, 1962.

——. *Camus and Sartre: Crisis and Commitment.* New York: Delta Books, 1972.

Carroll, David. *Albert Camus the Algerian: Colonialism, Terrorism, Justice.* New York: Columbia University Press, 2007.

Cruickshank, John. *Albert Camus and the Literature of Revolt.* London: Oxford University Press, 1959.

Devaux,André-A. "Albert Camus: Le christianisme et l'hellénisme." *Nouvelle Revue Luxemboureoise* (January–April 1970): 11–30.

Dostoyevsky, Fyodor. *The Brothers Karamazov.* Trans. Constance Garnett. New York: W.W. Norton, 1976.

Grenier, Jean. *Albert Camus: Souvenirs.* Paris: Gallimard, 1968.

Hamilton, William. "The Christian, the Saint, and the Rebel: Albert Camus." In *Forms of Extremity in the Modern Novel.* Ed. Nathan A. Scott Jr. Richmond: John Knox Press, 1965.

Isaac, Jeffrey C. *Arendt, Camus, and Rebellion.* New Haven: Yale University Press, 1992.

Jeanson, Francis. "Albert Camus ou l'âme révoltée." *Les Temps Modernes,* no. 79 (May 1952): 2070–90.

Judt, Tony. *The Burden of Responsibility: Blum, Camus, Aron, and the French Twentieth Century.* Chicago: University of Chicago Press, 1998.

Koestler, Arthur. *The Yogi and the Commissar, and Other Essays.* New York: Macmillan, 1967. Lewis,

R.W. B. *The Picaresque Saint.* London: Gollancz, 1960.

Merton, Thomas. "Camus: Journals of the *Plague* Years." *Sewanee Review* (Autumn 1967).

——. *The Plague: Introduction and Commentary.* New York: Seabury Press, 1968.

Murchland, Bernard. "The Dark Night before the Coming of Grace." In *Camus: A Collection of Critical Essays.* Englewood Cliffs, N.J.: Prentice-Hall, 1962.

Onimus, Jean. *Albert Camus and Christianity.* Trans. Emmett Parker. Montgomery: University of Alabama Press, 1970.

Plato. *The Republic of Plato.* Trans. Allan Bloom. New York: Basic Books, 1968.

——. *Symposium.* In *The Dialogues of Plato.* Trans. Seth Benardete. London: Bantam Books, 1986.

Sartre, Jean-Paul. *Existentialism and Humanism.* Trans. Philip Mairet. Brooklyn: Haskell House, 1977.

——. *Nausea.* Trans. Lloyd Alexander. New York: New Directions, 1964.

——. "Réponse à Albert Camus." *Les Temps Modernes,* no.82 (August 1952): 334–53.

——. *Situations IV: Portraits.* Paris: Gallimard, 1964.

Sprintzen, David. *Camus: A Critical Examination.* Philadelphia: Temple University Press, 1988.

——. *Sartre and Camus: A Historic Confrontation.* Ed. and trans. David Sprintzen and Adrian van den Hoven. New York: Humanity Books, 2004.

Srigley, Ronald D. *Albert Camus' Critique of Modernity.* Columbia: University of Missouri Press, 2011.

Thody, Philip. *Albert Camus, 1913–1960.* London: Hamish Hamilton, 1961.

Todd, Oliver. *Albert Camus: A Life.* New York: Alfred A. Knopf, 1997.

Voegelin, Eric. *The New Science of Politics.* Chicago: The University of Chicago Press, 1952.

Review: *The Originality and Complexity of Albert Camus's Writings*, edited by Emmanuelle Anne Vanborre

by Sylvia Crowhurst

Emmanuelle Anne Vanborre, the editor of *The Originality and Complexity of Albert Camus's Writings* states, "the different essays in this volume shed light on some of Camus's works; their richness, originality and complexity; and their relevance today" (p.3). Vanborre's volume is organized in three parts entitled, *Literary Consideration, Philosophical and Political Reflections, and Evolution and Influences.* The three parts of the volume are presented as ten essays written by scholastic international authors, with an Introduction establishing Albert Camus as a non conforming intellectual and a writer. The essays written by the authors and the editor in this volume have a fundamental feel of admiration towards Albert Camus. This is unsurprising as the author's research literature focuses on 20th century fiction, especially on Camus and his contemporaries such as Maurice Blanchot and Maryse Condeof, literary theory and Francophone literature. Camus's stylistic patterns and genres of writing, the difficulties Camus faced isolated from the French intellectual elite and his relationship he held with his contemporaries are examined in this volume. In addition, the authors of the essays discuss Camus's search for meaning, examine his volatile split with Jean-Paul Sartre, and consider his political view. Camus's uneasiness between insurgence and liberty, his existence and reflection on the other, and his philosophical work on the absurd nature of life are also covered. What makes Vanborre's volume so unique compared to other published articles concerning Albert Camus is that the wide-range of essays not only captures and encapsulate Camus's original thoughts and writings, but then further explores, re-examines and reveals why Camus's theoretical perspectives are still of relevance to us today, fifty years after his death. Vanborre's publication will greatly appeal to Camus scholars as an excellent source of contemporary academic discussion and debate.

In the opening essay, *"Camus, the Nouveau Roman, and the Postmodern,"* Edmund J. Smyth immerses readers into the world of Camus's style of writing and his relationship to the nouveau roman and the postmodern movement. Smyth examines Camus's writing style in *The Stranger, The Plague, The Fall, and Exile and the Kingdom* and suggests Camus's style of writing had considerable impact on modernist and post modern literature. Essays written by Alain Robbe-Grillet and Roland Barthes recognizing Camus as the instigator advocating *'écriture blanche'* are examined in Smyth's essay. Smyth reasons that the political stance and anti-Marxists position Camus adopted fifty years ago put Camus out of favor amongst his intellectuals peers and distrusted by his readers. Thus, Smyth contests Camus was often excluded from the emerging post modern theory, *nouveau roman* and the style and techniques of the post modern literary view. Fifty years later, Smyth desires Camus's writing to be re-examined and acknowledged for his fictional experimentation. It is well known that Camus's stylistic shift of writing differs from novel to novel. The change in Camus's stylistic writing may have led to misreading and misunderstanding by the *nouveaux romanciers* and the *nouvelle critique* of Camus's novels. However, how a reader interprets Camus's writing is purely of a personal nature and Camus cannot be blamed for their interpretation. Smyth's call for re-examination of Camus's fictional experimentation should indeed show the honor and respect Camus is entitled to.

The second and third essays of the first part concern two of Camus novels, *The Plague* and *The Fall*. In the second essay, *"The Complexity and Modernity of The Plague,"* Aurélie Palud continues Smyth's interpretation of Camus's style of writing and postmodern theory with reference to *The Plague* and how for fifty years critics have either admired or reproached the novel. Palud draws upon the analogy of contemporary fictions such as Gabriel García Márquez's *Love in the Time of Cholera* and Stewart O'Nan's *A Prayer for the Dying* and in doing so realizes *The Plague* has many postmodern features. Palud not only considers Camus's neutral, flat or white style of writing in *The Plague* to be that of modernity, but also considers the narrator in *The Plague* to be a sign of modernity. It is common knowledge amongst scholars of Camus that *The Plague* included an allegory of the rise of Nazism. Palud clarifies this by including text from Camus's letter addressed to Roland Barthes dated January 11th 1955. However, Palud argues whether *The Plague* metaphor has more meaning and is more complex than the allegory of Nazism. The last part of Palud's article focuses upon how Camus, over fifty years ago, describes our contemporary way of life today.

The third and final essay in the first part is written by the editor Emmanuelle Anne Vanborre and is titled "*Albert Camus's The Fall: The Vertiginous Fall into Language, Representation, and Reality.*" Vanborre analyzes *The Fall* delving into Camus's writing at the particular time of his life, his role of language, and explores Camus's relationship of self with the other. There have been numerous analyses of *The Fall* and its philosophical discourse, such as guilt, justice, punishment, good and evil. What makes Vanborre's evaluation of Camus's *The Fall* more appealing than other analyses is the addition of her interpretation of Camus's writing, form of text, and the context and role of language. Delving deep into the form of the text of *The Fall* Vanborre gives the reader a reflective insight into the remarkable flexibility of Camus's thoughts and penmanship. His text in *The Fall* is as apparent today as it was fifty years ago, and it invites us to challenge our contemporary relationship with language and our text, the other and our reality. Camus's basic philosophical issues such as his theory of Absurdism may be similar throughout his novels, but his ability to use differing forms of literary genres never cease to amaze.

Part two of this volume includes essays based on the "*Philosophical and Political Reflections*" of Camus's works. This part of the volume gives Camus readers an alluring insight into Camus philosophy, thoughts, and relationships with other writers. In the first essay of this part, "*Camus's Unbeknownst Legacy: Or, "I'm Having an Existential Crisis!" Don't You Really Mean A Camusian Crisis?"* Michael Y. Bennett give us a unique look into defining the meaning of "existential crisis"(p.54) and what we interpret existentialism to be. He starts by giving readers the *Urban Dictionary* versus *Oxford English Dictionary* definition of "existential crisis" (p.53). The definitions differ from one another in terms of development, essence, acts and meaning. Bennett then examines the ideas Jean-Paul Sartre's nihilistic existentialism portrays to the philosophy of Albert Camus. Bennett reasons when "the average person" (p.54) considers existentialism he/she considers Camus's philosophy of the absurd. Of course, who Bennett construes as an average person is left to the interpretation of the reader. Bennett briefly contrasts Alasdair Macintyre's idea of epistemological crisis in Macintyre's book *The Tasks of Philosophy* to Sartre's idea of existential crisis in *No Exit*. He then launches into a lengthy explanation of the Camusian Crisis drawing upon Camus's *The Myth of Sisyphus*. He examines Camus's volatile split with Jean-Paul Sartre and the presumptions fifty years ago to Camus's view of absurdity made by his contemporaries and readers. Bennett's essay is uncomplicated to follow and offers the reader a convincing, clearly defined prose showing the differences and contributions Sartre and Camus made to philosophy and letters in the twentieth century. He ends his essay with an astute and amusing quote, "So next time you hear someone say, "I'm having an existential crisis" make sure you ask them, "Don't you *really* mean a Camusian crisis?"(p.60).

In the fifth essay in this volume, "*Sisyphean (Out)rage and the Refusal to Mourn,*" Matthew H. Bowker's offers contemporary readers the idea that Camus's philosophical opinions, written in his major works fifty years ago, assist us today in our understanding of our grieving processes, both on cultural and individual levels. In doing so, readers understand Camus's comprehensive belief of his philosophy of the Absurd. Bowker draws upon the Sisyphean struggle described in Camus's philosophical essay, *The Myth of Sisyphus* and compares this to Camus's philosophy that we should prolong our absurd suffering. As readers of Camus will be aware, the characteristics of Camus's philosophy of the Absurd is based upon our active struggle and the only course open to us to win our struggle is refusing to give in. Bowker's essay certainly does not concede or struggle and details the two choices Camus offers readers when faced with grief. It is an interesting essay even if it does end on a sad note.

"*Albert Camus's Warring Twentieth Century From His Ancestral Spain To His Mediterranean Utopias,*" is the sixth essay in this volume written by Araceli Hernández-Laroche. Hernández-Laroche analyzes how the impact of a multitude of wars Camus experienced, affected and influenced his life and his writing. Hernández-Laroche describes Camus as a "moralist writer" (p.81) as Camus implored and warned his contemporaries against the rise of fascism in Italy and Nazism in Germany. Hernández-Laroche's essay sheds an interesting light upon Camus's relationships with other authors of different religions and nationalities, particularly writers of the *Ecole d'Alger.*

The final part of Vanborre's volume leads the reader to the" *Evolution and Influences*" of Camus's writing and the effect other authors had on Camus's work. Camus's *The Plague* is revisited once again in Jennifer Stafford Brown essay, "*Prison, Plague and Piety Medieval Dystopia in Albert Camus's The Plague.*" Brown asserts authors during wars and conflicts are more likely to use mythography in their prose. She suggests Camus's forced separation from his family during WWII reflects in his writing of *The Plague* which Camus started to write during the war. Brown argues Camus's use of medieval imagery within *The Plague* is a result of the political fascism Camus observed and the medieval trope and misery asserted in the Vichy regime. Readers of this essay would find it useful to have some prior knowledge of the rise of the Vichy regime in France, Marshal Philippe Pétain's rule and the French government during WWII. Brown's essay provides a unique comparison of the medieval imagery shown in *The Plague* to that of the medieval trope Pétain and his government used during their rule.

In essay eight in this volume, *"Summer by Albert Camus The Essay in the Mirror of Fiction,"* Mamadou Abdoulaye Ly continues with the theme of Camus's use of myth. Ly's essay differs from the other essays in this volume as Ly asserts Camus's text in *Summer* "is more the text of a poet" (p.119). Myth and autobiography is used by Camus on his reflections, observations and perceptions of human freedom. Through Ly's analysis of *Summer,* readers are given the opportunity to experience Camus's almost pithy and poetic in nature text of "childhood's lost paradise" (p.120).

In the penultimate essay, *"Affliction, Revolt, and Love A Conversation between Camus and Weil,"* Sophie Bourgault's essay contrasts two quite similar contemporaries Albert Camus and Simone Weil. Bourgault draws upon the admiration and affection Camus had for Weil's works, particularly in relation to Weil's depiction of the deplorable working conditions in factories and the silence of the afflicted proletariat. Bourgault asserts Camus thoughts are influenced by various of Weil's work, such as *L'Enracinement* and *Ecrits de Londres* and provides comparisons in Camus work and Weil's. She shows the way in which both contemporaries are concerned for the working conditions of the proletariat within factories, and how they play an active role for justice of the afflicted. Various scholarly articles have been written on the political thoughts, or social transformation of Camus and Weil; however, this essay has a freshness about it. Bourgault's essay shows the reader how fifty years ago Camus and Weil were dealing with the same issues protesters, such as Occupy Wall Street are today.

In the final and tenth essay in this volume, *"Tormented Shade Camus's Dostoevsky,"* Thomas Epstein thoughtfully considers Camus's relationship with the Russian novelist Fyodor Dostoevsky and how Camus's outlook towards Dostoevsky altered throughout Camus's life. Epstein explores Camus's voracious interest in Russian literature and how Dostoevsky's influence appears not only in Camus's fiction and drama such as *The Myth of Sisyphus,* but in his diaries, letters, interviews and essays throughout his life. Epstein attests that as Camus's art and literature matures so does his open, recurrent references to Dostoevsky. Epstein's essay is an interesting prose taking the reader through Camus relationship with Dostoevsky, from his development of existentialist, to Camus's appreciation of Dostoevsky's Western progressive ideology, and Camus's realization of Dostoevsky's *modernity* of writing. Epstein's essay differs from the numerous studies adherent to Dostoevsky's influence on Camus. He suggests Camus's tacit silence tells us more about his relationship with Dostoevsky than to what Camus declares to us.

Overall, Vanborre's volume is an informative worthwhile read and supplies an intriguing postmodern insight into Camus's world and his writings fifty years after his death, and provides the reasons Camus's writing still applies to us today. A prior understanding and knowledge of Camus's writings and his philosophy would be beneficial to the reader before embarking on the complexity of the arguments set forth in the essays. Vanborre has pulled together a comprehensive volume of well written, individualistic and analytical essays, which will undoubtedly leave inquisitive readers and enthusiasts of Camus exhilarated and enlightened.

The Originality and Complexity of Albert Camus's Writings. Edited by Emmanuelle Anne Vanborre. (New York. Palgrave Macmillan Publishers Limited, October 2012, Acknowledgments, Bibliography, Notes, Index, Pp.184. $85.00 paper).

Journal of Camus Studies – Manuscript Submission Guidelines

Mission & Scope

The Journal of Camus Studies is an interdisciplinary forum for scholarly conversation about the life and work of Albert Camus. The goal of the Journal of Camus Studies is to provide a genuinely international and interdisciplinary scholarly resource for exploration and examination of the thought of Albert Camus and his contemporaries.

The *Journal of Camus Studies* was founded in 2008 as the *Journal of the Albert Camus Society* by Simon Lea. The inaugural volume represented the work of international authors exploring the life and work of Camus from a variety of philosophical and theoretical perspectives. In 2010, Peter Francev was appointed General Editor in an effort to focus more intentionally on reaching an academic audience.

Manuscripts

Abstracts: Prior to manuscript submission, authors are asked to submit the following: full contact information along with a brief, one-paragraph biography detailing current affiliation, research interests and recent publications, as well as an abstract of no more than 250 words.

Manuscript Preparation: Manuscripts should be no longer than 10,000 words (text and notes). The entire paper must be double-spaced, with one-inch margins and 12-point font, in MS Word. Both the paper and notes must conform to the *MLA Style Manual and Guide to Scholarly Publishing*, 3rd edition. They must avoid sexist and ethnic biases. Also, manuscripts must not be under consideration by another publication. Along with the manuscript, the author must prepare a separate file as a cover letter. This file will include a history of the manuscript, whether it is derived from an M.A. or Ph.D. thesis with the advisor's name, whether it has been presented at a conference, or other pertinent information about its development. Authors are encouraged to submit all materials using MS Word to the General Editor who, then, will forward the materials to the review committee.

Review Process

The *Journal of Camus Studies* follows a policy of blind, peer review; please ensure that the main body of the manuscript contains no identifying remarks. All comments by reviewers are confidential and shall not be published. Final judgment with regard to publication is made by the General Editor.

When the editor receives a submission, the manuscript will undergo a peer review. At least, two reviewers will provide evaluative comments for each submission. On the basis of this review, the manuscript may be unconditionally rejected, conditionally accepted, or unconditionally accepted for publication. Each submitter will be provided with the peer review statements and may respond to the comments, ask questions, or seek clarification as desired. Evaluations, typically, will be complete within 6-8 weeks. Standard evaluation forms are used by the reviewers. If a particular reviewer cannot complete a review within a timely manner, the editor will seek an alternative, qualified reviewer. Sometimes the opinion of a reviewer is important enough that the editor must wait a little longer.

Conference Announcements

Announcements and correspondence regarding conferences, panels, papers, and other news of interest should be sent to the Editor, *Journal of Camus Studies*, at the following address:

Professor Peter Francev
General Editor, *Journal of Camus Studies*
Dept. of English
Mount San Antonio College
1100 N. Grand Ave
Walnut, California 91789-1399

pfrancev@mtsac.edu

Book Reviews

Book Review Preparation: Book Reviews should be a minimum of 750 words and no longer than 2,500 words. The entire review must be double-spaced, with one-inch margins and 12-point font, in MS Word. The review must conform to the MLA Style Manual and Guide to Scholarly Publishing, 3rd edition, or The Chicago Manual of Style, 15th edition. They must avoid sexist and ethnic biases, be written in English. Reviews must not be under consideration by another publication. The conclusion of the review should state the author's name and affiliation or current city, state, and country of residence.

Upon receipt of submission, the Book Review Editor will conduct an initial review to determine that the review is suitable for publication in the Journal. The Book Review Editor may then decline to pass the manuscript on for publication. The Editor and Associate Editors always seek to find the most qualified reviewers to evaluate books.

Deadline: Submission deadline: 30th September of each year. This allows the Editors ample time to review submissions, and still permit for revisions prior to publication.

Books to be Reviewed: Books relevant to the life and times of Albert Camus should be sent to the Book Review Editor, *Journal of Camus Studies*, at the following address:

Eric B. Berg
Book Review Editor, *Journal of Camus Studies*
Associate Professor of Philosophy
MacMurray College
447 East College Avenue
Jacksonville, IL 62650

Books sent from within the UK should be sent to:

BM Camus Mail,
London WC1N 3XX